| DATE | | | |
|---|---|---|---|
| | | | |
| | | | |
| | | | |
| | | | |
| | | | |
| | | | |
| | | | |
| | | | |
| | | | |
| | | | |
| | | | |
| | | | |

# Massachusetts Broadsides of the American Revolution

# Massachusetts Broadsides of the American Revolution

Edited by Mason I. Lowance, Jr., & Georgia B. Bumgardner

The University of Massachusetts Press Amherst 1976

LIBRARY OF CONGRESS CATALOG CARD NUMBER 75–32488
ISBN 0–87023–208–8
PRINTED IN THE UNITED STATES OF AMERICA
DESIGNED BY MARY MENDELL
LIBRARY OF CONGRESS CATALOGING IN PUBLICATION DATA APPEAR
ON THE LAST PRINTED PAGE OF THE BOOK.

For Marcus McCorison, Susan and Tim

# Contents

# Preface

FOR IF THE TRUMPET GIVE AN UNCERTAIN SOUND,
WHO SHALL PREPARE HIMSELF TO THE BATTLE?
I CORINTHIANS 14:8

NEARLY everyone has seen a broadside, but few people are aware of either the history of these documents or the wide variety of uses to which they have been put. Literary history may justifiably include the broadside as a subject for study, because this vehicle of expression has carried some unique examples of literature, both prose and verse. Perhaps the universality and frequency of broadside printing have contributed to contemporary neglect of the broadside as a cultural artifact. Only a small percentage of the total number of broadsides from the era of the American Revolution has survived; these survivors are nevertheless so numerous that saturation with the documents and their messages comes easily for the literary historian. Repositories like the Library of Congress and the American Antiquarian Society house literally thousands of revolutionary broadsides, but little has been done to catalogue, describe, or evaluate these unusual windows into the past. Unfortunately, the broadside is neither a "genre" nor conventional in any literary sense, and its failure to fit conveniently into a literary classification has no doubt contributed to its neglect by cultural and literary historians. The revolutionary broadsides, however, contain some of our most precious insights into popular culture, because they were designed to reach society quickly, dramatically and effectively.

As a means of inspiring public reaction, the broadside and its relatives, the newspaper and the periodical, have not even today been superseded by other media. The printed word remains a sort of final authority, and broadsides or pamphlets are particularly well suited for editorializing, moralizing, or offering commentary on events as they occur. For example, when the colonists finally declared their independence from Great Britain on July 4, 1776, the original manuscript document was quickly printed as a broadside, which was circulated throughout the colonies and England. It was the official way of publicly stating the case. It is significant that the first examples of printing in Europe and New England are broadsides rather than books, an understandable fact if one considers the role of the broadside: to spread messages quickly and dramatically, leaving the resolution of problems to authors and philosophers. As Ola Winslow has noted, the earliest dated specimen of printing from movable type is a broadside "Letter of Indulgence" granted by Pope Nicholas V, in aid of John II against the Turks, April 12, 1451, only a short time after the invention of printing in 1450. In New England, the Stephen Daye press in Cambridge issued "The Freeman's Oath" in 1639, one year prior to the printing of the famous *Bay Psalm Book*, the first book published in the American colonies.

Not only did the broadside faithfully record the events of the revolutionary era and the resulting formation of the independent United States, but as a cultural medium it also contributed significantly to the development of revolutionary sentiment in the period immediately prior to the Declaration of Independence, from the publication of Paul Revere's extraordinary engraving of the Boston Massacre in 1770 to the widespread broadside publication of the Declaration itself in 1776. Broadsides not only provided inflammatory calls to arms, but they were also a call to thought and judgment. For the study of the American Revolution, their presence offers modern readers an unusual mirror of the times, in which may be read the opinions of leaders on the events of the day, as well as more urgent messages designed to alert citizens to the dangers of British tyranny. During the era of the American Revolution, 1765 to 1789, the use of broadsides for the dissemination of revolutionary sentiment was widespread, and there was a corresponding growth in the number and frequency of broadsides produced. The broadside became a medium for revolutionary debate, a vehicle for carrying declarations and responses that were immediate and urgent, and occasionally both sides of an argument would appear on the same day, the second a response to ideas contained in the first. This represents a significant change from the use of the broadside in colonial America before 1760. Until revolutionary sentiment grew strong enough to support an insurgent press, the New England colonies received broadsides which were primarily official proclamations or public announcements of a noncontroversial nature. In Puritan New England, for example, the broadside was often used to carry funeral elegies or proclamations announcing forthcoming days of thanksgiving and fasting. But as the Revolution approached, the content of broadsides reflected a shift away from these routine declarations toward a new interest in the future glory of America once the tyranny of the British beast had been overcome. On December 19, 1775, the governor of Connecticut, Jonathan Trumbull, proclaimed a day of public fasting and prayer because of the troubles that were afflicting the colonies, and in this broadside, he called upon colonists to resist those forces that "threaten us with general Destruction, for no other Reason known to us, than that we will not surrender our Liberties, Properties, and Privileges, which we believe God and *Nature*, the British Constitution, and our Sacred Charters give us a just right to enjoy." In Massachusetts, the pattern was similar. The rhetoric of the typical thanksgiving proclamation was official and formal from 1691, when the new charter was granted to the Massachusetts Bay Colony, until the 1760's, when resistance to "taxation without representation," and the pressures that had been developing against the colonial governors since the Andros regime, erupted in emotional outbursts that were made public by pamphlets and broadsides. The quantitative expansion of broadside production from 1763 to 1789 is one measure of the importance of this vehicle during the Revolution, but the dramatic messages contained on broadsides offer an even more revealing view of the role of these documents.

The purpose of this collection is to gather under one cover a representative group of Massachusetts broadsides published during the Revolution that will depict, fully and dramatically, prominent historical moments from 1765 to 1789. The editors have restricted this selection to broadsides published in Massachusetts alone, because not only was Massachusetts the geographical center for many of the most dramatic episodes of the American Revolution, such as Paul Revere's famous ride and the Boston Tea Party, but it was also an important center of the colonial printing industry. Many broadsides were published in Massachusetts as part of an underground movement that preceded the eruption of hostilities in 1775, and for years, Massachusetts printers published documents for their revolutionary neighbors in Vermont and New Hampshire, where local printing only began after the events of 1776. Most of the broadsides in this collection are political; a few are ballads and poetry, but the most intriguing ones are concerned with the politics of the revolutionary conflict. The introductory essay further explores the role of the broadside in colonial America during the Revolution, drawing examples from Massachusetts and her neighbors to the south. The arrangement of the broadsides is chronological, and the notes have been designed to provide a running narrative describing the evolving crisis that resulted in American independence. Bibliographical information for each broadside has also been provided; however, we have given as a location for each document only that collection from which the facsimile copy was taken, though we realize that most of these broadsides are available in a number of libraires and historical collections.

We are indebted to Marcus McCorison, Director of the American Antiquarian Society, for permission to publish thirty-five of these unusual documents; to Curator Carey Bliss and Director James Thorpe of the Huntington Library, San Marino, California, for permission to use six from their fine collection of American broadsides; and to the John Carter Brown Library, the Massachusetts Historical Society, the New-York Historical Society, the Historical Society of Pennsylvania, the Essex Institute, the Boston Public Library, and the Bostonian Society, for permission to publish selected broadsides from their collections. We are particularly indebted to Walter Muir Whitehill and the Colonial Society of Massachusetts and to the University of Massachusetts' Bicentennial Committee, which generously provided a subvention for the production of this book. Our appreciation to Marcus McCorison for encouragement and friendship is expressed elsewhere in this volume. Gail Smith, Malcolm Call, Rodman Paul, Ray Billington, Claude Simpson, and J. A. Leo Lemay have provided invaluable assistance throughout the various stages of this project; their conversation as well as their careful reading give precision to reflection on the American Revolution. Finally, our thanks go to Susan Lowance and Tim Bumgardner, who have spent part of the past year revisiting, with us, the decades of the 1760's and 1770's.

Georgia B. Bumgardner and Mason I. Lowance, Jr.

# Massachusetts Broadsides of the American Revolution

# Introduction

IN purely technical terms, a broadside is a single sheet of paper printed on one side only. When printed on both sides, documents are usually designated broadsheets, and when folded and printed on four sides, a pamphlet or newspaper. But this definition describes very little of the broadside's role as a cultural artifact. If the verse that frequently appeared on a broadside cannot be considered a genre in literature, perhaps the broadside itself can be discussed as a particular literary type with a history and function not unlike that of the newspaper or periodical essay, both well-recognized and culturally significant literary forms.

The broadside is, therefore, one sheet and occasional in nature. While not all of the information it carries is urgent (though some broadsides were printed to "scoop" newspaper stories that would be published in periodical form later), the broadside is usually associated with a particular event or occasion. Moreover, the broadside has eluded the literary historians partly because the conventions of authorship do not conveniently follow the usual patterns of literary attribution. There are few well-recognized "broadside authors" (Martin Parker and William Elderton are well-known broadside ballad-writers) because many broadsides are composed by more than one writer or represent the views of a committee or government. Since some are not signed at all, there was no risk of legal repercussions for authors of controversial essays. Printers were therefore generally held responsible for content, and the penalties for printing revolutionary attacks on the colonial government were usually severe. Isaiah Thomas, a colonial printer who was associated with insurgent sentiment, risked personal safety and jeopardized his business each time his press was identified as the source of revolutionary propaganda. Eventually, he moved from Boston to Worcester to prevent the British from destroying his press and the beginnings of his personal library, which now forms the core of the American Antiquarian Society collection. Seditious libel was usually the charge against colonial printers who supported the revolutionary cause, and there were frequent prosecutions for this political crime in the years just before the Revolution. Alexander McDougall, for example, was jailed in December, 1770, for printing an inflammatory broadside. With such a strong opposition to revolution in the colonies, all of these printers faced serious charges for their association with the insurgent cause. In spite of these risks, most "signed" or attributable broadsides are political and controversial rather than literary.

While broadsides containing elegies or occasional poems have been common in all periods since the invention of printing, the broadside of the revolutionary era offered opposing political adversaries a single vehicle for dramatic expression, which resulted in a unique record of the political, military, and economic events of the period. The spectrum of expression ranges from the most polite and commendatory proclamation to the most inflammatory kind of political and personal invective. In most cases, the declarations were intended to generate a public response, and a good example of the broadside as a predecessor of our modern underground newspapers is provided by the following text, which appeared at the time of the Tea Act, in 1774:

BRETHREN AND FELLOW CITIZENS

> You may depend that those odious Miscreants and detestable Tools to the Ministry and Governor, the *Tea Consignees* (those traitors to their Country, Butchers, who have done, and are doing everything to Murder and Destroy all that shall stand in the way of the private Interest) are determined to come and reside again in the Town of Boston. I therefore give you this early Notice, that you may hold yourselves in Readiness, on the shortest Notice to give them such a Reception as such vile ingrates deserve.
>
> Joyce, Jun.
> Chairman of the Committee
> of Tarring and Feathering [1]

Although this example was "signed," many such broadsides were published under pseudonyms, to indicate a group sentiment or to protect the actual author. Others, like the Paul Revere engraving of the Boston Massacre, achieved for both designer and printer a reputation for patriotism that gave the new nation pride and hope.

Revere's well-known, masterful engraving of the massacre became the accepted version of events on that tragic day in 1770. But ultimately, the Revere document and the story became more than a simple documentary account of the tragic murders. Brief and one-sided, the narrative and its picture evolved into a symbol of British tyranny, and the publication of the document became an act of highest patriotism. Subsequent to its original publication as a print, the engraving was issued in broadside form accompanied by prose accounts of the massacre. The broadside as artifact and the broadside as cultural symbol, characteristic of a system of values and attitudes shared by the colonial insurgents, are both dissolved into one moment, which is captured like a word-picture on the printed side of the Revere proclamation. And it is clear that Revere did by no means intend that the engraving be used only once. The original version is titled "The Bloody Massacre perpetrated in King-Street, Boston, on March 5, 1770, by a party of the 29th Regt." Further investigation of its provenance suggests that the engraving may never have been intended to be merely a hastily printed broadside. As Sinclair Hitchings points out, "many copies from the

[1] See Samuel Tower, "Broadsides for the Revolution," *New York Times*, Sunday, March 25, 1973, where the text of this broadside is printed in full.

original printing survive; many of them are in their original frames with the original glass still in place. Revere apparently sold them framed and glazed. You could issue a broadside framed, of course, but the value obviously placed upon the *Boston Massacre* seems to identify it first as a picture, and one meant to last. Not all broadsides were throwaways, but almost by definition, they are printed for the moment." [2]

The importance Revere attached to the massacre engraving clearly indicates the kind of cultural response he anticipated, and this is a good example of the broadside's important interaction with the audience for which it was specifically designed. It is this moment of interaction that modern readers must capture in order to appreciate fully the true significance of the broadside in its historical and cultural context. As a literary form which responds to a need for immediacy and urgency, and requires stylistic compression, the broadside must be viewed with concern for the specific circumstances out of which it generates. Viewed from this historical perspective, the broadside can become a window to much larger and wide-ranging events, and in some cases, can provide insight into the attitudes and values of a local group.

The Revolutionary broadsides which date from 1773 to 1776 are not only the most numerous but also the most interesting, from a historical and cultural point of view. Together, they form a dramatic narrative of the events in the Boston area at the time of the Revolution, and a number of printings of the broadside Declaration of Independence are included in this group. By isolating a series of these colonial broadsides and setting them against a background of contemporary events, the modern reader can gain a clear sense of the excitement that was generated when these original announcements were made. The following selection is neither arbitrary nor complete; it is, rather, representative of those thousands of broadside documents that were issued on both sides of the controversy during the brief but intense prelude to the Revolution, and, like the Revere account of the Boston Massacre, it offers a paradigm for similar investigations of the revolutionary age through this urgent medium. The accompanying discussion gives an indication of the response in other colonies (as well as that in Massachusetts) to the events taking place in the Commonwealth.

An early example is a proclamation issued "By the Direction of the Committee of Correspondence for the Town of Boston," dated March 30, 1773, written by William Cooper and printed by Isaiah Thomas, "by order of the Town of Boston." [3] The proclamation records a meeting held on

[2]For a full discussion of the original production of the Revere engraving, see Sinclair Hitchings, "A Broadside View of America," *Lithopinion* (Spring, 1970), Issue 17, Volume 5, No. 1, p. 69, and Clarence S. Brigham, *Paul Revere's Engravings* (New York, 1969), 52–78.

[3]"*Boston, March 30, 1773*/ Sir (Autograph) By Direction of the Committee of Correspondence for the Town of Boston I now Transmit to you/ an attested Copy of the Proceedings of said Town on the 8th Instant, and am with due Respect/ your most humble Servant,/ William Cooper (autograph), Clerk of the Committee." Printed by

March 8, 1773, in Faneuil Hall, Boston, where Samuel Adams, the fiery revolutionary agitator, led the Committee of Correspondence to adopt a long resolution that included this notice:

> It is notorious to all the world, that the liberties of this continent and especially of this province, have been *systematically* and successfully invaded from step to step: Is it not then, to say the least, justifiable in any town, as *being part of the great whole,* when the last effort of tyranny is about to be made, to spread the earliest notice of it far and wide, and hold up the *iniquitous system* in full view. It is a great satisfaction to us, that so many of the respectable towns in the province, and we may add, gentlemen of figure in other colonies, have expressed, and continue to express themselves much pleased with the measure: And we encourage ourselves, that from the *manifest discovery* of an union of sentiments in this province, which has been one happy fruit of it, there will be the united efforts of *the whole* in all constitutional and proper methods to prevent the entire ruin of our liberties." (National Index 12688, CSmH. 82914)

Another record of a meeting in Faneuil Hall, dated December 1, 1773, [plate 10] carries news of a gathering "for the purpose of consulting, advising, and determining upon the most proper and effectual method to prevent the unloading, receiving, or vending of the detestable *Tea* sent out by the East India Company, part of which just being arrived in this Harbour." This broadside records the celebrated *Dartmouth* debate, which was an occasion marked by the appearance of Francis Rotch, the twenty-three year old son of the vessel's owner, Joseph Rotch, and its captain, a Mr. Hall, before the Faneuil Hall meeting. It is a synopsis account of the several meetings that took place over the following few days, resulting in a strongly-worded resolution by the Town demanding that:

> if any Person or Persons shall hereafter import Tea from Great Britain, or if any Master or Masters of any Vessel or Vessels in Great-Britain shall take the same on Board to be imported to this Place, until the said unrighteous Act shall be repeal'd, he or they shall be deem'd by this Body an Enemy to his Country; and we

---

Isaiah Thomas, 41 x 33.5 cm., four columns. Evans 12688, CSmH. 82914. Henceforth in this essay, broadsides will be identified in the text by standard classification numbers. I have used the *Evans Bibliography of American Imprints before 1800*, the Clifford Shipton-James Mooney *National Index of American Imprints Through 1800: The Short-Title Evans,* and the Huntington Library accession numbers. Some broadsides are identified by more than one number; the CSmH. designation is the Huntington Library classification. I am very grateful to Mr. Bruce Henry, research librarian at the Henry E. Huntington Library and Art Gallery, for his assistance in the preparation of this essay. Not only did he secure bibliographical information on the broadsides held by the Huntington, he also provided some historical notes on the contexts out of which several were produced.

must prevent the Landing and sale of the same, and the Payment of any Duty thereon. And we will effect the Return thereof to the Place from whence it shall come.

Mr. Samuel Adams,
Hon. John Hancock, Esq;
William Phillips, Esq;
John Rowe, Esq;
Jonathan Williams, Esq.

As Benjamin Labaree has shown, this heated declaration was a response to the series of Parliamentary Acts and taxes which had been levied on the American colonies during the previous two decades. England had imposed a variety of tax measures on colonial commerce, with mixed success, including the hated Stamp Tax, and the Townshend Act of 1767, which proposed that commissioners be stationed in an American port to oversee the collection of customs throughout the colonies. Benjamin Franklin and other revolutionary leaders had always opposed Britain's right to levy taxes in the colonies, and the Tea Tax was viewed as a final attempt following a long succession of efforts by Parliament to bring the colonies to heel. The outrage expressed in the December 1 broadside resulted in an action against British arrogance on the night of December 16, 1773, when a few patriots disguised vaguely as Indians dumped 340 chests of the dutied tea into the Boston harbor. Although this was a minor event considering the long history of hostilities that would follow, it set the pattern for future episodes of violent resistance resulting from the deteriorating relations between Britain and the colonies.

Revenge was not swift, but it was harsh. A contemporary broadside titled "Supplement to the *Pennsylvania Journal*" and issued on May 14, 1774, contains the full text of Britain's "*Act to discontinue, in such manner and for such time as are therein mentioned, the landing and discharging, lading or shipping of Goods, Wares, or Merchandize, at the Town, and within the Harbour of Boston, in the Province of Massachusetts-Bay, in North-America.*" The document also includes a chronology of the debate over the enactment of the hated "Port Act," as the bill authorizing the harbor blockade was later to be called. Because this broadside from the *Pennsylvania Journal* contains urgent information that was also printed in the newspaper itself, the supplement is a good example of the relation between broadside publication and periodical circulation. Several versions of this broadside exist; one was printed in Boston in the spring of 1774, probably just after the declaration by Parliament (in March) to close the Boston harbor as of June 1 [plate 12]. The handsome title of the broadside reads emphatically, "An Act to Block up the Harbour of Boston!" The document, however, contains no date.

Reaction to the Port Act was strong and immediate. Two interesting broadsides chronicle the "Proceedings of the Committee of Correspondence in New York Committee Chamber, July 13, 1774" (National Index 13477; CSmH. 109101). The second document is dated July 19, 1774, but both were issued by Isaac Low, Chairman of the Committee, and both contain the ten "resolves" adopted by the committee to signal resistance to Britain's unjust retaliation in Massachusetts Bay (National Index 13479; CSmH. 82890). The "resolves" are a balanced statement of the problem, since the first resolve declares allegiance to "his most sacred Majesty *George* the Third, King of Great Britain," as "liege, lawful and rightful Sovereign, and that it is our indispensible duty to the utmost of our Power, by all constitutional Means to maintain and support his Crown and Dignity. . . . That we therefore view with inexpressible Concern and Grief, some late Acts of the British Parliament, claiming and exercising Rights which we humbly conceive are replete with Destruction, and may be attended with the most fatal Consequences to the Colonies, and their parent State." This gentle beginning, however, is followed by subsequent resolutions that are clear declarations of colonial outrage at the English reaction to the Boston Tea Party:

> *Resolved:* That particularly the Act for Blocking up the Port of Boston is, in the highest Degree arbitrary in its Principles, oppressive in its Operation, unparallelled in its Rigor, indefinite in its Exactions, and subversive of every Idea of British Liberty; and therefore justly to be abhorred and detested by all good Men.
>
> *Resolved:* That the Destruction of the Tea at Boston, was not the *Only* Motive for bringing such unexampled Distress on that People; because the Alternative of suffering it, or paying for the Tea, had otherwise been left in their Option. It is therefore truly to be lamented by all the Colonies; that Administration were furnished with any Pretext for the Violent Measures now carrying into Execution.
>
> *Resolved:* That Vengeance separately directed, has more a dangerous Tendency, and is more Destructive of the Liberties of America, than conjunctively; and that therefore it is the indispensible Duty of all the Colonies, according to their different Circumstances, to afford every reasonable Assistance to a Sister-Colony in Distress; especially when that Distress is evidently calculated to intimidate others from Contributing what may be their Power, to procure the desired Relief.

The practical result of this committee meeting was to adopt a resolution to meet in a Congress of Delegates to "consult on the Mode of procuring Relief from our Difficulties." Even here, however, the proposers were aware of the delicate balance between open hostility toward Britain and preservation of liberty on the one hand, and the ever-present commercial ties with the mother country on the other. The seventh resolution states "that nothing less than dire Necessity can justify, or ought to induce the Colonies to unite in any Measure that might materially injure our Brethren the Manufacturers, Traders, and Merchants in Great Britain; but that the Preservation of our inestimable Rights and Liberties, as enjoyed and exercised, and handed down to us by our Ancestors, ought to supersede all other Considerations. . . ." Finally, the eighth resolve contains the most emphatic declaration of the committee: "That if a Non-Importation Agreement of Goods from Great Britain, should be adopted by the Congress, it ought to be *very general* and *faithfully* adhered to; and that a Non-importation *partially* observed, like that last, would answer no good Purpose; but on the contrary, only serve to *expose* all the Colonies to further injuries." The Cold War was on, and it was only a matter of time before a more active conflict would follow.

The next meeting was to be the suggested Congress of Delegates, or "Provincial Congress," and it was held in Philadelphia in September and October, 1774. A number of broadsides were printed during this period of early congressional association, and two are particularly intriguing. The first is a chronicle of some of the congressional resolutions, and is titled "The Following Extracts from the Votes and Proceedings of the American Continental Congress we are Induced to Publish thus early purely to ease the Impatience of our Readers" (National Index 13708; CSmH. 19354). Besides giving modern readers a clear sense of the extreme urgency with which broadsides were often printed during the revolutionary era, this document is also of interest because of its similarity to the earlier "Suffolk Resolves," the publication of which marked the beginning of the colonists' movement to declare themselves an independent organization with specific rights and privileges. Originally adopted by a convention in Suffolk County, Massachusetts, on September 9, 1774, the resolves were carried to the Congress by Paul Revere, where they were adopted on September 17. Both versions were written with a strong feeling for independence. They advise Massachusetts to form a provisional government, pronounce the Coercive Acts unconstitutional, urge the Commonwealth's citizens to arm themselves, and recommend non-importation, non-consumption, and non-exportation. Some copies of the later broadside reprintings carry the names of the delegates from twelve of the thirteen colonies (Georgia was excluded), as well as that of the president of the Congress, Peyton Randolph of Virginia.

The text of this congressional document is exceedingly important. The summer of 1774, during which the Port Act was in effect, was a crucial period for radical organizers like Samuel Adams. Each colony had met separately to decide, among other things, whether or not they should meet as a united body to discuss the Coercive Acts that were being imposed on them by Great Britain. Finally, in September of that year, the delegates gathered in Carpenter's Hall, in Philadelphia, to forge the resolutions contained ultimately in this broadside account. The determination of this small group of men is clearly seen in the Congress's prefatory declaration: ". . . having taken under our most serious deliberation, the state of the whole continent, (we) find that the present unhappy situation of our affairs, is occasioned by a ruinous system of colony administration adopted by the British Ministry about the year 1763, evidently calculated for enslaving these Colonies, and, with them, the British Empire. . . ." Bernard Bailyn, in *The Ideological Origins of the American Revolution*, cites this declaration as an example of "the logic of rebellion," reflecting the theory held among colonists that Britain was conspiring to enslave them and destroy liberty. Moreover, the resolutions themselves are strong. They essentially terminate all trade with Britain as of December 1, 1774, and even cite specifically certain very lucrative areas of commerce, such as the slave trade. But they also provide alternative ways of surviving this non-importation agreement: "that we will in our several stations encourage frugality, economy, and industry; and promote agriculture, arts, and the manufactures of this country, especially that of wool. . . ." Soon afterwards, on October 26, 1774, a provincial congress met in Cambridge, Massachusetts, to prepare for the now inevitable hostilities.

The second congressional broadside contains an account of this meeting and commences with a conditional statement which lays the blame squarely on Great Britain:

> Whereas in Consequence of the present unhappy Disputes between Great-Britain and the Colonies, a formidable Body of Troops with warlike Preparations of every Sort are already arrived at, and others destined for the Metropolis of this Province (Boston), and the expressed Design of their being sent is to execute Acts of the British Parliament, utterly subversive of the Constitution of the Province. . . . It is RESOLVED, and hereby commended to the several Companies of Militia in this Province, who have not already chosen and appointed officers, that they meet forthwith, and elect Officers to Command their respective Companies." (National Index 13416, CSmH. 109109)

And in what was to be an early declaration of the deterrant principle, the broadside concludes by noting that "the security of the Lives, Liberties, and Properties of the Inhabitants of this Province depends under Providence on their Knowledge and Skill in the Art Military, and in their being properly and effectually armed and equipt. . . ." The stage was now set, and it was just a short time before these mutually antagonistic preparations would escalate into armed conflict.

But not all of the colonists were sympathetic with the cause so eloquently heralded by Samuel Adams and his followers. It has been estimated that in 1774 fewer than one-third of the colonial subjects favored armed resistance against Great Britain, and even fewer favored termination of allegiance to the King. The Quakers, for example, frequently protested against war of any kind. In a curious broadside issued on January 24, 1775, James Pemberton, clerk of the Quaker meeting at Philadelphia, recorded some resolutions adopted by that group. The basic attitude expressed here is that peace should be sought regardless of the circumstances, but the meeting also adopted resolutions favoring the British or Tory cause:

> The Divine Principle of grace and truth which we profess, leads all who attend to its dictates, to demean themselves as peaceable subjects, and to discountenance and avoid every measure tending to excite disaffections to the king, as supreme magistrate, or to the

legal authority of his government; to which purpose many of the late political writings and addresses to the people appearing to be calculated, we are led by a sense of duty to declare our entire disapprobation of them—their spirit and temper being not only contrary to the nature and precepts of the gospel, but destructive of the peace and harmony of civil society, disqualify men in these times of difficulty, for the wise and judicious consideration and promoting of such measures as would be most effectual for reconciling differences, or obtaining redress of grievances. (National Index 14052, CSmH. 108514)

In contrast, American revolutionaries published accounts of the first battle, Lexington and Concord, in the inflammatory and emotional rhetoric that characterized their cause, as exhibited in a patriotic broadside entitled "The American Crisis. Let God, and the World Judge Between us" (National Index 42764; CSmH. 108275). This broadside appeared in response to the engagement of April 19, 1775, which was viewed at first as another British massacre of American patriots, rather than as an historic moment of American heroism. In May of 1774, General Thomas Gage had been sent to Boston as Commander-in-Chief for the second time. During the following year he tried to enforce the Coercive Acts and to cope with the inevitable resistance. Under pressure from England to take some decisive action, Gage ordered a raid upon the colonial munitions depot at Concord. The resulting clash with the defenders provided an incomparable opportunity for the revolutionaries to drive home their view of the oppressive situation, and this they did in numerous broadsides that defended the colonists' righteous cause. According to the patriots:

> a handful of inoffensive Men, collected at Lexington, Eight of whom, without the least Provocation, (the British troops) laid dead on the Spot. . . . The Inhuman Murderers (then) fled with Precipitation, but marked the Road with more than savage Cruelty, by burning Houses, stabbing sick old Men, and murdering Women and Babes. . . . We have sinned against God, but we have not sinned against our King, or his Ministers, we have ever, and uniformly, been the most faithful Subjects in the World. . . . What Phrenzy, then, has possessed the Hearts of a very few haughty Ministers, who rule the Nation, to drive such a people as this to Desperation. . . . Rouse, then, ye Inhabitants of Britain. . . . and save this Land, and save yourselves from the most tremendous of all Evils, the dreadful Curse of absolute Slavery. . . .

The "Sun and Center of all Plagues," this curse of slavery, was no longer challenged by the weak voice of a few dissidents howling in the American wilderness; it was now a focus of resistance to British domination over all the colonies, first graphically portrayed in Revere's engraving of the Boston Massacre, now vividly demonstrated in the word-pictures created by accounts of the attack at Lexington and Concord.

The British viewed the Lexington-Concord incident in a different way altogether, and to answer the revolutionaries' version published a broadside of their own entitled, "A Circumstantial Account Of an Attack . . . on his Majesty's Troops" [plate 17]. A comparison of this account with those issued by the revolutionaries shows clearly that the British had no rhetorical or ideological framework to equal their adversaries' very alarming and inflammatory posture. This broadside contains only a few bland censures in what is basically a simple narrative of the sequence of events as remembered by the troops. However, the account does stress the restraint of the British forces. British officers "gave Orders, that the Troops should not fire, unless fired upon." Even when it became obvious that there existed "a preconcerted Scheme to oppose the King's Troops, whenever there should be a favorable Opportunity for it," the officers still emphatically instructed the troops "on no Account to fire, nor even to attempt it without Orders." Further, when the well-behaved and disciplined English discovered an atrocity committed against one of their own, "a Sight which Struck the soldiers with Horror," they apparently did not retaliate, and the officers took "all Pains to convince the Inhabitants that no Injury was intended them, and that if they [the citizens] opened their Doors when required, to search for said stores, not the slightest Mischief should be done; neither had any of the People the least Occasion to complain, but they were sulky." The broadside also reveals the British pique at being fired upon by an enemy that took cover and would not fight face to face, and it ends by scolding, "this unfortunate Affair has happened through the Rashness and Imprudence of a few People."

The Lexington-Concord clash made clear to British officials that further measures would have to be taken in order to discourage resistance. Therefore, on June 12, 1775, General Gage issued a proclamation, "By His Excellency, The Hon. Thomas Gage, Esq. Governor, Commander in Chief, in and over His Majesty's Province of Massachusetts-Bay, and Vice-Admiral of the same. A Proclamation" [plate 20], written by "Gentleman Johnny" Burgoyne. It opens with the allegation, "the infatuated Multitudes . . . have long suffered themselves to be conducted by certain well-known Incendiaries and Traitors, in a fatal Progression of crimes, against the constitutional authority of the State." The latest crimes were "the Actions of the 19th of April . . . of such Notoriety." Since "the good Effects which were to arise from the Patience and Lenienty of the King's Government, have often been frustrated, and are now rendered hopeless . . . , it only remains for those who are entrusted with supreme Rule . . . to prove they do not bear the Sword in vain." Then follows a declaration of martial law and an offer of royal pardon to all who would lay down their arms, all, that is, except Samuel Adams and John Hancock, "whose offences are of too flagitious a Nature to admit of any other consideration than that of a condign Punishment." Many Americans and some Britons greeted the proclamations with understandable derision. No doubt all rebels would have echoed in chorus a remark which one of their fellows inscribed on one copy of the document: "Mr. Gage, you have forgot the Congress" (National Index 14184; CSmH. 82888).

Mr. Gage, though, had not forgotten Congress, nor the armed citizenry. Realizing that martial law could not be enforced by mere proclamation, he, with Generals Henry Clinton, William Howe, and Burgoyne, drew up a plan for the military occupation of the peninsulas of Charlestown and Dorchester, control of which would give them mastery of Boston. Careless talk, however, alerted the patriots to British intentions and the Americans dug into Breed's Hill on Charlestown peninsula at night, before the British knew what had happened. Gage and the generals judged the American presence there to be an intolerable threat. Thus the stage was set for the famous battle of Bunker Hill, on June 17, 1775.

Although the Americans were eventually driven out for lack of ammunition, the battle demonstrated the vulnerability of the Redcoats and provided a dramatic episode that lent itself to patriotic exploitation. Broadsides, again, were the principle vehicles of propaganda. Two important revolutionary broadsides were immediately printed. Both are in verse, very amateurish but quite characteristic in form and style. In his "Poem on the Bloody Engagement that was fought on Bunker Hill" [plate 24], the Rev. Elisha Rich wrote the following lines:

> New-England search and know the cause,
> Has thou not broken *God*'s best laws,
> For which thy God doth thee chastise,
> And turns thy Friends to Enemies.
>
> Would thou obtain thy *Liberty*,
> Then break all bands of slavery,
> And do thou *Liberty* proclaim
> To all that have a human frame.

In the second of these broadsides, "The American Hero" [plate 22], the brave Patriot is depicted as spurning death, asking, "Why should vain mortals tremble at the sight of death and destruction in the field of battle?" These two broadsides taken together offer an oversimplified explanation of the cause of the war, advice on how to respond to it, and great flourishes of inspirational rhetoric to build confidence among the hesitant. They are clear examples of the patriotic impulse generated by British attacks on colonial insurgents, as the Revere engraving of the Boston Massacre had been five years earlier.

The Battle of Bunker Hill also occasioned a British broadside [plate 23], most of which was a simple narrative summary of events. This untitled broadside contains a single appeal to British patriotism, but it lacks the fiery conviction of its American counterpart: "This Action has shown the Bravery of the King's Troops, who under every Disadvantage, gained a compleat Victory over Three Times their Number, strongly posted, and covered by Breastworks. But they fought for their *King*, their *Laws*, and *Constitution*." Despite these loyal sentiments, the British were suspicious of Gage. Even when they sent him back to America in May of 1775, British officials in London had doubts about Gage's ability. The Bunker Hill episode confirmed their suspicion and moved them to recall Gage in September, replacing him with General William Howe as Commander-in-Chief.

This superb opportunity to satirize Gage openly was not lost to the rebels. They eventually published a remarkable broadside entitled "Gage's Folly; or, The Tall Fox Out-witted" [plate 29], which taunts Gage and his abortive attempts to stem the tide of revolution:

From Briton's shore Gage sailed o'er
    To Massachusetts-Bay,
Quite void of fear he landed here
    About the first of May.
With courage stout he made no doubt
    But he should win the field,
Tho' Rebels call'd, he thought for all,
    To make those Rebels yield

. . .

But now poor Gage seems in a rage,
    To think he cross'd the sea,
Because he finds the People's minds
    Are bent on Liberty.

Appropriately enough, this broadside, published in January, 1776, also carries an advertisement for the twelfth edition of Thomas Paine's *Common Sense,* the Revolution's most eloquent appeal for independence.

In the same month, a broadside disclosing just how far colonial opinion had travelled was issued by the General Court of Massachusetts. Entitled "By the Great and General Court of the Colony of *Massachusetts Bay, A Proclamation*" [plate 27], it announced that a provisional, revolutionary government had been freely elected and organized, and, because "no reasonable Prospect remains of a speedy Reconciliation with *Great Britain,*" obedience to the British officials was indefinitely suspended. Just one step short of proclaiming independence, this broadside is also notable for its preamble, which in substance parallels much of the Declaration of Independence. "As the Happiness of the People is the sole End of Government, so the Consent of the People is the only foundation of it." Unlike the more secular Declaration, however, the broadside reflected the powerful Puritan tradition in Massachusetts Bay. It continues: "That Piety and Virtue, which alone can secure the Freedom of any People, may be encouraged, and Vice and Immorality suppressed, the Great and General Court have thought it fit to issue this Proclamation, commanding and enjoining it upon the good People of this Colony, that they lead sober, religious and peacable Lives. . . ." Finally, making no pretence of loyalty to George III, the authors of the proclamation concluded with *"God Save the People."* Surely the climax of the antagonism was very near.

As the broadsides from this three-year period suggest, conditions had reached an intolerable level of tension and misunderstanding. Finally, North Carolina took the ultimate step in April, 1776, when she announced her readiness to separate from Britain. Following suit the next month were

Rhode Island, Massachusetts, and Virginia. The latter colony instructed its congressional delegates to propose officially that independence be declared. Thus on June 7, Richard Henry Lee submitted a resolution to that effect, and Congress voted to have a formal document drafted.

The subsequent drafting and publication of the Declaration of Independence forms the most exciting chapter in the history of American broadside printing, because the first "clean" copy of the document was a broadside printed by Philadelphia printer John Dunlap rather than a holograph manuscript. The Declaration's principal author, Thomas Jefferson, produced a document ideally suited to the broadside form of publication. The inherently exciting message was made even more electrifying by its transmission through widely circulated broadsides which, by their very nature, imported something special, something of unusual urgency and great significance. In a few months' time, the inflammatory proclamation came out in nineteen separate broadside printings as well as in countless newspapers. Copies numbering in the thousands circulated throughout the new states.

Only a few of these early broadsides of the Declaration of Independence have survived. The original broadside announcing Jefferson's intentions for the colonies appeared in the early morning hours of Friday, July 5, 1776, but most of the surviving documents date from later that month. The Dunlap printing, however, is a classic example of the importance of broadside printing during times of critical political and social change. The genetic history of the Declaration's evolution has been traced many times; however, the critical role of Dunlap's broadside in maintaining the original language of the document has not been sufficiently acknowledged.

Having adopted the Declaration on July 4, two full days after independence had actually been voted, Congress now arranged for its promulgation. Early in the morning on Friday, July 5, John Dunlap published at least 500 copies to be distributed to the colonial legislatures and various units of the army. These copies contained only the printed signatures of John Hancock, president of the Continental Congress, and Charles Thompson, secretary. If, as some believe, the members of Congress ever signed a copy on the fourth of July, they would have signed the working copy, now lost, which Dunlap used to print his broadside. Thus the Dunlap broadside survives as the most authoritative version of the original Declaration, despite the existence of manuscript fragments and revisions in Jefferson's own hand (National Index 15185).

One of the Dunlap broadsides became one of three authoritative copies inserted into the rough draft of the *Journal of the Continental Congress*, and a handwritten copy was inserted into the corrected edition of the *Journal*. Thus the version most often considered to be the "original manuscript" of the Declaration, the engrossed parchment housed in the elevator vault of the National Archives, is actually a document prepared by a scribe from the Dunlap broadside specifically for the purpose of gathering the remaining congressional signatures. It was not ordered by Congress until July 19, 1776, was not first signed until August 2, and was not completely signed until November or possibly even later.

In subsequent months, the broadside played an even more significant public role in spreading the eloquent message of the original Jefferson manuscript printed by Dunlap. Hundreds of copies were made, and each colony published its own edition of the original text. Predictably, the British responded with scorn and refutation. In his study, *The Declaration of Independence*, Carl Becker lists the British pamphlets which appeared in reply to the Declaration, including John Lind's *An Answer to the Declaration of the American Colonies* (1776), Thomas Hutchinson's *Strictures Upon the Declaration of the Congress in Philadelphia* (1776), and *A Declaration of Independence Published by the Congress at Philadelphia in 1776 With a Counter-Declaration Published at New-York in 1781*. Public locations, such as taverns and meeting-houses, became sites for the posting of broadsides from Whigs and Tories, and as post-riders arrived in the villages from such regional centers as Boston, New York, Hartford, and Charleston, the innkeepers and town officials could effectively control the dissemination of information by posting only those broadsides that reflected their own views or the views of their customers. But the war was on, and many announcements carried information that would be of great interest to both sides.

Broadsides were used, of course, for a wide variety of purposes during the revolutionary era, as in more settled times. The narrative history traced here shows how selected documents may tell the developing dramatic story of historical episodes. But the collection contains a variety of broadside subjects, such as broadside ballads and songs which celebrate significant moments during the conflict. "The American Hero, Made on the Battle of Bunker Hill" [plate 22] and "The Yankey's Return from Camp" [plate 18] are examples illustrating how the earlier tradition of broadside balladry was adapted to the circumstances of the American Revolution. Ballads, or nartarive songs, had been printed on broadsides in England for two centuries, and the custom of hawking the "penny-broadside" in the streets of London had been practiced by "balladmongers" equally as long. Thus a ready-made custom was simply continued by the colonials to celebrate their victories and to create folk-heroes. Moreover, "General Washington, A New Favourite Song, at the American Camp" [plate 30], is an excellent example of the borrowing of an entire tune and stanza structure in the creation of a "new song" from the earlier "British Grenadiers." Similarly, "The Yankey's Return from Camp," or "Yankee Doodle," had been a popular tune in England before being adopted by the colonials, and the moment of this adoption has actually been cited: at the Battle of Lexington and Concord, the British marched in singing the tune, and the victorious colonials marched away with it. The musical setting for "The American Hero," on the other hand, is found in *A Select Number of plain Tunes* of Andrew Law (Cheshire, Connecticut, 1781), and has been called "the War Hymn of the American Revolution."

Execution proclamations and announcements of death were common broadside subjects throughout the seventeenth and eighteenth centuries in America. We have included "A Poem in Memory of the Fifth of March, 1770" [plate 6] to illustrate how the tradition of the funeral broadside was also adopted to help promote the colonial cause. But two broadsides announcing public executions, "The Last Words and Dying Speech of Ezra Ross, James Buchanan, and William Brooks" [plate 39] and "The Last Words and Dying Speech of Robert Young, Executed for Rape of an Eleven Year Old Child" [plate 40], are good examples of the way in which the execution of a felon would be turned into a moral example for the community at large, by the publication of his execution confessional and repentance. Even in these cases, as the notes for the broadsides show, the conflict between England and America was still central to the issues treated in the broadside accounts.

All fifty of the documents which follow cannot be treated in the introductory essay. The notes, however, provide a historical context for each broadside, and the bibliographical information should make access to each relatively easy. We also urge readers to consider the hundreds of newspapers, pamphlets, and sermons printed during the same period as supporting documents which can add to the enjoyment of these dramatic and visual broadside accounts.

Traditionally, the period of the American Revolution is brought to an end with the inauguration of George Washington in 1789. The Inaugural Address was published in broadside form, as was his Farewell Address—both reprinted hundreds of times in the years that followed the first presidency and the drafting of the Constitution. Broadside printing proliferated during the federal period, because the formation of a new government by the consent of the governed meant that all decisions were to be given full public exposure. These broadsides continue to give a rich sense of historic moments and episodes as they occurred. For example, the documents tracing the evolution of the Constitution and its ratification by the separate states, or those military and political broadsides chronicling the events of the War of 1812, offer an exciting time capsule for the modern reader which is not available in the more discursive histories written about these episodes. The neglected broadsides provide an exciting and more intimate documentary history of public responses to each movement, and a dramatic narrative of each episode as it developed. As social and cultural historians turn to computers for an analysis of town records and military lists, they should remember the public broadside as the primary vehicle for many proclamations and commentaries concerning the American Revolution. The dramatic language of these documents, and the compression of arguments into a single printed sheet, offers a unique perspective on the historical period and a vivid record of this unusually exciting time.

Mason I. Lowance, Jr.

# Bibliographical Notes

ALONG with the notes providing an historical context for each broadside, are references to several standard bibliographies. These are useful because they point out the existence of additional copies of some broadsides, and supply other helpful information. Charles Evans' *American Bibliography* (13 vols., Chicago and Worcester, 1903–1955) lists chronologically American books, pamphlets, broadsides, and serials, and locates copies in various repositories. In 1970, the University Press of Virginia published Roger Bristol's *Supplement to Charles Evans' American Bibliography.* This volume corrects some of the entries in the earlier compilation and adds several thousand new ones. *The National Index of American Imprints,* edited by Clifford K. Shipton and James E. Mooney, was published by the American Antiquarian Society and Barre Publishers in 1969. This author index provides easy access to Evans and Bristol and to the Readex Microprint Corporation *Early American Imprints Series,* which reproduces the imprints listed in Evans and Bristol in microform. Bristol's compilation has its own numbering system but each entry also includes the number which is used in the Readex Microprint project.

The Wegelin numbers refer to the revised and enlarged edition of Oscar Wegelin's *Early American Poetry,* published by Peter Smith in 1930. Many of the poetic broadsides, however, have come to light since the publication of this pioneering work. *Broadsides, Ballads &c. Printed in Massachusetts 1639–1800,* compiled by Worthington C. Ford and published by the Massachusetts Historical Society in 1922, is another helpful volume. Copies in other libraries and collections are noted, and several of the broadsides and vignette illustrations are reproduced. A perusal of this volume will attest to the variety and number of broadsides produced during the seventeenth and eighteenth centuries in Massachusetts.

The measurements of the broadsides in our collection are in centimeters, height preceding width, and the location of the copy reproduced is also noted.

## 1. Liberty, Property, and No Excise
[Boston, 1765]

HOSTILE reaction to Parliament's attempts to tax the colonies generated from feelings deeper than resentment of unjustified taxes; the colonists genuinely feared that taxes could lead to a loss of individual property ownership, a principle which, they believed, had historically distinguished them from England. Thus liberty, less an abstract conception than a concrete reality, became one of the central issues in pre-revolutionary America, and its symbols proliferated throughout the colonies. In 1765, Thomas Paine, the author of *Common Sense* and *The Age of Reason*, wrote a ballad called "Liberty Tree," which was later published in the *Pennsylvania Magazine* for July, 1775, when he was editor. Paine's ballad celebrated the famous tree, an elm located in front of a house near the Boylston market in Boston.

During the Stamp Act crisis, the Liberty Tree became a focus for expression of public sentiment. Broadsides were posted to its trunk, and on August 14, 1765, an effigy representing Andrew Oliver, distributor of the hated stamps in Boston, was hanged from the tree's branches. On another part of the tree a worn boot was suspended, a common graphic pun on the name of the Earl of Bute, first Lord of the Treasury. Though Chief Justice Hutchinson directed the sheriff to remove this spectacular exhibition, the figures were not removed until later in the evening when patriots took them down to carry them through the streets of Boston. Later that night, the crowd destroyed the Stamp Office and burned the effigy in front of Oliver's house. The legendary Liberty Tree was victimized when the British army took possession of Boston in 1774, but other "Liberty Trees" promptly were dedicated elsewhere in the Boston area. See Frank Moore, *Ballads and Songs of the American Revolution* (Boston, 1886).

NATIONAL INDEX 41554
BRISTOL 2589
FORD 1348
RARE BOOK DEPARTMENT, BOSTON PUBLIC LIBRARY
35.6 x 47 cm.

*Liberty, Property, and no Exciſe.*

# A Poem,

Compos'd on occaſion of the SIGHT ſeen on the GREAT TREES, (ſo called) in BOSTON, NEW-ENGLAND, on the 14th of AUGUST, 1765.

LET *Albion*'s ſons in praiſe their tongues employ ;
*New-England* ſmile, and *Boſton* ſhout for joy :
In ſpite of knaves, their politics and wit,
She ſtill enjoys her *LIBERTY* and *PITT*.
She reſts ſecure from ev'ry foreign foe,
Derides their plots, and ſees their overthrow ;
And ſoon ſhall ſee the wretch completely curs'd
Who ſtrove to *STAMP* her glory in the duſt.
" Freedom, (ſhe cries) I cannot cringe to knaves,
" My ſons are free, and never will be ſlaves :"
Let tyrants rule with arbitrary ſway,
Villains command, and whining fools obey :
Let daſtards live in infamy and ſhame,
While *Britons* fight for liberty and fame :
Let all her foes like bees prepare to ſwarm ;
Old *Pluto* rage, and *Purgatory* ſtorm :
Let *Charon* raiſe his oars and long-boat take,
And force with fury down the torrid lake.
Speak *Proſerpine*, thy will ſhall be obey'd,
Bid ev'ry fiend forſake the gloomy ſhade :
Give theſe commands to each infernal ghoſt,
" Go ſpit your venom on the *Britiſh* coaſt ;
" Haſte there and ſpread contention wide and far,
" Perplex her iſle, and ſet her ſons at war :
" Then to *America* with vengeance go,
" Let them in ſlavery own the powers below."
Suppoſe this done, and all the winged bands
At this new world with thunder in their hands :
Our hardy youth would ſtill their force repel,
Defeat their wiles and drive them back to hell ;
Theſe ſons of *Mars* their courage would confound,
A conqueſt gain and ſtill maintain their ground.
Then would' e'en devils be compell'd to own
Our ſovereign lives and God ſupports his throne :
Thus blaſt his foes in ev'ry baſe deſign
All-gracious heaven, and bleſs the royal line.
O give us favor in our monarch's eyes,
Defend our rights, remove the late *EXCISE*:
Let truth prevail and fierce oppreſſion ceaſe,
And bid our Prophet ſpeak the words of peace.
Lo ! here he comes, ſoftly he ſeems to tread,
Now rolls his eyes, now bows his rev'rend head :
He like a God appears in form divine,
Whoſe very aſpect ſpeaks ſome deep deſign ;
Hither he comes, on purpoſe to relate
Each ſacred truth and tell ſome hidden fate,
" *Boſton*, (he cries) your woes are at an end,
" Your foe ſhall fall and times ſhall quickly mend ;
" With ſhame o'erwhelm'd he ſoon ſhall hide his face,
" Then hark while I predict the time and place.
" The day now dawns, the gloomy night is ſpent,
" And ſoon your eyes ſhall ſee the grand event.
" See fair *Aurora* from her couch ariſe,
" Whoſe chearful bluſhes paints the morning ſkies :
" The ſhades are chac'd, the ling'ring ſtars are fled,
" And yonder *Phœbus* lifts his golden head :
" (Then cries the Prophet) I muſt haſte away,
" The Gods command and mortals muſt obey."
No more I heard from out his ſacred mouth,
He took his leave and went towards the *South* :
Then I beheld amazing wonders there,
Saw human ſhapes and monſters in the air.
A ſtately elm appear'd before my eyes,
Whoſe lofty branches ſeem'd to touch the ſkies ;
It's limbs were bent with more than common fruit,
It bore the Devil, *O——r*, and *B--te*.
Well then, ſaid I, my doubts are wholly fled,
I find the truth of what the father ſaid :
But while I ſtood to gaze upon the tree,
Another and another came to ſee ;
Each moment I beheld a diff'rent face,
For on they preſt 'till thouſands fill'd the place,
Here ſtands a child and looks with wond'ring eyes,
And there a champion of gigantic ſize ;
Yonder a maid at humbler diſtance ſtands,
And here a jilt with lifted eyes and hands.
This pleaſing proſpect entertains the throng,
All join as one, and thus begin their ſong,
" With grateful joy, O *Boſton*, now behold
" Thoſe truths fulfill'd, which lately were foretold !
" With thankful hearts now ſee the villains ſwing,
" Who hate their country, and would ſell their king :
" Behold the man, *whoſe heart* was ſet on gain
" And view the wretch, who wiſh'd ſome tyrant's reign."
Thus I obſerv'd they entertain'd the day,
In ſongs and chat they paſt the hours away ;
Now *Sol* retires, and journies down the Weſt,
And weary nature ſeems in ſable dreſt.
And now a hero lifts his voice aloud,
Stretches his hand, and ſpeaks to all the crowd.
" Hear me, (he cries) and be not too ſevere,
" Curſt be the man that leaves the bodies here
" Expos'd to all the dangers of the night,
" Then bear them hence with every fun'ral right."
Thus having ſpoke, they all with willing hands
Began to execute their chief's commands :
With rapid haſte ſome to the tree repair,
And on their ſhoulders bear a ladder there.
One draws his knife, and running to their aid,
Aſcends the limbs, that bear each lifeleſs ſhade ;
Then cuts the ropes in preſence of them all,
And as he cuts the ghaſtly *objects* fall.
Down on the earth in horrid form they lie ;
A frightful ſight to each beholding eye :
What now, (ſaid I) is all compaſſion fled ?
Can none be found, that will relieve the dead ?
Their chief reply'd, " Go place them on the bier ;
" Prepare yourſelves and quickly bring them here."
This done, he cries, " Let ev'ry man reſort
" In ſolemn order with the corps to *court*.
" March then, (ſaid he) in one united throng,
" And as you march, be this the fun'ral ſong.
" *Great* Jove *decrees, and go theſe mortals muſt* ;
" *'Tis earth to earth, and STAMP 'em in the duſt.*"
Then as they move, the words are ſung by all,
Down to the *court* and thro' the pompous *hall* :
Soon after this aroſe a grand debate,
(Such oft' attend the fun'rals of the great)
And wild diſorder ſeizes all the band ;
Forth ſome advance, while others make a ſtand.
One bids them halt, another " ſtill march forth
" And viſit all the region of the *North*."
A third proclaims, " Let theſe be firſt convey'd
" In peaceful ſilence to the dreary ſhade."
Then ſpake their head, (the regent of the night)
" Alas ! our hoſt is in a ſhameful plight :
" Is this the way to get a hero's name ?
" The road to honor and immortal fame ?
" Ceaſe wrangling then, let each in order ſtand,
" Join arm to arm, like one eternal band ;
" Then here (he cries) be all contention fled,
" Come follow on, your chief is at the head."
Thus having ſpake, all hear the wond'rous *man*,
And forth they move ; (the champion leads the van)
All ſeem impatient to obey his will,
And bend their courſe for the appointed *hill*,
Whoſe lofty ſummit once contain'd a *fort*,
To this they haſte and quickly leave the *court*.
Freedom and friendſhip centers in each ſoul,
They ſhout and ſing without the leaſt controul :
Here then we find no obſtacles aroſe,
Noiſe could offend, and nothing dare oppoſe,
(Nothing) except a ſtately *EDIFICE**,
This ſtops their courſe, but ſoon they down with this ;
Low in the duſt they made the ſtructure lay,
Then *STAMPT* the bricks, and bore the wood away ;
Now from the ruins ev'ry one retire,
Up to the *mount* and raiſe the fun'ral fire.

* Suppoſed to be built for a STAMP-OFFICE.

## 2. A Catalogue of Books
[Boston, 1765?]

ANDREW Barclay is best recalled for his bookbinding, for he was one of the few eighteenth-century binders who signed his work with elegantly engraved labels; but he was also a publisher, as well as an importer of books. Barclay came to the colonies from Scotland, probably in the early 1760's. A Loyalist, he joined the Loyal North British Volunteers and left Boston when the town was evacuated in March of 1776. From there he went to New York, where he began selling and binding books in 1777. After the Revolution he moved to Shelburne, Nova Scotia, where he added farming to his other activities. He died there in 1823. (See Hannah D. French, "The Amazing Career of Andrew Barclay, Scottish Bookbinder, of Boston," *Studies in Bibliography*, Bibliographical Society of the University of Virginia, XIV (1961), 145–162.)

This broadside not only lists titles of works that were being sold and read in Massachusetts Bay a decade before the Revolution; it also illustrates the degree of cultural dependence between the colonies and England. Although printing had been established very early in Massachusetts Bay, with the opening of Stephen Daye's little press in Cambridge in 1639, the publication of the broadside "Freeman's Oath," and the 1640 publication of the first book printed in the colonies, the *Bay Psalm Book*, native American literature was not to flourish until long after the Revolutionary era, in the American Renaissance of the mid-nineteenth century.

Titles included in Barclay's shipment reflect very wide, if traditional, tastes in reading among his customers. Congreve's *Poems*, *Gulliver's Travels*, *Robinson Crusoe*, and *Don Quixote* suggest a far richer literary diet, with a greater diversity of focus, than we sometimes assume the early colonists enjoyed. More typical are *Cromwell's Life*, the Bible, Bunyan's *Pilgrim's Progress*, John Flavel's *Navigation Spiritualized* and *Husbandry Spiritualized*, and Watson's *Body of Divinity*.

NATIONAL INDEX 41516
BRISTOL 2549
FORD 1340
AMERICAN ANTIQUARIAN SOCIETY
36.2 x 22 cm.

# A Catalogue of BOOKS,

## Lately imported from Britain;

And to be Sold by *A. BARCLAY,*

Second Door North of the three King's

## Corn-hill *BOSTON.*

ADdinfon's Evidence.
Ambrofe's looking to Jefus.
ditto Primæ Media et ultima.
Allen's Works 2 Vol.
Afflicted Man's Companion.
Allen's Allarm,
Adventures of a black Coat.
Arabian Night's Entertainment.
Argal[illegible]s & Parthema.
Bowman's principals of Chriftianity.
Britifh Letter Writer.
Bells Travels 2 Vol.
Bofton's four fold State.
Bofton on the Covenant.
Bofton's crook of the Lot.
Bofton's Catechifm.
Balm of Gilead.
Boyle's Voyages.
Bruces Life.
Brook's Remedies.
Buckanniers of America.
Barren fig Tree.
Congreave's Poems.
Cloud of Witneffes.
Calvin's Inftitutions, 4o
Crook-fhank's Hiftory 2 Vol.
Cole on God's Sovereignty.
Crawford's dying Thoughts.
Cromwell's Life.
Charles 12th.
Companion for the Altar.
Cocker's Arethmetick.
Col Jack
Cyrus's Travels.
Countryman's Jewell.
Cynthiæ.
Crawford's Catechifm.
Craighead on the Sacrament.
Clark on Baptifm.
12 Cæfers.
Confeffion of Faith, large.
ditto Small.
Doddridge's Rife and Progrefs.
Death of Abel.
Durham on Death, ditto Ifaiah.
Durham on the unfearchable riches of Chrift. Dyer's Works.
Don Quixot.
Drake's Voyages.
Devil on two St[illegible]ks.
Doddridge on Regeneration.
Erfkin's Sermons 4 Vol.
Eæfops Fables.
Flavel's Works, Folio.
ditto on Reformation.
ditto Navigation fpiritualiz'd.
ditto on Providence.
ditto Saint indeed.
Fisher's Englifh Grammer.
Foucault's Maxims.
French Convert.
Francis Spira.
Fortunate Villager.
Fisher's Arethmatick.
Firmin's real Chriftian.
Fenlon on Eloquence.
Gofpel Sonnets.
Gaudentia di Lucca.
Gray on Prayer.
ditto precious Promifes.
Gulliver's Travels. Guardian,
Guthry's Tryal.
Grace abounding.
Gray's Sermons.
Goofe's Tales.
Hervey's Dialogues, 2 Vol.
Hervey's Meditations
Hales Contemplations, 2 Vol.
Hill's Arethmatick.
Heaven's Glory.
Heavenly Footman.
Hiftory of Scotland.
Hocus, Pocus
Heaven upon Earth.
Joe Miller's Jeft.
Knoxe's Hiftory.
Laugh and be Fat.
Lark.
Lennet.
London Jefts.
Mafon on Self-Knowledge.
Marfhal on Sanctificatian.
Myftery of Faith.
Montague's Letters.
Mair's Book-keeping.
Mair's Geography.
New Book of Knowledge.
Owen on Communion.
Œconomy of human Life.
Papers concerning the Rebellion.
Pocket Dictionary.
Parifh Girl.
Pennetential Cries.
Pilgrim's Progrefs.
Prefent for an Apprentice
ditto a Servant Maid
Ralph Erfkin's Works 2 Vol Folio
Row's Letters,
Row's devout Exercifes.
Ramfey's Songs.
Ramfay's Poems,
Review of America.
Reynard the Fox.
Reading made Eafy.
Ruffell's Seven Sermons.
Robin Red Breaft.
Robinfon Crufo.
Sherlock on Death.
Sherlock on Judgment
Spiritual Warfare
Scougal's Life of God
Secretary's Guide.
Seven wife mafters,
Seven wife miftreffes,
Telemachus 2 Vol.
Tell tale
Triumphs of Love.
Truth, Victory over Error
Thomfon's Seafons
Tanfur's royal Melody.
Univerfal Dictionary.
Whole duty of Man
Watt's Lyrick Poems
Willifon's Catechifms
Willifon's Example
Willifon's Sacramental Meditations
Watfon's Body of Divinity
Week's Preperation
Warden on the Lord's Supper
Wifes Companion
Webfter's Book-keeping.
Vincents Catechifm
Young's Night Thoughts.

At the faid Shop may be had, Bibles Gilt or Plain, Teftaments, Prayer-Books, Tate & Brady's Pfalms, gilt or plain, Watts' Pfalms & Hymns, with or without Tunes, Accidences, Dilworth's and other Spelling Books, Primers, Pfalters, Singing-Books, Account-Books, Receipt Books, Morocco letter Cafes Plays, Pamphlets, Paper, Pens, Ink, Ink Powder, Wax, Wafers, &c. &c.

*N. B.* All Sorts of Books bound, gilt or plain, in the neateft Manner by faid *Barclay*. Gentlemen in Town and Country, who pleafe to favour him with their Cuftom, may depend upon being ferved with Fidelity and Difpatch.

☞ Cafh given for Sheep-fkins fit for Book-binding, at the fame Place.

## 3. Glorious News. Boston, 1766
## [Boston: Drapers, Edes & Gill, Green & Russell, and Fleets]

THIS broadside is a prelude to the period of jubilation in Boston over the repeal of the Stamp Act. Printed by the publishers of the four Boston newspapers, it was distributed free of charge to their subscribers, while others presumably had to pay for it. News traveled slowly, for it took two months for notice of the repeal of the Stamp Act to reach Boston, although American ships were ready to leave England on a moment's notice with news.

"No taxation without representation" was the battle-cry of the insurgents who wanted fair treatment from Britain. Mark Boatner notes that the infamous Stamp Act, which was in effect from November 1, 1765 until May 1, 1766, was designed to raise £60,000 per year to help defray the costs of maintaining British troops in America. It taxed various types of printed matter, like newspapers, broadsides, and pamphlets, most legal documents, and luxury items like dice and playing cards. Most printers, like Isaiah Thomas, opposed the tax, but we may assume that part of the opposition arose from the burden it placed upon their businesses. However, taxation as a principle stirred discontent because the colonists feared a "domino theory" of taxation, and viewed the Stamp Tax and later Tea Tax as preludes to property tax, by which they might lose their status as freemen. A majority of American farmers, for example, owned their farmland, while in England exactly the opposite was true. Thus any taxation that might eventually lead to a loss of property was viewed with apprehension and suspicion, and the failure of Britain to allow colonial representation in Parliament only added fuel to the flame. The "right" of England to tax America became the focus, and it was a debate that England eventually lost.

In Parliament, the Stamp Act was advocated by George Grenville. Although Grenville advised enforcement of his act by military force, wisdom prevailed in Parliament and on March 18, the decision was made to repeal the unpopular Act as of May 1, 1766.

NATIONAL INDEX 10317
FORD 1371
AMERICAN ANTIQUARIAN SOCIETY
33.5 x 20.9 cm.

# Glorious News.

BOSTON, Friday 11 o'Clock, 16th *May* 1766.

THIS Instant arrived here the Brig Harrison, belonging to *John Hancock*, Esq; Captain *Shubael Coffin*, in 6 Weeks and 2 Days from LONDON, with important News, as follows.

From the LONDON GAZETTE.

*Westminster, March* 18th, 1766.

THIS day his Majesty came to the House of Peers, and being in his royal robes seated on the throne with the usual solemnity, Sir Francis Molineux, Gentleman Usher of the Black Rod, was sent with a Message from his Majesty to the House of Commons, commanding their attendance in the House of Peers. The Commons being come thither accordingly, his Majesty was pleased to give his royal assent to

An ACT to REPEAL an Act made in the last Session of Parliament, intituled, an Act for granting and applying certain Stamp-Duties and other Duties in the British Colonies and Plantations in America, towards further defraying the expences of defending, protecting and securing the same, and for amending such parts of the several Acts of Parliament relating to the trade and revenues of the said Colonies and Plantations, as direct the manner of determining and recovering the penalties and forfeitures therein mentioned.

Also ten public bills, and seventeen private ones.

Yesterday there was a meeting of the principal Merchants concerned in the American trade, at the King's Arms tavern in Cornhill, to consider of an Address to his Majesty on the beneficial Repeal of the late Stamp-Act.

Yesterday morning about eleven o'clock a great number of North American Merchants went in their coaches from the King's Arms tavern in Cornhill to the House of Peers, to pay their duty to his Majesty, and to express their satisfaction at his signing the Bill for Repealing the American Stamp-Act, there was upwards of fifty coaches in the procession.

Last night the said gentleman dispatched an express for Falmouth, with fifteen copies of the Act for repealing the Stamp-Act, to be forwarded immediately for New York.

Orders are given for several merchantmen in the river to proceed to sea immediately on their respective voyages to North America, some of whom have been cleared out since the first of November last.

Yesterday messengers were dispatched to Birmingham, Sheffield, Manchester, and all the great manufacturing towns in England, with an account of the final decision of an august assembly relating to the Stamp-Act.

---

When the KING went to the House of Peers to give the Royal Assent, there was such a vast Concourse of People, huzzaing, clapping Hands, &c. that it was several Hours before His Majesty reached the House.

Immediately on His Majesty's Signing the Royal Assent to the Repeal of the Stamp-Act the Merchants trading to America, dispatched a Vessel which had been in waiting, to put into the first Port on the Continent with the Account.

There were the greatest Rejoicings possible in the City of London, by all Ranks of People, on the TOTAL Repeal of the Stamp-Act,—the Ships in the River displayed all their Colours, Illuminations and Bonfires in many Parts. — In short, the Rejoicings were as great as was ever known on any Occasion.

It is said the Acts of Trade relating to America would be taken under Consideration, and all Grievances removed. The Friends to America are very powerful, and disposed to assist us to the utmost of their Ability.

Capt. Blake sailed the same Day with Capt. Coffin, and Capt. Shand a Fortnight before him, both bound to this Port.

*It is impossible to express the Joy the Town is now in, on receiving the above, great, glorious and important NEWS—The Bells in all the Churches were immediately set a Ringing, and we hear the Day for a general Rejoicing will be the beginning of next Week.*

---

PRINTED for the Benefit of the PUBLIC, by
*Drapers, Edes & Gill, Green & Russell*, and *Fleets*.
The Customers to the Boston Papers may have the above gratis at the respective Offices.

4. By His Excellency Francis Bernard, Esq.
[Boston: Richard Draper, 1769]

EVER since the appointment of Royal Governors for Massachusetts Bay Colony had been established in the seventeenth century, colonists had viewed the presence of royal authority as an intrusion into their affairs. Colonial Massachusetts governors like Edmund Andros and Francis Bernard were resented not only because they symbolized the presence of the English king and the arbitrary authority of Parliament, but also because their power was often asserted without regard for colonial feeling. In *The Stamp Act Crisis,* Edmund Morgan observes that although Bernard was not aware of the extent to which his administration was abhorred by the colonists, he was realistic enough to understand that reform was necessary in order to insure colonial cooperation with Parliament. In the middle colonies, Bernard was regarded as a symbol of the inadequacy of British authority, and he made the serious mistake of interpreting colonial opposition to the tyranny of Parliament as a personal insult to his administration. He saw his own ambition for personal power and prestige as a patriotic desire for British supremacy, and had visions of "a new colonial empire of which he should be the guiding genius, or in which at least his own dignity would be firmly established under the aegis of a supreme Parliament."

The present proclamation is harmless enough. It is a declaration announcing a day of general fasting, a practice in the Massachusetts Bay Colony dating from the early seventeenth century, when citizens would be reminded of the goodness of God's providence in guiding the colony on the errand into the wilderness. Blessings for the King, however, are also included, and the royal seal decorating the broadside is paralleled by *God Save the King,* a marked contrast to later broadsides that call upon the Almighty for salvation of the *American States,* or display the motto *God Save the People.* The apostrophe to God was a common motif on early broadsides and suggests a continuity of belief about the divine purpose in accordance with which America was founded, and through which she continued to grow.

NATIONAL INDEX 11329
FORD 1487
AMERICAN ANTIQUARIAN SOCIETY
38.4 x 30.1 cm.

By His EXCELLENCY

# *FRANCIS BERNARD*, Esq;

Captain-General and Governor in Chief, in and over His Majesty's Province of the *Massachusetts-Bay*, in *New England*, and Vice-Admiral of the same.

# A PROCLAMATION

## *For a General Fast.*

AS the Time is now approaching wherein it has been usual, according the laudable Custom of this Country, for the People on a Day appointed to humble themselves before Almighty GOD, and implore his Blessing upon the Business of the ensuing Year:

I HAVE thought fit to appoint, and I do, by and with the Advice and Consent of His Majesty's Council, appoint Thursday the Sixth Day of *April* next ensuing, to be a Day of Fasting and Prayer throughout this Province, that the Ministers of God's holy Word, with their several Congregations, may thereon prostrate themselves before the Throne of Grace, meekly confessing their Sins, and beseeching Almighty GOD, that notwithstanding our Unworthiness He would be pleased to continue his gracious Providence over us: And especially that He would be pleased to bless our most Gracious Sovereign the KING, in the Maintainance of his Health, Wealth, Peace and Honor, in the Preservation of his Royal Consort, their Issue, and all the Royal Family, and in the Prosperity of the whole British Empire, and all its Members and Dependencies; that He would be pleased to regard the People of this Province with the Eye of his Mercy, to prosper them in their Husbandry, Fishery and Trade, and to bless the Works of their Hands, and that they may reap the Fruits of the Earth in due Season and a sufficient Plenty; and above all, that He would be pleased to give us true Repentance, to forgive us all our Sins, and endue us with his Grace that we may amend our Lives according to his Word, and finally be accepted by him through the Merits and Mediation of his Son *JESUS CHRIST*.

And I command and enjoin all Magistrates and Civil Officers to see that the said Day be observed, as a Day set apart for Religious Worship, and that no servile Labour nor Recreation be permitted thereon.

*GIVEN at the Council-Chamber in* Boston, *the Eighth Day of* March, *in the Ninth Year of the Reign of our Sovereign Lord* GEORGE *the* Third, *by the Grace of GOD, of* GREAT-BRITAIN, FRANCE, *and* IRELAND, KING, *Defender of Faith*, &c. *and in the Year of our Lord* 1769.

By His Excellency's Command,
A. OLIVER, Secr'y.

*Fra. Bernard.*

## *GOD* Save the KING.

---

*BOSTON*: Printed by RICHARD DRAPER, Printer to His Excellency the Governor, and the Honourable His Majesty's Council, 1769.

## 5. The Tom-Cod Catcher
[Boston, 1769]

THIS broadside was printed soon after Governor Francis Bernard's departure for England on July 25, 1769. Bernard's arrogant administration and his policy of coercive despotism had been climaxed by his insistence that British troops be quartered in Boston at colonial expense. This was tantamount to requiring that hostile forces be treated as guests, and the colonists voiced such strong opposition that Bernard was recalled to England. The position of Royal Governor continued after his departure, but its authority had been reduced considerably.

Although Bernard is not directly identified as the subject of the poem, there can be no doubt of the poem's intended criticism of his administration. "Go, B[ernar]d, thou minion!—to thy country go/ For *Boston*, loud proclaims you, Freedom's foe; . . ." The "B——r——t" represents "Baronet," and throughout the poem, Bernard is compared to a devil, oppressive slave master, and tyrant. It is an important broadside because of the illustration as well, a clear woodcut depicting Bernard as a "Tom-Cod," or young cod, which was a term of ridicule. The famous Boston cod-catcher is here analagous to Britain's recall of the "young cod," and the poem was not the only way in which colonists celebrated Bernard's departure. Ola Winslow notes that "his departure, July 25, 1769, was the occasion for a noisy demonstration in Boston. Bells were rung, cannon fired, the Liberty Tree decked with flags, and a great bonfire built on Fort Hill. Various abusive verses were published, and, for a time, the word "baronet" became a term of ridicule and opprobrium. Bernard had received the title in April, 1769."

All of "The Tom-Cod Catcher" can be found in *Oppression. A Poem. By an American. With Notes, by a North Briton*, first printed in London and reprinted in Boston in 1765 as a pamphlet. The broadside's first twenty-four lines are on page 6 of *Oppression.* Of several changes the most important are "B——d" for "B——" and "Boston" for "England." Lines 25–36 are on page 8; in line 33 the broadside changes "it has" to "you have." The next lines (through "And make lost Liberty once more to reign") are from page 13. Lines 39–48 follow page 7 with two lines of the original dropped. The next fifteen lines (to "With arms a-kimbo, deal to each its fate") are from page 9 of the pamphlet, omitting one verse. Lines 64–79 are on page 11, with two verses dropped and the line "And be a Tyrant, Verres, or a Devil" revised from "And be a B——R——N, Cartouch or a Devil." The broadside continues from page 11 through "To make you love them, and to fear their frown." The only significant changes in the final verses, from pages 15–16, are "****" and "*****" to "K***" and "C****." The chance discovery of this adaptation leads one to ponder how many ballads or poems are "borrowed." Even a first-line index would not solve the problem.

NATIONAL INDEX 42013
BRISTOL 3084
FORD 1505
WEGELIN 701
AMERICAN ANTIQUARIAN SOCIETY
37.5 x 25 cm.

The Tom-Cod Catcher.

ON

# The DEPARTURE of an infamous B-R---T.

Gov.r

GO B------d, thou minion !--- to thy country go,
For BOSTON, loud proclaims you, Freedom's foe ;
Why will you ſtay, where mankind ſcorns your name
Where ev'ry year adds blackneſs to your fame,
Where if you die, few friends your deeds will bawl,
In Britiſh cries, or ditties of Fingall ?
Haſte, haſte O B------d, and betake your way,
Where ſnows eternal chill the face of Day :
Where torped rocks and mountains threat' the ſkies,
And hills o're hills in barren pomp ariſe ;
Where poverty ſupreme for ever reigns,
Nor envy'd wealth, diſturb the peaſants brains.
E'en croaking ravens, will rejoice your flight,
And join in chorus with the birds of night :
The rav'nous tyger, with the hind will play,
And glad with joy, th' unfeeling aſs will bray.
If thus all nature for your abſence long,
What wonder then, if I ſhould join the throng :
When yet of evils, I more feel can name,
Enough to blaſt you to the lateſt fame :
Of ills ! that half the northern world annoys,
That mars their trade, their liberty deſtroys,
That makes them ſlaves, or meer mechanick tools,
To work for nought, as fools do work for fools.
Go on ye Pilferer, with all the rage
That half-ſtarv'd ſpani'ls for a bone engage,
Be like your brothers here, a tyrant crew,
Do all that fell rapacious ſouls can do ;
Make right and wrong an equal ballance hold,
And prove or diſapprove, as weighs the gold.
Like theſe, in all the majeſty of deſk,
Look big, command, and flout, and jeer the beſt.
As you have done, the laſt paſſing year,
Made the new world in anger ſhed the tear ;
Unmindful, of their native once lov'd iſle,
They'll bid All-g--nce ceaſe her peaceful ſmile,
While from their arms, they tear Oppreſſion's chain,
And make loſt LIBERTY once more to reign.
Could thoſe brave heroes, who now ſleep in reſt,
But know how much their children are oppreſs'd,
Methinks they'd riſe and murmur from their graves,
" Were we not wretched ! muſt our ſons be ſlaves !
" Are there no ſtores of vengeance for that race ?
" That long have dar'd th' Almighty to his face,
" Who to half earth have prov'd ſo fell a peſt,
" That living, dying, and the dead can't reſt ;"
And as they vaniſh'd, pray ; " Hear, oh my God !
" Preſerve this country from a TYRANT's rod."
Shall ſuch low vagrants, whom ſome L--D has raiſ'd,
For ſuch harſh conduct be eſteem'd or praiſ'd ?
Are they more faithful to the S-te or C-- n,
Than thoſe whoſe honeſty, with friendſhip join ?
No ! I proclaim that man at once a knave,
Who ſcorns thoſe virtues which adorn the brave :
Honour can't bind him, that no friendſhip knows,
He's ſure a villain, that delights in woes,
And proves or diſapproves as profit flows.
Muſt it not fill all men of ſenſe with ſcorn,
To ſee a muckworm of the earth, low born,
The chance production of ſome am'rous ſpark,
In ignorance ſupreme, profoundly dark ?
To ſee him ſeat his mighty ſelf in ſtate,
With arms a-kimbo, deal to each its fate.
Fly cringing minion ! from all converſe fly,
Den with the wolves, and learn the wolv'rins cry,
Go join in concert with the croaking frogs,
Or howl in chorus with a pack of dogs ;
With monkeys go, and chatter on a ſtage,
Or turn a maſtiff, and each curr engage.
Better do worſe ! turn pandor, pimp or ſlave,
Turn highway-man, turn murderer, or knave ;
All do, that thy fell ſoul can think as evil,
And be a Tyrant, Verres, or a Devil.
What are ſuch crimes ? when ballanc'd with the woes,
That from the vagrant ! to thy country flows ;
Meer nought and trifling, light as empty air,
They harm but few, but theſe whole countries ſhare ;
On one on all, th' oppreſſive evil lights,
And like a tyrant robs them of their rights.
Can jealouſy extend its horrid ſway
To harm the tender offspring of a day,
To hurt a country, but in opening bud,
A people link'd by ſtrongeſt ties of blood ?
It can, it does, all kindred ties begone ?
Nought here but riches pleaſe the rav'nous throng ;
A golden fury, rages in each breaſt,
Let ſink who will, or ſwim, they will be bleſt.
Like fools they've plan'd, it is to keep you down,
To make you love them, and to fear their frown.
Were I a K*** ! I'd think it noble ſport.
To kick ſuch mongril tyrants from my C****.
No knaviſh ſoul, that's aggrandiz'd by wealth,
Obtain'd by force, or got by meaneſt ſtealth ;
Should tread the threſhold of the R---l dome,
But like a robber, be exil'd from home ;
Or ſhare, what beſt becomes a thieviſh wretch,
A Tyburn ſalutation from a Ketch.

## 6. A Poem, in Memory of the Fifth of March, 1770 [Boston, 1770]

THE Boston Massacre has been the subject of considerable academic and political controversy ever since the tragic evening when Britain's Twenty-Ninth Regiment killed or wounded many of the determined colonists in King Street. An "official" account was published soon after, the result of an extensive investigation involving both British and American testimony, which was called *A Short Narrative of the Horrid Massacre in Boston Perpetrated in the Evening of the Fifth Day of March, 1770, by Soldiers of the XXIXth Regiment.* This document was printed by order of the town of Boston, and it was sold by a well-known revolutionary printer, Benjamin Edes, in Queen Street. It was also distributed widely in London.

The information contained in the main body of this booklet is straightforward; it was obtained from lengthy courtroom depositions which were taken from witnesses to the massacre and from some of its participants. But the conclusions expressed here are clearly biased in favor of colonial views: "they were deeply impressed and affected by the tragedy of the preceding night, and were unanimously of opinion, it was incompatible with their safety that the troops should remain any longer in the town." A more objective account, and by far the most comprehensive version of the events surrounding the Boston Massacre, is provided in Hiller Zobel's recent book, *The Boston Massacre.* One chapter is devoted to the detailed events of that specific, historical moment, and a dramatic, but accurate narrative explains how Colonel Preston, the officer in charge of the Twenty-Ninth Regiment, escaped culpability for the order to fire.

The illustrations on this broadside are noteworthy. Coffins had been used to decorate elegies and funeral sermons since the late seventeenth century, and here, they serve a double purpose, for they are also intended to stir resentment and hostility toward English rule. The propagandistic purpose of this funeral elegy for those five young men slain in the Boston Massacre is reinforced by the language of the poem itself. Christopher Seider, the young boy who was killed by Ebeneezer Richardson, is also mentioned, further emphasizing the atrocities of British rule. Divine vengeance is invoked to restore justice, and the poem concludes with a quatrain reminding colonists that their free land has been invaded by tyrants, and that unless it is defended, freedom will disappear from the face of the earth. Though the poem and the broadside retain the form of a funeral elegy, the narrative is less about the virtues of the deceased, the usual subject of earlier funeral elegies, than about the injustice of the massacre as a historical event.

NATIONAL INDEX 42156
BRISTOL 3251
MASSACHUSETTS HISTORICAL SOCIETY
33.5 x 20.5 cm.

A

# P O E M,

## IN MEMORY of the (never to be forgotten)

# FIFTH of MARCH,

## 1770.

On the Evening of which, a Party of the 29th. Regiment commanded by Capt. Preston, fired upon the Inhabitants in King-Street, by which five persons were Killed Viz.

SAMUEL GRAY, JAMES CALDWELL, PATRICK CARR.
SAMUEL MAVERICK, CRISPUS ATTUCKS, and

I.

THE rising sun bespeaks the mournful day,
When youth's, (though innocent) in blood did lay,
When bloody men shot forth the darts of death,
FIVE of our fellow-creatures drop'd their breath.

II.

Look into king-street! there with weeping eyes
Repair O Boston's sons----there hear the cries!
There see the men lie in their wallow'd gore!
There see their bodies, which fierce bullets tore!

III.

There hear their dying shrieks! their dying cries,
(Though but a few) before they clos'd their eyes!
Before the living took the dead away,
Those barb'rous monsters pierc'd them as they lay.

IV.

Down in the dark and silent graves they lye,
Their bodies rests, but vengeance is the cry.
O! may this day then never be forgot;
Remember well the place;—the bloody spot,

V.

Where, like a current, christians blood did flow,
No one can tell what they did undergo.
Step to the burying-ground, and there behold
The bones of FIVE, which now in dust are roll'd,

VI.

Who fell a prey to wicked treach'rous men,
But all the Murd'rers will be judg'd again.
Is it consistent with the laws of GOD,
To see such guilty Murd'rers go abroad?

VII.

Young SEIDER's fate we ought now to bemoan,
And drop a tear on his unhappy tomb;
He was the first that fell in a just cause;
His Murd'rer now must dye by Heaven's laws.

VIII.

Justice demands, and vengeance loud doth cry,
Come forth, O! RICHARDSON, for thou must die.
You acted then against the laws of GOD,
And now must feel the scourges of his rod.

IX.

Ho! all ye Murd'rers, hear what GOD doth say,
"Vengeance belongs to me, I will repay."------
Though you are clear'd on earth, you are not free,
The GOD of glory soon will summons thee.

X.

Young MONK, whose wounds afflict his body sore,
He feels great pain, and soon will be no more.
O! may he find some gen'rous friends to give,
So that he may not want while he does live.

XI.

If bloody men intrudes upon our land,
Where shall we go? or whither shall we stand?
Then may I wander to some distant shoar,
Where man nor beast had never trod before.

Printed and Sold next to the Writing-School, in Queen-Street.

## 7. An Account of a Late Military Massacre at Boston
[Boston: Edes & Gill?, 1770]

ACCORDING to Hiller Zobel's *The Boston Massacre*, the Paul Revere engraving of the Boston Massacre is a "demonstrably and designedly inaccurate propaganda piece." The massacre was perhaps the most celebrated event of the Revolutionary era before Lexington and Concord. This large broadside incorporates both the engraving by Revere and the extensive newspaper account of the event which was published in the *Boston Gazette*. The engraving was originally published in an edition of 800 copies, late in March of 1770, and then was used again on this broadside. Some historians feel that Revere originally intended his engraving of the massacre to be sold independently, aside from its later use as a broadside decoration, since some extant copies were mounted in contemporary frames.

Whether this broadside is considered propaganda, a news story, or simply a graphic reminder of the tensions that existed between Great Britain and Massachusetts Bay, it was an important document in its time, providing a visual if distorted account of the incident. The presence of coffins with the initials of the victims would certainly have stirred public sentiment, the coffin motif being a commonplace for elegies and broadsides announcing public executions or accidents, so the Revere picture offered a unique and most unusual view of the British atrocity—as the colonists understood it.

NATIONAL INDEX 42050
BRISTOL 3156
NEW-YORK HISTORICAL SOCIETY
48.2 x 39 cm.

# [A]n Account of a late Military Massacre at Boston, or the Consequences of Quartering Troops in a populous well-regulated Town, taken from the [Bo]ston-Gazette, of March 12, 1770.

**BOSTON, March 12, 1770.**

THE Town of Boston affords a recent and melancholy Demonstration of the destructive Consequences of quartering Troops among Citizens in a Time of Peace, under a Pretence of supporting the Laws and aiding Civil Authority; every considerate and unprejudic'd Person among us was deeply imprest with the Apprehension of these Consequences when it was known that a Number of Regiments were ordered to this Town under such a Pretext, but in Reality to inforce oppressive Measures; to awe and controul the legislative as well as executive Power of the Province, and to quell a Spirit of Liberty, which however it may have been basely oppos'd and even ridicul'd by some, would do Honor to any Age or Country. A few Persons amongst us had determin'd to use all their Influence to procure so destructive a Measure with a View to their securely enjoying the Profits of an American Revenue, and unhappily both for Britain and this Country they found Means to effect it.

It is to Governor Bernard, the Commissioners, their Confidents and Coadjutors, that we are indebted as the procuring Cause of a military Power in this Capital—The Boston Journal of Occurrences, as printed in Mr. Holt's York Gazette, from Time to Time, afforded many striking Instances of the Distresses brought upon the Inhabitants by this Measure; and since those Journals have been discontinued, our Troubles from that Quarter have been growing upon us: We have known a Party of Soldiers in the face of Day fire off a loaden Musket upon the Inhabitants, others have been prick'd with their Bayonets, and even our Magistrates assaulted and put in Danger of their Lives, when Offenders brought before them have been rescued; and why those and other bold and base Criminals have as yet escaped the Punishment due to their Crimes, may be soon Matter of Enquiry by the Representative Body of this People—It is natural to suppose that when the Inhabitants of this Town saw those Laws which had been enacted for their Security, and which they were ambitious of holding up to the Soldiery, eluded, they should more commonly resent for themselves—and accordingly it has so happened; many have been the Squabbles between them and the Soldiery; but it seems their being often worsted by our Youth in those Rencounters, has only serv'd to irritate the former—What passed at Mr. Gray's Rope-walk, has already been given the Public, and may be said to have led the Way to the late Catastrophe—That the Rope-walk Lads when attaked by superior Numbers should defend themselves with so much Spirit and Success in the Club-way, was too mortifying, and perhaps it may hereafter appear, that even some of their Officers were *unhappily* affected with this Circumstance: Divers Stories were propagated among the Soldiery, that serv'd to agitate their Spirits; particularly on the Sabbath, that one Chambers, a Serjeant, represented as a sober Man, had been missing the preceeding Day, and must therefore have been murdered by the Townsmen; an Officer of Distinction so far credited this Report, that he enter'd Mr. Gray's Rope-walk that Sabbath; and when required of by that Gentleman as soon as he could meet him, the Occasion of his so doing, the Officer reply'd, that it was to look if the Sergeant said to be murdered had not been hid there; this sober Sergeant was found on the Monday unhurt, in a House of Pleasure—The Evidences already collected shew, that many Threatnings had been thrown out by the Soldiery, but we do not pretend to say that there was any preconcerted Plan, when the Evidences are published, the World will judge—We may however venture to declare, that it appears too probable from their Conduct, that some of the Soldiery aimed to draw and provoke the Townsmen into Squabbles, and that they then intended to make Use of other Weapons than Canes, Clubs or Bludgeons.

Our Readers will doubtless expect a circumstantial Account of the tragical Affair on Monday Night last; but we hope they will excuse our being so particular as we should have been, had we not seen that the Town was intending an Enquiry and full Representation thereof.

On the Evening of Monday, being the 5th Current, several Soldiers of the 29th Regiment were seen parading the Streets with their drawn Cutlasses and Bayonets, abusing and wounding Numbers of the Inhabitants.

A few minutes after nine o'clock, four youths, named Edward Archbald, William Merchant, Francis Archbald, and John Leech, jun. came down Cornhill together, and seperating at Doctor Loring's corner, the two former were passing the narrow alley leading to Murray's barrack, in which was a soldier brandishing a broad sword of an uncommon size against the walls out of which he struck fire plentifully. A person of a mean countenance armed with a large cudgel bore him company. Edward Archbald admonished Mr. Merchant to take care of the sword, on which the soldier turned round and struck Archbald on the arm, then pushed at Merchant and pierced thro' his cloaths inside the arm close to the arm-pit and grazed the skin. Merchant then struck the soldier with a short stick he had, and the other Person ran to the barrack and bro't with him two soldiers, one armed with a pair of tongs the other with a shovel: he with the tongs pursued Archbald back thro' the alley, collar'd and laid him over the head with the tongs. The noise bro't people together, and John Hicks, a young lad, coming up, knock'd the soldier down, but let him get up again; and more lads gathering, drove them back to the barrack, where the boys stood some time as it were to keep them in. In less than a minute 10 or 12 of them came out with drawn cutlasses, clubs & bayonets, and set upon the unarmed boys and young folks, who stood them a little while, but finding the inequality of their equipment dispersed.—On hearing the noise, one Samuel Atwood, came up to see what was the matter, and entering the alley from dock-square, heard the latter part of the combat, and when the boys had dispersed he met the 10 or 12 soldiers aforesaid rushing down the alley towards the square, and asked them if they intended to murder people? They answered Yes, by G—d, root and branch! With that one of them struck Mr. Atwood with a club, which was repeated by another, and being unarmed he turned to go off, and received a wound on the left shoulder which reached the bone and gave him much pain. Retreating a few steps, Mr. Atwood met two officers and said, Gentlemen, what is the matter? They answered, you'll see by and by. Immediately after, those heroes appeared in the square, asking where were the boogers? where were the cowards? But notwithstanding their fierceness to naked men, one of them advanced towards a youth who had a split of a raw stave in his hand, and said damn them here is one of them; but the young man seeing a person near him with a drawn sword and good cane ready to support him, held up his stave in defiance, and they quietly passed by him up the little alley by Mr. Silsby's to Kingstreet, where they attacked single and unarmed persons till they raised much clamor, and then turned down Cornhill street, insulting all they met in like manner, and pursuing some to their very doors. Thirty or forty persons mostly lads, being by this means gathered in King street, Capt. Preston, with a party of men with charged bayonets, came from the main guard to the commissioners house, the soldiers pushing their bayonets, crying, Make way! They took place by the custom-house, and continuing to push to drive the people off, pricked some in several places; on which they were clamorous, and, it is said, threw snow-balls. On this, the Captain commanded them to fire, and more snow-balls coming, he again said, Damn you, Fire, be the consequence what it will! One soldier then fired, and a townsman with a cudgel struck him over the hands with such force that he dropt his firelock; and rushing forward aimed a blow at the Captain's head, which graz'd his hat and fell pretty heavy upon his arm: However, the soldiers continued the fire, successively, till 7 or 8, or as some say 11 guns were discharged.

By this fatal manœuvre, three men were laid dead on the spot, and two more struggling for life; but what shewed a degree of cruelty unknown to British troops, at least since the house of Hanover has directed their operations, was an attempt to fire upon or push with their bayonets the persons who undertook to remove the slain and wounded!

Mr. Benjamin Leigh, now undertaker in the Delph Manufactory, came up, and after some conversation with Capt. Preston, relative to his conduct in this affair, advised him to draw off his men, with which he complied.

The dead are Mr. Samuel Gray, killed on the spot, the ball entering his head and beating off a large portion of his skull.

A mulatto man, named Crispus Attucks, who was born in Framingham, but lately belonged to New-Providence and was here in order to go for North-Carolina, also killed instantly; two balls entering his breast, one of them in special goring the right lobe of the lungs, and a great part of the liver most horribly.

Mr. James Caldwell, mate of Capt. Morton's vessel, in like manner killed by two balls entering his back.

Mr. Samuel Maverick, a promising youth of 17 years of age, son of the Widow Maverick, and an apprentice to Mr. Greenwood, Ivory-Turner, mortally wounded, a ball went through his belly, and was cut out at his back: He died the next morning.

A lad named Christopher Monk, about 17 years of age, an apprentice to Mr. Walker, Shipwright; wounded a ball entered his back about 4 inches above the left kidney, near the spine, and was cut out of the breast on the same side; apprehended he will die.

A lad named John Clark, about 17 years of age, whose parents live at Medford, and an apprentice to Capt. Samuel Howard of this town; wounded, a ball entered just above his groin and came out at his hip, on the opposite side, apprehended he will die.

Mr. Edward Payne, of this town, Merchant, standing at his entry-door, received a ball in his arm, shattered some of the bones.

Mr. John Green, Taylor, coming up Leverett's Lane, received a ball just under his hip, and lodged in the under part of his thigh, which was extracted.

Mr. Robert Patterson, a seafaring man, who was the person that had his trowsers shot through in Richardson's affair, wounded; a ball went thro' his right arm, and he suffered great loss of blood.

Mr. Patrick Carr, about 30 years of age, who work'd with Mr. Field, Leather-Breeches-maker in Queen-street, wounded, a ball enter'd near his hip and went out at his side.

A lad named David Parker, an apprentice to Mr. Eddy the Wheelwright, wounded, a ball entered in his thigh.

The People were immediately alarmed with the Report of this horrid Massacre, the Bells were set a Ringing, and great Numbers soon assembled at the Place where this tragical Scene had been acted; their Feelings may be better conceived than express'd; and while some were taking Care of the Dead and Wounded, the Rest were in Consultation what to do in those dreadful Circumstances.—But so little intimidated where they, notwithstanding their being within a few Yards of the Main-Guard, and seeing the 29th Regiment under Arms, and drawn up in King-Street; that they kept their Station and appear'd as an Officer of Rank express'd it ready to run upon the very Muzzles of their Muskets.—The Lieut. Governor soon came into the Town-House, and there met some of his Majesty's Council, and a Number of Civil Magistrates; a considerable Body of the People immediately entered the Council Chamber, and expressed themselves to his Honor with a Freedom and Warmth becoming the occasion. He used his utmost Endeavours to pacify them, requesting that they would let the Matter subside for the Night, and promising to do all in his Power that Justice should be done, and the Law have its Course; Men of Influence and Weight with the People were not wanting on their part to procure their Compliance with his Honor's Request by representing the horrible Consequences of a promiscuous and rash Engagement in the Night, and assuring them that such Measures should be entered upon in the Morning as would be agreeable to their Dignity, and a more likely way of obtaining the best Satisfaction for the Blood of their Fellow-Townsmen.—The Inhabitants attended to these Suggestions, and the Regiment under Arms being ordered to their Barracks, which was insisted upon by the People, they then separated and returned to their Dwellings by One o'Clock, at 3 o'Clock Capt. Preston was committed, as were the Soldiers who fir'd, a few Hours after him.

Tuesday Morning presented a most shocking Scene, the Blood of our Fellow Citizens running like Water thro' King-Street, and the Merchants Exchange the principal Spot of the Military Parade for about 18 Months past. Our Blood might also be track'd up to the Head of Long-Lane, and through divers other Streets and Passages.

At eleven o'clock the inhabitants met at Faneuil-Hall, and after some animated speeches becoming the occasion, they chose a Committee of 15 respectable Gentlemen to wait upon the Lieut. Governor in Council, to request of him to issue his Orders for the immediate removal of the troops.

The Message was in these Words:

*THAT it is the unanimous opinion of this meeting that the inhabitants and soldiery can no longer live together in safety; that nothing can rationally be expected to restore the peace of the town and prevent further blood and carnage, but the immediate removal of the Troops; and that we therefore most fervently pray his Honor that his power and influence may be exerted for their instant removal.*

His Honor's Reply, which was laid before the Town then Adjourn'd to the Old South Meeting-House, was as follows,

Gentlemen,

*I AM extremely sorry for the unhappy differences between the inhabitants and troops, and especially for the action of the last evening, and I have exerted myself upon that occasion that a due enquiry may be made, and that the law may have its course. I have in council consulted with the commanding officers of the two regiments who are in the town. They have their orders from the General at New-York. It is not in my power to countermand those orders. The Council have desired that the two regiments may be removed to the Castle. From the particular concern which the 29th regiment has had in your differences, Col. Dalrymple who is the commanding officer of the troops has signified that that regiment shall without delay be placed in the barracks at the Castle until he can send to the General and receive his further orders concerning both the regiments, and that the main guard shall be removed, and the 14th regiment so disposed and laid under such restraint that all occasion of future disturbances may be prevented.*

The foregoing Reply having been read and fully considered—the question was put, Whether the Report be satisfactory? Passed in the Negative. (only 1 dissentient) out of upwards of 4000 Voters.

It was then moved & voted that John Hancock, Esq; Mr. Samuel Adams, Mr. William Molineux, William Phillips, Esq; Dr. Joseph Warren, Joshua Henshaw, Esq; and Samuel Pemberton, Esq; be a Committee to wait on his Honour the Lieut. Governor, and inform him, that it is the unanimous Opinion of this Meeting, that the Reply made to a Vote of the Inhabitants presented his Honor in the Morning, is by no means satisfactory; and that nothing less will satisfy, than a total and immediate removal of all the Troops.

The Committee having waited upon the Lieut. Governor agreeable to the foregoing Vote; laid before the Inhabitants the following Vote of Council received from his Honor.

His Honor the Lieut. Governor laid before the Board a Vote of the Town of Boston, passed this Afternoon, and then addressed the Board as follows.

*Gentlemen of the Council,*

"I lay before you a Vote of the Town of Boston, which I have just now received from them, and I now ask your Advice what you judge necessary to be done upon it.

The Council thereupon expressed themselves to be *unanimously* of opinion, "that it was absolutely necessary for his Majesty's service, the good order of the Town, and the Peace of the Province, that the Troops should be immediately removed out of the Town of Boston, and thereupon advised his Honor to communicate this Advice of the Council to Col. Dalrymple, and to pray that he would order the Troops down to Castle-William." The Committee also informed the Town, that Col. Dalrymple, after having seen the Vote of Council, said to the Committee, "That he now gave his word of Honor that he would begin his Preparations in the Morning, and that there should be no unnecessary delay until the whole of the two Regiments were removed to the Castle."

Upon the above Report being read, the Inhabitants could not avoid expressing the high Satisfaction it afforded them.

After Measures were taken for the Security of the Town in the Night by a strong Military Watch, the Meeting was Dissolved.

The 29th Regiment have already left us, and the 14th Regiment are following them, so that we expect the Town will soon be clear of all the Troops. The Wisdom and true Policy of his Majesty's Council and Col. Dalrymple the Commander appear in this Measure. Two Regiments in the midst of this populous City; and the Inhabitants justly incensed: Those of the neighbouring Towns actually under Arms upon the first Report of the Massacre, and the Signal only wanting to bring in a few Hours to the Gates of this City many Thousands of our brave Brethren in the Country, deeply affected with our Distresses, and to whom we are greatly obliged on this Occasion—No one knows where this would have ended, and what important Consequences even to the whole British Empire might have followed, which our Moderation and Loyalty upon so trying an Occasion, and our Faith in the Commander's Assurances have happily prevented.

Last Thursday, agreeable to a general Request of the Inhabitants, and by the Consent of Parents and Friends, were carried to their *Grave* in Succession, the Bodies of *Samuel Gray, Samuel Maverick, James Caldwell,* and *Crispus Attucks*, the unhappy Victims who fell in the bloody Massacre of the Monday Evening preceeding!

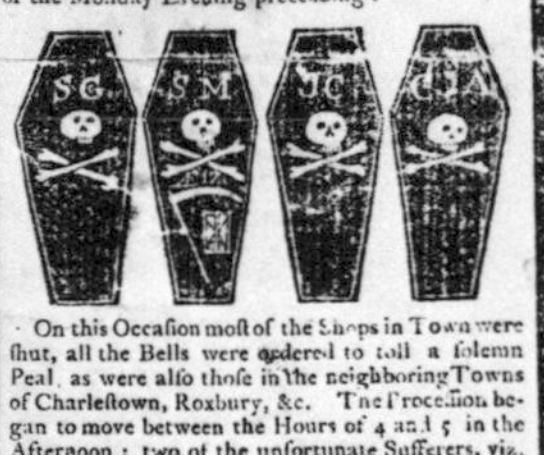

On this Occasion most of the Shops in Town were shut, all the Bells were ordered to toll a solemn Peal, as were also those in the neighboring Towns of Charlestown, Roxbury, &c. The Procession began to move between the Hours of 4 and 5 in the Afternoon; two of the unfortunate Sufferers, viz. Messi. *James Caldwell* and *Crispus Attucks*, who were Strangers, borne from Faneuil-Hall, attended by a numerous Train of Persons of all Ranks; and the other two, viz. Mr. *Samuel Gray*, from the House of Benjamin Gray, (his Brother) on the North-side the Exchange, and Mr. *Maverick*, from the House of his distressed Mother Mrs. *Mary Maverick*, in Union-Street, each followed by their respective Relations and Friends: The several Hearses forming a Junction in King-Street, the Theatre of that inhuman Tragedy! proceeded from thence thro' the Main-Street, lengthened by an immense Concourse of People, so numerous as to be obliged to follow in Ranks of six, and brought up by a long Train of Carriages belonging to the principal Gentry of the Town. The Bodies were deposited in one Vault in the middle Burying-ground: The aggravated Circumstances of their Death, the Distress and Sorrow visible in every Countenance, together with the peculiar Solemnity with which the whole Funeral was conducted, surpass Description.

**BOSTON, March 19.**

Last Wednesday Night died, *Patrick Carr*, an Inhabitant of this Town, of the Wound he received in King-Street on the bloody and execrable Night of the 5th Instant—He had just before left his Home, and upon his coming into the Street received the fatal Ball in his Hip which passed out at the opposite Side; this is the fifth Life that has been sacrificed by the Rage of the Soldiery, but it is feared it will not be the last, as several others are dangerously languishing of their Wounds. His Remains were attended on Saturday last from Faneuil-Hall by a numerous and respectable Train of Mourners, to the *same* Grave, in which those who fell by the *same* Hands of Violence were interred the last Week.

---

THE BLOODY MASSACRE perpetrated in King Street BOSTON on March 5th 1770 by a party of the 29th REGt.

Unhappy BOSTON! see thy Sons deplore,
Thy hallow'd Walks besmear'd with guiltless Gore:
While faithless P—n and his savage Bands,
With murd'rous Rancour stretch their bloody Hands;
Like fierce Barbarians grinning o'er their Prey,
Approve the Carnage and enjoy the Day.

If scalding drops from Rage from Anguish Wrung,
If speechless Sorrows lab'ring for a Tongue,
Or if a weeping World can ought appease
The plaintive Ghosts of Victims such as these;
The Patriot's copious Tears for each are shed,
A glorious Tribute which embalms the Dead.

But know, Fate summons to that awful Goal,
Where JUSTICE strips the Murd'rer of his Soul:
Should venal C—ts the scandal of the Land,
Snatch the relentless Villain from her Hand,
Keen Execrations on this Plate inscrib'd,
Shall reach a JUDGE who never can be brib'd.

*The unhappy Sufferers were Mess.rs* SAM.L GRAY, SAM.L MAVERICK, JAM.S CALDWELL, CRISPUS ATTUCKS & PAT.K CARR *Killed. Six wounded; two of them* (CHRIST.R MONK & JOHN CLARK) *Mortally*

8. An Address to the True-Born Sons of Liberty
[Boston?, 1772?]

THE "sons of Liberty" were the radicals of the American revolutionary era, but were not one single group whose membership was closed to outsiders. Apparently the criterion for meriting the designation was undeviating loyalty to the insurgent cause, and this broadside shows clearly that "whenever their constituents neglect to call them to account for such their neglect and breach of trust, they are not worthy the name of the SONS OF LIBERTY, the name of SLAVE is more suitable, for slaves they really are, and are fit for nothing else; for it plainly shews that they don't know they are imposed upon, or that they are such cowardly bastards they dare not assert their rights."

This may have been strong language, but the actions of these Liberty groups were even more threatening. Born accidentally in Sir Isaac Barre's 1765 speech in the House of Commons (in which he opposed the Stamp Act and referred to these "sons of liberty"), the radical groups formed ad hoc associations that were variously labeled Committees of Correspondence, Committees of Safety, "true-born Whigs," or simply "citizens," according to Mark Boatner's *Encyclopedia of the American Revolution.* "Their rhetoric was usually emotional, and their actions intimidating. Tars and feathers were instruments of persuasion, and Samuel Adams' group popularized the name 'Sons of Liberty,' giving it the authority and authenticity of a political party in the wings."

NATIONAL INDEX 42310
BRISTOL 3420
FORD 1605
AMERICAN ANTIQUARIAN SOCIETY
36.2 x 24.5 cm.

# An ADDRESS to the *True-born Sons of Liberty* in the Government of the *Maſſachuſetts-Bay.*

GENTLEMEN,

THE ſpirit with which you have of late oppoſed the ſtamp act, ſhews, that you have taken upon you, to think ſomething of ſtate affairs. Go on my friends, and inquire further: It is the proper buſineſs of every man, who is governed by laws, to ſtudy into the nature of thoſe laws; and wherever he finds an error, point it out, in order for amendment. I beg of you go on, and inquire into the conſtitution and oeconomy of this government: And if your rights and liberties are invaded, ſtudy what meaſures you muſt take for redreſs; and be, (as you were in the late caſe of the ſtamp act) united in thoſe meaſures, and you are morally certain of ſucceſs and remedy. The method you have taken to put a ſtop to the ſtamp act, (however exploded by ſome deſigning perſons) are, for aught I know, the only method to oppoſe deſpotiſm. But if all your conduct in oppoſing that hateful act of parliament cannot be approved of, ſome part of it may, without juſt offence to any body, viz. your giving particular inſtructions to your reſpective repreſentatives, how to act on that matter. And if this practice ſhould take place in general throughout this government, with reſpect to the common and ordinary buſineſs of government, it might relieve us from (near or quite) as great a tax, as the ſtamp act would have been, had it taken place, which no doubt will be obvious to you all, if you will inquire into the common and ordinary conduct of our own general court, in years paſt; for as a ſecret I can tell you, that all our oppreſſors are not on the other ſide the atlantic.

Within a few years paſt, (as I have been inform'd) it hath been a practice of ſome perſon or perſons, to draw money out of the publick treaſury of this province, without a vote or the conſent of the houſe of repreſentatives for ſo doing. And it hath alſo been a practice of our general court, to make very large grants of our money, and property, to particular perſons, which was as diſſatisfactory, (in the time of it) to many of you, as it would be to you now, to have the ſtamp act take place. And if any ſhould aſk, what grants thoſe were, it may be anſwered, the grant made to the honorable Edmond Trowbridge, Eſq; of about a Thouſand Dollars, to make up the loſſes he had ſuſtain'd by being in the office of attorney general; and there is not the leaſt doubt, but that he took that office for ſake of the profits of it, and that the profits are adequate to the ſervice, or a man of his underſtanding would never have taken it, and kept it, ſo long as he has done; for there is no penalty for refuſing to ſerve as an attorney. And other grants of large ſums made to ThomasGoldthwait, Eſq; ſecretary of war ſo called, an office quite new and unknown before, and of our G—r's coining, which made way for a grant to adjutant general Bratile, who, the court thought in juſtice ought to have one, as he had before ſerved longer and to great Acceptance in the ſame buſineſs, tho' not with the ſame title, & had neither charged or received one farthing therefor. And alſo ſeveral grants in money & land to the value of ſeveral hundred pounds, made to the hon. Timo. Ruggles, Eſq; for ſerving the province in the office of brigadier-general, &c. for which his wages was £.30 L. M. per month; and he very gratefully rewards the province by charging only a Guinea per day for his time, in going to New-York to the late Congreſs; (but to the honor of the preſent court, be it ſpoken, they did not allow his account) but however, he charg'd about eighty or ninety pounds for about a month's expence, to ſupport that delightful charmer, political dignity. Another grant the general court very generouſly made to each of the members of the court of a new law-book at the public expence. But the moſt extraordinary of all grants is, the granting ſuch extravagant fees to particular offices as are now eſtabliſh'd by the preſent fee table. And this is really making large grants to each other, which will appear very plain by anſwering truly theſe three queſtions.

Firſt, What offices in the government have thoſe fees?

Secondly, What offices have the majority of the members of the general court ſuſtain'd in the government?

Thirdly, Who granted them their fees; and in what manner were they granted?

To the firſt I anſwer, The ſheriffs, judge of probate, regiſter of probate, clerks of the courts, county-regiſter of deeds, and attorneys: Theſe are ſome of the offices that have thoſe fees.

To the ſecond I anſwer, That a great majority both in the council and houſe of repreſentatives have ſuſtain'd ſome one or other of the offices aforeſaid; or they were juſtices of the peace, or military officers; and theſe laſt were generally promoted according as they ſerv'd; ſerv'd w

The anſwer to the third queſtion is, They granted the fees themſelves, in the following manner; the houſe of repreſentatives prepar'd the fee table, and ſet the fees to the ſeveral offices that they each of them ſuſtain'd, high enough to pleaſe themſelves; and ſent it up to the council for their concurrence: and they very readily concur'd, if it pleas'd each of them; and then the governor was requeſted to ſign it, which he very readily did, if he was pleas'd; ſo that when the fee table was eſtabliſh'd, the court was pleas'd, with what? and the conſtituents was diſpleas'd, at what?

And thus it appears (that if they acted like other men in their circumſtances, and there is no doubt they did) that the preſent eſtabliſhment of fees are large grants of your money, which the members of the GeneralCourt made to each other. And in order to make a lucrative office for a court favourite, (for what other reaſon can be given for it?) it is but a few years ſince we had a ſtamp act eſtabliſhed by our own government, but then our own court could appoint their own favourite ſtamp maſter: But according to the late ſtamp act, the ſtamp maſter muſt be appointed by authority in OldEngland; and perhaps they might appoint their own favourite, who really has no right to the fleece of this country. I don't myſelf allow any body to rob me of the fleece of my own ſheep. I omit taking notice of officers fees relating to the cuſtom houſe, impoſt, &c. &c. and leave it to the almoſt ruined merchant to ſet thoſe matters in a proper light.

But gentlemen, I take it that the right of all appropriations of the public money is in the people. And when the governor or council, either ſeperately or together, appropriate any of the public money, without the conſent of the houſe of repreſentatives, they are liable to be called to account by the houſe of repreſentatives for ſuch miſconduct; and when the houſe of repreſentatives are remiſs in their duty in that reſpect, and allow the public money to be ſquandered away, or drawn out of the treaſury and appropriated unconſtitutionally, that then the repreſentatives are liable, and ought to be called to account by their conſtituents; and whenever their conſtituents neglect to call them to account for ſuch their neglect and breach of truſt, they are not worthy the name of the SONS OF LIBERTY, the name of *ſlave*, is more ſuitable, for ſlaves they really are, and are fit for nothing elſe; for it plainly ſhews that they don't know they are impoſed upon, or that they are ſuch cowardly baſtards they dare not aſſert their rights. And in order to prevent your being made the property of deſigning courtiers for the future, don't chuſe any of thoſe officers to repreſent you in the general court; they have an intereſt to ſerve diametrically oppoſite to yours; and for that reaſon ought not to be truſted. And when you have choſe a perſon to repreſent you in the general court (let his character or office be what it will) give him inſtructions for the rule of his conduct; it will give him boldneſs in court, and add weight to his arguments.

The following is humbly offered as proper inſtructions to be given for the preſent.

*Firſt.* That you uſe the whole of your influence, and endeavour that no perſon holding any fee or military office whatſoever, eſpecially judges of the ſuperiour court, ſecretary, &c. be choſen into his Majeſty's council of this province; and that you attend at the election of counſellors, and give your vote accordingly.

*Second,* That you endeavour as aforeſaid, that for the future the general court of this province be held in an open manner, that ſuch as are ſo minded, and behave agreeable to good order, may ſee and hear how affairs are conducted in ſaid court; and that this matter be determined by a vote of yeas and nays, that if the deſired end be not attain'd, we may not miſplace our reſentment; and if it be obtain'd, that a proper convenient houſe, both for the court and ſpectators be forthwith prepared.

*Third.* That you endeavour as aforeſaid, that the preſent fee table of this province be made null and void; and that a new fee table be made and eſtabliſhed inſtead thereof, which ſhall be more equal and impartial; not giving to any officer in the government, (except theGovernor) more, nor leſs, than you would be willing to do the ſame ſervice for yourſelf: And that you obſerve this rule in granting pay for contingent and occaſion ſervices

*Fourth,* That if there be any perſon or perſons who have taken money out of the treaſury of this province, without the conſent of the houſe of repreſentatives, that you call all ſuch perſons to account for the ſame, and order the ſaid perſons to replace all ſuch money in the ſaid treaſury again forthwith, and inform us your conſtituents of your ſucceſs, that if your order be not punctually complied with, the trueborn SONS OF LIBERTY may adviſe thereon.

*Fifth,* That you endeavour that there be no monopolizing of public offices in this government; and that one man be not inveſted with more than one office at one time, except it be compatible with the true intereſt of the people in general.

*Sixth,* That you take ſpecial care that we enjoy the free Liberty of the P R E S S, as well as all rights and liberties contain'd in theEngliſh conſtitution, and the charter of this province.

*Seventh,* That you make no grant of the public money or property, to make up the loſs any perſon or perſons have ſuſtained in the late tumults (raiſed by means of the ſtamp act) until we your conſtituents are made certain that the mob or mobs who have commited any outrages, were not raiſed on purpoſe to counteract and bring into diſgrace the true born SONS OF LIBERTY, and put a ſtop to their commendable proceeding.

*Eighth,* That you give diligent attendance at every ſeſſion of the general court of this province the preſent year, and adhere to theſeour inſtructions, (and the ſpirit of them) as you regard our friendſhip, and would avoid our juſt reſentment.

*N. B.* The author of the foregoing piece is not unaware that politicians may be inclin'd to pick flaws in his performance (and condemn right or wrong). But however, if they do, he appeals to the people in general for whom it was wrote, and deſires the SONS OF LIBERTY in every Town would inſiſt upon its being publickly read at the opening of their next May meeting for the choice of repreſentatives. And if he has done them good by writing it, he thinks himſelf well rewarded; if not, he hopes ſome abler hand will eſpouſe the cauſe, and do them all the good they ſtand in need of. And as this is the firſt time he hath ever appeared in print, he promiſes it ſhall be the laſt, without he ſhould think there is further occaſion.

A COUNTRYMAN.

## The following Gentlemen are Repreſentatives for the Towns following.

*Roxbury,* Joſeph Williams, Eſq;
*Dorcheſter,* John Robinſon, Eſq;
*Milton,* Stephen Miller, Eſq;
*Salem,* Andrew Oliver, Eſq;
——— William Brown, Eſq;
*Ipſwich,* Dr. John Calef,
*Newbury-Port,* Dudley Atkins, Eſq;
*Marblehead,* William Bourn, Eſq;
*Haverhill,* Richard Saltonſtall, Eſq;
*Cambridge,* Joſeph Lee, Eſq;
*Concord,* Charles Preſcott, Eſq;
*Reading,* Ebenezer Nichols, Eſq;
*Groton,* Abel Lawrence, Eſq;
*Chelmsford,* Sampſon Stoddard, Eſq;
*Medford,* Stephen Hall, Eſq;
*Sudbury,* John Noyes, Eſq;
*Lincoln,* Hon. Chambers Ruſſell, Eſq;
*Springfield,* John Worthington, Eſq;
*Northampton,* Timothy Dwight, Eſq;
*Plimouth,* Thomas Foſter, Eſq;
*Scituate,* Thomas Clapp, Eſq;
*Marſhfield,* John Winſlow, Eſq;
*Bridgwater,* Daniel Howard, Eſq;
*Middleboro',* Daniel Oliver, Eſq;
*Duxbury,* Briggs Alden, Eſq;
*Pembroke,* Joſiah Keen, Eſq;
*Wells,* Joſeph Sayer, Eſq;
*Falmouth,* Samuel Waldo, Eſq;
*Hardwick,* Hon. Timothy Ruggles, Eſq;
*Southboro',* Ezra Taylor, Eſq;
*Hardwich,* Chillingſworth Foſter, Eſq;
*Eaſtham,* Jonathan Doane, Eſq;

## 9. A Monumental Inscription on the Fifth of March
[Boston: Isaiah Thomas, 1772]

"THOU shalt take no satisfaction for the life of a MURDERER—he shall surely be put to death," reads the Biblical injunction; however, Ebenezer Richardson escaped this fate, was pardoned by the King and was confined in prison for only two years. In her *American Broadside Verse,* Ola Winslow notes that "Richardson was one of the most notorious criminals of the Revolutionary times for the reason that his crime was closely bound up with the events of the Boston Massacre of March 5, 1770." An officer in the Boston Custom House during the non-importation excitement of the late sixties, he was regarded to be an informer, and was accordingly an object of suspicion and hatred. On February 22, 1770, he attempted to remove a wooden image which some citizens had erected in front of the shop of Theophilus Lillie, an importer who traded with England. In the confusion which followed, Richardson fired a shot which fatally wounded Christopher Seider, a boy of eleven.

The Seider incident nearly cost Richardson his life, right on the spot. A mob of angry spectators gathered immediately and tried to lynch him, but he was saved by William Molineux and was later brought to trial in Faneuil Hall. Meanwhile, on Monday, February 26, young Seider's funeral was literally staged, "the largest perhaps ever known in America," according to Mark Boatner. Thousands attended, despite a severe snowstorm that had covered Boston only two days before. The funeral was used as an opportunity to generate sympathy for the insurgent cause, and to demonstrate the intensity of resentment the colonists felt toward British loyalists.

Richardson was tried on April 20, 1770, and though he was found guilty of murder, he was later pardoned because Governor Hutchinson, believing the crime to be manslaughter instead of murder, refused to sign the execution papers. Thus Richardson's name became synonymous with injustice, and he was the subject of several broadsides, including "The Life, and Humble Confession, of Richardson, the Informer," (National Index 12302), which is reprinted in Ola Winslow's study.

The "Monumental Inscription" broadside not only rails against the freedom enjoyed by Richardson, but commemorates the Boston Massacre. Isaiah Thomas included a very similar layout in the March 5, 1772, issue of the *Massachusetts Spy.* The illustration is clearly adapted from Paul Revere's engraving of the massacre and actually was executed by Revere for *The Massachusetts Calendar* for 1772, an almanac published by Isaiah Thomas.

NATIONAL INDEX 12302
FORD 1631
WEGELIN 646
AMERICAN ANTIQUARIAN SOCIETY
49 x 29.2 cm.

# A MONUMENTAL INSCRIPTION

ON THE

# Fifth of March.

Together with a few LINES

On the Enlargement of

## EBENEZER RICHARDSON,

Convicted of MURDER.

AMERICANS!
BEAR IN REMEMBRANCE
The HORRID MASSACRE!
Perpetrated in King-ftreet, BOSTON,
New-England,
On the Evening of March the Fifth, 1770.
When FIVE of your fellow countrymen,
GRAY, MAVERICK, CALDWELL, ATTUCKS,
and CARR,
Lay wallowing in their Gore!
Being *bafely*, and moft *inhumanly*
MURDERED!
And SIX others badly WOUNDED!
By a Party of the XXIXth Regiment,
Under the command of Capt. Tho. Prefton.
REMEMBER!
That Two of the MURDERERS
Were convicted of MANSLAUGHTER!
By a Jury, of whom I fhall fay
NOTHING,
Branded in the hand!
And *difmiffed*,
The others were ACQUITTED,
And their Captain PENSIONED!
Alfo,
BEAR IN REMEMBRANCE
That on the 22d Day of February, 1770.
The infamous
EBENEZER RICHARDSON, Informer,
And tool to Minifterial hirelings,
Moft *barbaroufly*
MURDERED
CHRISTOPHER SEIDER,
An innocent youth!
Of which crime he was found guilty
By his Country
On Friday April 20th, 1770;
But remained *Unfentenced*
On Saturday the 22d Day of February, 1772.
When the GRAND INQUEST
For Suffolk county,
Were informed, at requeft,
By the Judges of the Superior Court,
That EBENEZER RICHARDSON's *Cafe*
*Then lay before his* MAJESTY.
Therefore faid *Richardfon*
This day, MARCH FIFTH! 1772,
Remains UNHANGED!!!
Let THESE things be told to Pofterity!
And handed down
From Generation to Generation,
'Till Time fhall be no more!
Forever may AMERICA be preferved,
From weak and wicked monarchs,
Tyrannical Minifters,
Abandoned Governors,
Their Underlings and Hirelings!
And may the
Machinations of artful, *defigning* wretches,
Who would ENSLAVE THIS People,
Come to an end,
Let their NAMES and MEMORIES
Be buried in eternal oblivion,
And the PRESS,
For a *SCOURGE* to Tyrannical Rulers,
Remain FREE.

AWAKE my drowfy Thoughts! Awake my mufe!
Awake O earth, and tremble at the news!
In grand defiance to the laws of God,
The Guilty, Guilty murd'rer walks abroad.
That city mourns, (the cry comes from the ground,)
Where law and juftice never can be found:
Oh! fword of vengeance, fall thou on the race
Of thofe who hinder juftice from its place.
O MURD'RER! RICHARDSON! with their lateft breath
Millions will curfe you when you fleep in death!
Infernal horrors fure will fhake your foul
When o'er your head the awful thunders roll.
Earth cannot hide you, always will the cry
Of Murder! Murder! haunt you 'till you die!
To yonder grave! with trembling joints repair,
Remember, SEIDER's corps lies mould'ring there;
There drop a tear, and think what you have done!
Then judge how you can live beneath the Sun.
A PARDON may arrive! You laws defy,
But Heaven's laws will ftand when KINGS fhall die.
Oh! Wretched man! the monfter of the times,
You were not hung "by reafon of *old* Lines,"
*Old* Lines thrown by, 'twas then we were in hopes,
That you would foon be hung with *new made* Ropes;
But neither *Ropes nor Lines*, will fatisfiy
For SEIDER's blood! But GOD is ever nigh,
And guilty fouls will not unpunifh'd go
Tho' they're excus'd by judges here below!
You are enlarg'd but curfed is your fate
Tho' †*Cufhing*'s eas'd you from the prifon gate
The ⁑*Bridge* of *Tories*, *it* has borne you o'er
Yet you e'er long may meet with HELL's dark fhore.

\+ "Lines" - the name of one of the Judges
* Name of another Judge [illegible]
† Do. of another of the Judges
⁑ Trowbridge another Judge.

## 10. Boston, December 1, 1773
[Boston: Edes and Gill, 1773]

ANYONE reading this broadside carefully will see clearly that the "Sons of Liberty" (including such signatories as Samuel Adams and John Hancock) had every intention of doing violence to those who traded with the enemy. The opening declaration states that the Faneuil Hall meeting was held "for the Purpose of consulting, advising, and determining upon the most proper and effectual Method to prevent the unloading, receiving, or vending the detestable TEA sent out by the East India Company, Part of which being just arrived in this Harbour. . . ." The subsequent events of the Boston Tea Party should have come as no surprise. The signers of this public proclamation declared their intentions "to carry their Votes and Resolutions into execution, at the Risque of their Lives and Property."

This broadside is not as significant visually as it is important historically. Although groups had been meeting for years and resolutions had been drafted many times before, the record of the meeting at Faneuil Hall provided clear testimony regarding the determination of the colonists to resist Britain's attempts to enforce the Tea Tax. Once again, the principle of enforced taxation was more important than the actual cost of the tax duty, though this was no longer regarded as an insignificant levy. Outbursts like these became more common, and the colonists stated the principles on which their resistance would rest.

NATIONAL INDEX 12694
FORD 1657
AMERICAN ANTIQUARIAN SOCIETY
43.2 x 35 cm.

# BOSTON, December 1, 1773.

*At a Meeting of the* PEOPLE *of* Boston, *and the neighbouring Towns, at* Faneuil-Hall, *in said* Boston, *on Monday the 29th of* November 1773, *Nine o'Clock, A. M. and continued by Adjournment to the next Day; for the Purpose of consulting, advising and determining upon the most proper and effectual Method to prevent the unloading, receiving or vending the detestable* TEA *sent out by the East-India Company, Part of which being just arrived in this Harbour:*

IN Order to proceed with due Regularity, it was moved that a Moderator be chosen, and

JONATHAN WILLIAMS, Esq;
Was then chosen Moderator of the Meeting.

A MOTION was made that as the Town of Boston had determined at a late Meeting legally assembled, that they would to the utmost of their Power prevent the landing of the Tea, the Question be put, Whether this Body are absolutely determined that the Tea now arrived in Capt. Hall shall be returned to the Place from whence it came at all Events. And the Question being accordingly put, it passed in the Affirmative. Nem. Con.

It appearing that the Hall could not contain the People assembled, it was Voted, that the Meeting be immediately Adjourned to the Old South Meeting-House, Leave having been obtained for this Purpose.

The People met at the Old South according to Adjournment.

A Motion was made, and the Question put, viz. Whether it is the firm Resolution of this Body that the Tea shall not only be sent back, but that no Duty shall be paid thereon; & pass'd in the Affirmative. Nem. Con.

It was moved, that in order to give Time to the Consignees to consider and deliberate, before they sent in their Proposals to this Body, as they had given Reason to expect would have been done at the opening of the Meeting, there might be an Adjournment to Three o'Clock, P. M and the Meeting was accordingly for that Purpose adjourned.

THREE o'Clock, P. M. met according to Adjournment.

A Motion was made, Whether the Tea now arrived in Captain Hall's Ship shall be sent back in the same Bottom—Pass'd in the Affirmative, *Nem Con.*

Mr. Rotch the Owner of the Vessel being present, informed the Body that he should enter his Protest against their Proceedings.

It was then moved and voted, *nem. con.* That Mr. Rotch be directed not to enter this Tea; and that the Doing of it would be at his Peril.

Also Voted, That Captain Hall the Master of the Ship, be informed that at his Peril he is not to suffer any of the Tea brought by him, to be landed.

A Motion was made, That in Order for the Security of Captain Hall's Ship and Cargo, a Watch may be appointed——and it was Voted that a Watch be accordingly appointed to consist of 25 Men.

Capt. Edward Procter was appointed by the Body to be the Capt. of the Watch for this Night, and the Names were given in to the Moderator, of the Townsmen who were Volunteers on the Occasion.

It having been observed to the Body, that Governor Hutchinson had required the Justices of the Peace in this Town to meet and use their Endeavours to suppress any Routs or Riots, &c. of the People that might happen.—It was Moved and the Question put—Whether it be not the Sense of this Meeting, that the Governor's Conduct herein carries a design'd Reflection upon the People here met; and is solely calculated to serve the Views of Administration—Passed in the Affirmative, nem. con.

The People being informed by Col. Hancock, that Mr. Copley, Son-in Law to Mr. Clarke, Sen. had acquainted him that the Tea Consignees did not receive their Letters from London till last Evening, and were so dispersed, that they could not have a joint Meeting early enough to make their Proposals at the Time intended; and therefore were desirous of a further Space for that Purpose,

The Meeting out of great Tenderness to these Persons, and from a strong Desire to bring this Matter to a Conclusion, notwithstanding the Time they had hitherto expended upon them to no Purpose, were prevailed upon to adjourn to the next Morning Nine o'Clock.

TUESDAY Morning Nine o'Clock,
Met according to Adjournment.

THE long expected Proposals were at length brought into the Meeting, *not* directed to the Moderator, but to John Scollay, Esq; one of the Selectmen—It was however voted that the same should be read, and they are as follow, viz.

*Monday, Nov. 29th, 1773.*

*SIR,*

WE are sorry that we could not return to the Town satisfactory Answers to their two late Messages to us respecting the Teas; we beg Leave to acquaint the Gentlemen Selectmen that we have since received our Orders from the Honorable East-India Company.

We still retain a Disposition to do all in our Power to give Satisfaction to the Town, but as we understood from you and the other Gentlemen Selectmen at Mess. Clarkes Interview with you last Saturday, that this can be effected by nothing less than our sending back the Teas, we beg Leave to say, that this is utterly out of our Power to do, but we do now declare to you our Readiness to Store the Teas until we shall have Opportunity of writing to our Constituents and shall receive their further Orders respecting them; and we do most sincerely wish that the Town considering the unexpected Difficulties devolved upon us will be satisfied with what we now offer.

We are, SIR,
Your most humble Servants,
*Tho. & Elisha Hutchinson,*
*Benja. Faneuil,* jun. for Self and
*Joshua Winslow,* Esq;
*Rich'd Clarke & Sons.*

*John Scollay,* Esq;

Mr. Sheriff Greenleaf came into the Meeting, and begg'd Leave of the Moderator that a Letter he had received from the Governor, requiring him to read a Proclamation to the People here assembled might be read; and it was accordingly read.

Whereupon it was moved, and the Question put, Whether the Sheriff should be permitted to read the Proclamation—which passed in the Affirmative, nem. con.

The Proclamation is as follows, viz.

*Massachusets-Bay.* } By the Governor.

TO JONATHAN WILLIAMS, Esq; acting as Moderator of an Assembly of People in the Town of Boston, and to the People so assembled:

*WHEREAS printed Notifications were on Monday the 29th Instant posted in divers Places in the Town of Boston and published in the News-Papers of that Day calling upon the People to assemble together for certain unlawful Purposes in such Notifications mentioned: And whereas great Numbers of People belonging to the Town of Boston, and divers others belonging to several other Towns in the Province, did assemble in the said Town of Boston, on the said Day, and did then and there proceed to chuse a Moderator, and to consult, debate and resolve upon Ways and Means for carrying such unlawful Purposes into Execution; openly violating, defying and setting at nought the good and wholsome Laws of the Province and the Constitution of Government under which they live: And whereas the People thus assembled did vote or agree to adjourn or continue their Meeting to this the 30th Instant, and great Numbers of them are again met or assembled together for the like Purposes in the said Town of Boston,*

IN Faithfulness to my Trust and as His Majesty's Representative within the Province I am bound to bear Testimony against this Violation of the Laws and I warn exhort and require you and each of you thus unlawfully assembled forthwith to disperse and to surcease all further unlawful Proceedings at your utmost Peril.

*Given under my Hand at Milton in the Province aforesaid the 30th Day of November 1773 and in the fourteenth Year of His Majesty's Reign.*

By His Excellency's Command, T. Hutchinson.
THO'S FLUCKER, Secr'y.

And the same being read by the Sheriff, there was immediately after, a loud and very general Hiss.

A Motion was then made, and the Question put, Whether the Assembly would disperse and surcease all further Proceedings, according to the Governor's Requirement——It pass'd in the Negative, nem. con.

A Proposal of Mr. Copley was made, that in Case he could prevail with the Mess. Clarkes to come into this Meeting, the Question might now be put, Whether they should be treated with Civility while in the Meeting, though they might be of different Sentiments with this Body; and their Persons be safe until their Return to the Place from whence they should come——And the Question being accordingly put, passed in the Affirmative, Nem. Con.

Another Motion of Mr. Copley's was put, Whether two Hours shall be given him, which also passed in the Affirmative.

Adjourn'd to Two o'Clock, P. M.

TWO o'Clock P. M. met according to Adjournment.

A Motion was made and passed, that Mr. Rotch and Capt. Hall be desired to give their Attendance.

Mr. Rotch appeared, and upon a Motion made the Question was put, Whether it is the firm Resolution of this Body, that the Tea brought by Capt. Hall shall be returned by Mr. Rotch to England in the Bottom in which it came; and whether they accordingly now require the same, which passed in the Affirmative, Nem. Con.

Mr. Rotch then informed the Meeting that he should protest against the whole Proceedings as he had done against the Proceedings on Yesterday, but that tho' the returning the Tea is an involuntary Act in him, he yet considers himself as under a Necessity to do it, and shall therefore comply with the Requirement of this Body.

Capt. Hall being present was forbid to aid or assist in unloading the Tea at his Peril, and ordered that if he continues Master of the Vessel, he carry the same back to London; who reply'd he should comply with these Requirements.

Upon a Motion, Resolved, That John Rowe, Esq; Owner of Part of Capt. Bruce's Ship expected with Tea, as also Mr. Timmins, Factor for Capt. Coffin's Brig, be desired to attend.

Mr. Ezekiel Cheever was appointed Captain of the Watch for this Night, and a sufficient Number of Volunteers gave in their Names for that Service.

VOTED, That the Captain of this Watch be desired to make out a List of the Watch for the next Night, and so each Captain of the Watch for the following Nights until the Vessels leave the Harbour.

Upon a Motion made, Voted, that in Case it should happen that the Watch should be any Ways molested in the Night, while on Duty, they give the Alarm to the Inhabitants by the tolling of the Bells—and that if any Thing happens in the Day Time, the Alarm be by ringing of the Bells.

VOTED, That six Persons be appointed to be in Readiness to give due Notice to the Country Towns when they shall be required so to do, upon any important Occasion. And six Persons were accordingly chosen for that Purpose.

John Rowe, Esq; attended, and was informed that Mr. Rotch had engaged that his Vessel should carry back the Tea she bro't in the same Bottom, & that it was the Expectation of this Body that he does the same by the Tea expected in Capt. Bruce; whereupon he reply'd that the Ship was under the Care of the said Master, but that he would use his utmost Endeavour, that it should go back as required by this Body, and that he would give immediate Advice of the Arrival of said Ship.

VOTED, That it is the Sense of this Body that Capt. Bruce shall on his Arrival strictly conform to the Votes passed respecting Capt. Hall's Vessel, as tho' they had been all passed in Referrence to Capt. Bruce's Ship.

Mr Timmins appeared and informed that Capt. Coffin's Brig expected with Tea was owned in Nantucket, he gave his Word of Honor that no Tea should be landed while she was under his Care, nor touched by any one untill the Owner's Arrival.

It was then Voted, That what Mr. Rowe and Mr. Timmins had offered was satisfactory to the Body.

Mr. Copley returned and acquainted the Body, that as he had been obliged to go to *the Castle*, he hoped that if he had exceeded the Time allowed him they would consider the Difficulty of a Passage by Water at this Season as his Apology: He then further acquainted the Body, that he had seen all the Consignees, and tho' he had convinced them that they might attend this Meeting with safety, and had used his utmost Endeavours to prevail upon them to give Satisfaction to the Body; they acquainted him, that believing nothing would be satisfactory short of re-shipping the Tea, which was out of their Power, they thought it best not to appear, but would renew their Proposal of storing the Tea, and submitting the same to the Inspection of a Committee, and that they could go no further, without incurring their own Ruin; but as they had not been active in introducing the Tea, they should do nothing to obstruct the People in their Procedure with the same.

It was then moved, and the Question put, Whether the return made by Mr. Copley from the Consignees, be in the least Degree satisfactory to this Body, & pass'd in the Negative. Nem. Con.

*Whereas a Number of Merchants in this Province have inadvertently imported Tea from Great Britain, while it is subject to the Payment of a Duty imposed upon it by an Act of the British Parliament for the Purpose of raising a Revenue in America, and appropriating the same without the Consent of those who are required to pay it:*

*RESOLVED*, That in thus importing said Tea, they have justly incurr'd the Displeasure of our Brethren in the other Colonies.

*And Resolved further*, That if any Person or Persons shall hereafter import Tea from Great-Britain, or if any Master or Masters of any Vessel or Vessels in Great-Britain shall take the same on Board to be imported to this Place, until the said unrighteous Act shall be repeal'd, he or they shall be deem'd by this Body, an Enemy to his Country; and we will prevent the Landing and Sale of the same, and the Payment of any Duty thereon. And we will effect the Return thereof to the Place from whence it shall come.

RESOLVED, That the foregoing Vote be printed and sent to England, and all the Sea-Ports in this Province.

Upon a Motion made, Voted, That fair Copies be taken of the whole Proceedings of this Meeting, and transmitted to New York & Philadelphia, And that
Mr. SAMUEL ADAMS,
Hon. JOHN HANCOCK, Esq;
WILLIAM PHILLIPS, Esq;
JOHN ROWE, Esq;
JONATHAN WILLIAMS, Esq
Be a Committee to transmit the same.

Voted, That it is the Determination of this Body, to carry their Votes and Resolutions into Execution, at the Risque of their Lives and Property.

Voted, That the Committee of Correspondence for this Town, be desired to take Care that every other Vessel with Tea that arrives in this Harbour, have a proper Watch appointed for her —— Also Voted, That those Persons who are desirous of making a Part of these Nightly Watches, be desired to give in their Names at Messieurs Edes and Gill's Printing-Office.

Voted, That our Brethren in the Country be desired to afford their Assistance upon the first Notice given; especially if such Notice be given upon the Arrival of Captain Loring, in Messieurs Clarkes' Brigantine.

Voted, That those of this Body who belong to the Town of Boston do return their Thanks to their Brethren who have come from the neighbouring Towns, for their Countenance and Union with this Body in this Exigence of our Affairs.

VOTED, That the Thanks of this Meeting be given to JONATHAN WILLIAMS, Esq; for his good services as Moderator.

VOTED, That this Meeting be Dissolved—— And it was accordingly Dissolved.

---

Printed by EDES and GILL, 1773.

## 11. Tea, Destroyed by Indians [Boston, 1773?]

THE broadside verse here is iambic pentameter, and the form of this poem suggests that it was a song. Iambic pentameter is difficult, though not impossible, to sing, especially if the work is intended to be sung by large groups. Probably the authors intended the verses to be more inspirational than vocally effective, but our speculation is inconclusive. As Benjamin Labaree pointed out in *The Boston Tea Party,* Governor Hutchinson was completely surprised by the violence of the event, despite insurgent warnings. In his *History of Massachusetts Bay,* Hutchinson tries to explain why he did not order marines to board the vessels and arrest the patriots. Apparently fearing another incident like the Boston Massacre, he reasoned that it would be better to seek justice after the fact than to confront the insurgents directly, particularly since the colonists had already occasioned the removal of two regiments from Boston.

Ola Winslow's account of the evening of December 16, 1773, is particularly dramatic. "Under cover of night some fifty residents of Boston, disguised as Indians, emptied the entire cargo of three tea ships into Boston harbor, thereby ending a long controversy as to the enforcement of the tea tax, so obnoxious to the colonists. This tax, imposed by Townshend six years before, had not been repealed April 2, 1770, when the duty on certain other articles was withdrawn. This occurrence, which was the subject of much comment in the press and in other contemporary annals, was also frequently memorialized in verse, most of which was printed in the newspapers during the early months of 1774, rather than in broadside form." The Tea Party thus provided the revolutionary patriots with the stuff of myth and legend, and with the Boston Massacre, it assumed a cultural importance that exceeded its momentary historical value, because it attracted many colonists to the insurgent cause.

NATIONAL INDEX 42517
BRISTOL 3656
MASSACHUSETTS HISTORICAL SOCIETY
32 x 20.5 cm.

[1773?]
Bass

# T E A,

## *DESTROYED BY INDIANS.*

YE GLORIOUS SONS OF FREEDOM, brave and bold,
That has ſtood forth----fair LIBERTY to hold;
Though you were INDIANS, come from diſtant ſhores,
Like MEN you acted-----not like ſavage Moors.

*CHORUS.*

*Boſtonian's SONS keep up your Courage good,*
*Or Dye, like Martyrs, in fair Free-born Blood.*

Our LIBERTY, and LIFE is now invaded,
And FREEDOM's brighteſt Charms are darkly ſhaded!
But, we will STAND---and think it noble mirth,
To DART the man that dare oppreſs the Earth.
*Boſtonian's SONS keep up your Courage good,*
*Or Dye, like Martyrs, in fair Free-born Blood.*

How grand the Scene!----(No Tyrant ſhall oppoſe)
The T E A is ſunk in ſpite of all our foes.
A NOBLE SIGHT---to ſee th' accurſed TEA
Mingled with MUD----and ever for to be;
For KING and PRINCE ſhall know that we are FREE.
*Boſtonian's SONS keep up your Courage good,*
*Or Dye, like Martyrs, in fair Free-born Blood,*

Muſt we be ſtill--- and live on Blood-bought Ground,
And not oppoſe the Tyrants curſed ſound?
We Scorn the thought----our views are well refin'd
We Scorn thoſe ſlaviſh ſhackles of the Mind,
"We've Souls that were not made to be confin'd."
*Boſtonian's SONS keep up your Courage good,*
*Or Dye, like Martyrs, in fair Free-born Blood.*

Could our Fore-fathers riſe from their cold Graves,
And view their Land, with all their Children SLAVES;
What would they ſay! how would their Spirits rend,
And, Thunder-ſtrucken, to their Graves deſcend.
*Boſtonian's SONS keep up your Courage good,*
*Or Dye, like Martyrs, in fair Free-born Blood.*

Let us with hearts of ſteel now ſtand the task,
Throw off all darkſome ways,. nor wear a Mask.
Oh! may our noble Zeal ſupport our frame,
And brand all Tyrants with eternal SHAME.
*Boſtonian's SONS keep up your Courage good,*
*And ſink all Tyrants in their GUILTY BLOOD.*

## 12. An Act to Block Up the Harbour of Boston [Boston, 1774]

REACTION to the Boston Tea Party was predictable. Governor Thomas Hutchinson called together the Council of the Massachusetts Bay Colony to determine a course of action, but the council did not agree on a method for determining responsibility or for punishing those found guilty. Benjamin Labaree, in his study *The Boston Tea Party,* observes that some patriots announced public support of the tea incident, and most Bostonians approved of the tea's destruction. On 24 December, most of the committee members pledged in a solemn pact "to support and vindicate each other, and any Person or Persons who may be likely to suffer for any noble Effort *they have made* to serve their country." Paul Revere carried the news from Boston to New York, where broadside versions were published and circulated. The news was then spread to Philadelphia by broadsides, post riders, and news accounts.

The colonists were pleased with this example of patriotic resistance, but Parliament took a different view. Adopting a policy of coercion toward the Massachusetts Bay Colony, largely prompted by the resistances met earlier by the Stamp Act and other tax proposals, England established a blockade of the port of Boston with the Port Bill of March 25, 1774. Debate over the Port Bill had arrived at the conclusion that only through force would the obedience of Bostonians be secured. This broadside account carries the actual text of the Port Act, and occasioned vitriolic responses throughout the colonies from the Committees of Correspondence, some of which voted to close their own ports in sympathy with Boston.

NATIONAL INDEX 42612
BRISTOL 3755
HENRY E. HUNTINGTON LIBRARY
41.5 x 26.5 cm.

1774

# An Act to block up the Harbour of BOSTON!

Anno Regni GEORGII III. Regis Magnæ Britanniæ, Franciæ, & Hiberniæ.

*An Act to discontinue, in such Manner, for such Time as is therein mentioned, the landing and discharging, lading or shipping, of Goods, Wares, and Merchandise, at the Town, and within the Harbour of Boston, in the Province of Massachusetts-Bay, in North-America.*

WHEREAS dangerous commotions and insurrections have been fomented and raised in the town of Boston, in the province of Massachusetts-Bay, in New-England, by divers ill affected persons, to the subversion of his Majesty's government, and to the utter destruction of the public peace, and good order of the said town; in which commotions and insurrections certain valuable cargoes of teas, being the property of the East-India Company, and on board certain vessels lying within the bay or harbour of Boston, were seized and destroyed: And whereas, in the present condition of the said town and harbour, the commerce of his Majesty's subjects cannot be safely carried on there, nor the customs payable to his Majesty duly collected; and it is therefore expedient that the officers of his Majesty's customs should be forthwith removed from the said town: May it please your Majesty that it may be enacted; and be it enacted by the King's most excellent Majesty, by and with the advice and consent of the Lords spiritual and temporal, and Commons, in this present Parliament assembled, and by the authority of the same, That from and after the FIRST DAY OF JUNE, one thousand seven hundred and seventy-four, it shall not be lawful for any person or persons whatsoever to lade or put, or cause or procure to be laden or put, off or from any quay, wharff, or other place, within the said town of Boston, or in or upon any part of the shore of the bay, commonly called the harbour of Boston, between a certain headland or point called NAHANT POINT, on the eastern side of the entrance into the said bay, and a certain other headland or point called ALDERTON POINT, on the western side of the entrance into the said bay, or in or upon any island, creek, landing-place, bank, or other place, within the said bay or headlands, into any ship, vessel, lighter, boat, or bottom, any goods, wares, or merchandise whatsoever, to be transported or carried into any other country, province, or place whatsoever, or into any other part of the said province of the Massachusetts-Bay, in New-England; or to take up, discharge, or lay on land, or cause or procure to be taken up, discharged, or laid on land, within the said town, or in or upon any of the places aforesaid, out of any boat, lighter, ship, vessel, or bottom, any goods, wares, or merchandise whatsoever, to be brought from any other country, province or place, or any other part of the said province of the Massachusetts Bay, in New-England, upon pain of the forfeiture of the said goods, wares, and merchandise, and of the said boat, lighter, ship, vessel, or other bottom into which the same shall be put, or out of which the same shall be taken, and of the guns, ammunition, tackle, furniture, and stores, in or belonging to the same: And if any such goods, wares, or merchandise, shall, within the said town, or in any the places aforesaid, be laden or taken in from the shore into any barge, hoy, lighter, wherry, or boat, to be carried on board any ship or vessel outward bound to any other country or province, or other part of the said province of the Massachusetts-Bay, in New-England, or be laden or taken into such barge, hoy, lighter, wherry, or boat, from or out of any ship or vessel coming in and arriving from any other country or province, or other part of the said province of the Massachusetts-Bay, in New-England, such barge, hoy, lighter, wherry, or boat, shall be forfeited and lost.

And be it further enacted by the authority aforesaid, That if any wharfinger, or keeper of any wharff, crane, or quay, or their servants, or any of them, shall take up or land, or knowingly suffer to be taken up or landed, or shall ship off, or suffer to be waterborne, at or from any of their said wharffs, cranes, or quays, any such goods, wares, and merchandise; in every such case, all and every such wharfinger, and keeper of such wharff, crane, or quay, and every person whatever who shall be assisting, or otherwise concerned in the shipping, or in the loading or putting on board any boat, or other vessel, for that purpose, or in the unshipping such goods, wares, and merchandise, or to whose hands the same shall knowingly come after the loading, shipping, or unshipping thereof, shall forfeit and lose treble the value thereof, to be computed at the highest price which such sort of goods, wares, and merchandise, shall bear at the place where such offence shall be committed, at the time when the same shall be so committed, together with the vessels and boats, and all the horses, cattle, and carriages whatsoever, made use of in the shipping, unshipping, landing, removing, carriage or conveyance of any of the aforesaid goods, wares, and merchandise.

And be it further enacted by the authority aforesaid, That if any ship or vessel shall be moored or lie at anchor, or be seen hovering within the said bay, described and bounded as aforesaid, or within one league from the said bay so described, or the said headlands, or any of the islands lying between or within the same, it shall and may be lawful for any Admiral, Chief Commander, or commissioned officer of his Majesty's fleet or ships of war, or for any officer of his Majesty's customs, to compel such ship or vessel to depart to some other port or harbour, or to such station as the said officer shall appoint, and to use such force for that purpose as shall be found necessary: And if such ship or vessel shall not depart accordingly, within six hours after notice for that purpose given by such person as aforesaid, such ship or vessel, together with all the goods laden on board thereon, and all the guns, ammunition, tackle, and furniture, shall be forfeited and lost, whether bulk shall have been broken or not.

Provided always, That nothing in this act contained shall extend, or be construed to extend, to any military or other stores for his Majesty's use, or to the ships or vessels whereon the same shall be laden, which shall be commissioned by, and in the immediate pay of, his Majesty, his heirs, or successors; nor to any fuel or victual brought coastwise from any part of the continent of America, for the necessary use and sustenance of the inhabitants of the said town of Boston, provided the vessel wherein the same are to be carried shall be duly furnished with a cocket and let-pass, after having been duly searched by the proper officers of his Majesty's customs at Marblehead, in the port of Salem, in the said province of Massachusetts-Bay; and that some officer of his Majesty's customs be also there put on board the said vessel, who is hereby authorised to go on board, and proceed with the said vessel, together with a sufficient number of persons, properly armed, for his defence, to the said town or harbour of Boston; nor to any ships or vessels which may happen to be within the said harbour of Boston on or before the first day of June, one thousand seven hundred and seventy-four, and may have either laden or taken on board, or be there with intent to load or take on board, or to land or discharge, any goods, wares, and merchandise, provided the said ships and vessels do depart the said harbour within fourteen days after the said first day of June, one thousand seven hundred and seventy-four.

And be it further enacted by the authority aforesaid, That all seizures, penalties and forfeitures, inflicted by this act, shall be made and prosecuted by any Admiral, Chief Commander, or commissioned officer of his Majesty's fleet, or ships of war, or by the officers of his Majesty's customs, or some of them, or by some other person deputed or authorised, by warrant from the Lord High Treasurer, or the Commissioners of his Majesty's Treasury for the time being, [illegible] other person whatsoever: And if any such officer, or other person authorised as aforesaid, shall, directly or indirectly, take or receive any bribe or reward, to connive at such lading or unlading, or shall make or commence any collusive seizure, information, or agreement for that purpose, or shall do any other act whatsoever, whereby the goods, wares, or merchandise, prohibited as aforesaid, shall be suffered to pass either inwards or outwards, or whereby the forfeitures and penalties inflicted by this act may be evaded, every such offender shall forfeit the sum of FIVE HUNDRED POUNDS for every such offence, and shall become incapable of any office or employment, civil or military; and every person who shall give, offer or promise, any such bribe or reward, or shall contract, agree, or treat with any person, so authorised as aforesaid, to commit any such offence, shall forfeit the sum of FIFTY POUNDS.

And be it further enacted by the authority aforesaid, That the forfeitures and penalties inflicted by this act shall and may be prosecuted, sued for, and recovered, and be divided, paid and applied, in like manner as other penalties and forfeitures inflicted by any act or acts of Parliament, relating to the trade or revenues of the British colonies or plantations in America, are directed to be prosecuted, sued for, or recovered, divided, paid and applied, by two special acts of Parliament, the one passed in the fourth year of his present Majesty (intituled, An act for granting certain duties in the British colonies and plantations in America; for continuing, amending, and making perpetual, an act passed in the sixth year of the reign of his late Majesty King George the Second, intituled, An act for the better securing and encouraging the trade of his Majesty's sugar colonies, in America; for applying the produce of such duties, and of the duties to arise by virtue of the said act, towards defraying the expences of defending, protecting, and securing, the said colonies and plantations; for explaining an act made in the twenty-fifth year of the reign of King Charles the Second, intituled, An act for the encouragement of the Greenland and Eastland trades, and for the better securing the plantation trade; and for altering and disallowing several drawbacks on exports from this kingdom, and more effectually preventing the clandestine conveyance of goods to and from the said colonies and plantations, and improving and securing the trade between the same and Great-Britain) the other passed in the eighth year of his present Majesty's reign (intituled, An act for the more easy and effectual recovery of the penalties and forfeitures inflicted by the acts of Parliament relating to the trade or revenues of the British colonies and plantations in America.)

And be it further enacted by the authority aforesaid, That every charter party, bill of lading, and other contract for consigning, shipping, or carrying any goods, wares, and merchandise whatsoever, to or from the said town of Boston, or any part of the bay or harbour thereof, described as aforesaid, which have been made or entered into, or which shall be made or entered into, so long as this act shall remain in full force, relating to any ship which shall arrive at the said town or harbour, after the first day of June, one thousand seven hundred and seventy-four, shall be, and the same are hereby declared to be, utterly void, to all intents and purposes whatsoever.

And be it further enacted by the authority aforesaid, That whenever it shall be made to appear to his Majesty, in his Privy Council, that peace and obedience to the laws shall be so far restored in the said town of Boston, that the trade of Great-Britain may safely be carried on there, and his Majesty's customs duly collected, and his Majesty, in his Privy Council, shall adjudge the same to be true, it shall and may be lawful for his Majesty, by proclamation, or order of Council, to assign and appoint the extent, bounds and limits, of the port or harbour of Boston, and of every creek or haven within the same, or in the islands within the precinct thereof; and also to assign and appoint such and so many open places, quays and wharffs, within the said harbour, creeks, havens and islands, for the landing, discharging, lading, and shipping of goods, as his Majesty, his heirs or successors, shall judge necessary and expedient; and also to appoint such and so many officers of the customs therein, as his Majesty shall think fit; after which it shall be lawful for any person or persons to lade or put off from, or to discharge and land upon, such wharffs, quays, and other places, so appointed within the said harbour, and none other, any goods, wares, and merchandise whatever.

Provided always, That if any goods, wares, or merchandise, shall be laden or put off from, or discharged or landed upon, any other place than the quays, wharffs, or places, so to be appointed, the same, together with the ships, boats, and other vessels employed therein, and the horses, or other cattle and carriages used to convey the same, and the person or persons concerned or assisting therein, or to whose hands the same shall knowingly come, shall suffer all the forfeitures and penalties imposed by this or any other act on the illegal shipping or landing of goods.

Provided also, and it is hereby declared and enacted, That nothing herein contained shall extend, or be construed, to enable his Majesty to appoint such port, harbour, creeks, quays, wharffs, places, or officers, in the said town of Boston, or in the said bay or islands, until it shall sufficiently appear to his Majesty that full satisfaction hath been made, by or on behalf of the inhabitants of the said town of Boston, to the united Company of Merchants of England trading to the East-Indies, for the damage sustained by the said Company, by the destruction of their goods sent to the said town of Boston, on board certain ships or vessels as aforesaid; and until it shall be certified to his Majesty, in Council, by the Governor, or Lieutenant-Governor, of the said province, that reasonable satisfaction hath been made to the officers of his Majesty's revenue, and others, who suffered by the riots and insurrections above mentioned, in the months of November and December, in the year one thousand seven hundred and seventy-three, and in the month of January, in the year of one thousand seven hundred and seventy-four.

And be it further enacted by the authority aforesaid, That if any action or suit shall be commenced, either in Great-Britain or America, against any person or persons, for any thing done in pursuance of this act of Parliament, the defendant or defendants, in such action or suit, may plead the general issue, and give the said act, and the general matter, in evidence, at any trial to be had thereupon, and that the same was done in pursuance and by the authority of this act: And if it shall appear to have been done, the jury shall find for the defendant or defendants; and if the plaintiff shall be nonsuited, or discontinue his action, after the defendant or defendants shall have appeared; or if judgment shall be given upon any verdict or demurrer, against the plaintiff, the defendant or defendants shall recover treble costs, and have the like remedy for the same, as defendants have in other cases by law.

Sold at the Printing-Office, near the Court-House.

## 13. We the Subscribers
[Boston, June, 1774]

COLONIAL response to the Port Bill was heated. Some Committees of Correspondence advocated the closing of all American ports as a display of sympathy with Boston. As Benjamin Labaree has noted, Massachusetts merchants were united in their opposition to England, and urged the adoption of a strong boycott retaliation. The plan devised within two days after the Port Bill was announced was not carried out for several months, but it promised to cut off trade with not only Great Britain, but the West Indies as well.

Communities and districts like Charlton drafted responses to the outrageous Port Bill, most of which censured any persons doing business with England. Like the tea consignees earlier, merchants who continued to trade with Britain did so at their own jeopardy. This broadside protest from the "subscribers" in Charlton District (just west of Worcester, Massachusetts), is typical of many forms that were circulated to all the towns in the province, in order to elicit support for the opposition to the Port Bill. It bears the signatures of one hundred and thirty-two citizens, headed by that of the Rev. Caleb Curtis and his wife, and is unusual because of the number of women represented among the signers. The risks involved in publicly declaring opposition to English authority were well known; but the colonials had begun to mete out punishments of their own, and great risks were now taken by those who continued to trade with Britain.

NATIONAL INDEX 13163
FORD 1778
AMERICAN ANTIQUARIAN SOCIETY
51 x 20.2 cm.

WE the Subſcribers, inhabitants of the ~~town~~ Deſtrict of Charlton having taken into our ſerious conſideration the precarious ſtate of the liberties of North-America, and more eſpecially the preſent diſtreſſed condition of this inſulted province, embarraſſed as it is by ſeveral acts of the Britiſh parliament, tending to the entire ſubverſion of our natural and charter rights ; among which is the act for blocking up the harbour of Boſton : and being fully ſenſible of our indiſpenſable duty to lay hold on every means in our power to preſerve and recover the much injured conſtitution of our country ; and conſcious at the ſame time of no alternative between the horrors of ſlavery, or the carnage and deſolation of a civil war, but a ſuſpenſion of all commercial intercourſe with the iſland of Great Britain : Do, in the preſence of God, ſolemnly and in good faith, covenant and engage with each other, 1ſt, That from henceforth we will ſuſpend all commercial intercourſe with the ſaid iſland of Great Britain, until the ſaid act for blocking up the ſaid harbour be repealed, and a full reſtoration of our charter rights be obtained. And,

2dly, That there may be the leſs temptation to others to continue in the ſaid, now dangerous commerce, we do in like manner ſolemnly covenant that we will not buy, purchaſe or conſume, or ſuffer any perſon, by, for or under us to purchaſe or conſume, in any manner whatever, any goods, wares or merchandize which ſhall arrive in America from Great Britain aforeſaid, from and after the laſt day of Auguſt next enſuing. And in order as much as in us lies to prevent our being interrupted and defeated in this only peaceable meaſure, entered into for the recovery and preſervation of our rights, we agree to break off all trade, commerce and dealings whatever with all perſons, who perfering their own private intereſt to the ſalvation of their now periſhing country, ſhall ſtill continue to import goods from Great Britain, or ſhall purchaſe of thoſe who do import.

3dly, That ſuch perſons may not have it in their power to impoſe upon us by any pretence whatever, we further agree to purchaſe no article of merchandize from them, or any of them, who ſhall not have ſigned this, or a ſimilar covenant, or will not produce an oath, certified by a magiſtrate to be by them taken to the following purpoſe ; *viz.* I of in the county of do ſolemnly ſwear that the goods I have now on hand, and propoſe for ſale, have not, to the beſt of my knowledge, been imported from Great Britain, into any port of America ſince the laſt day of Auguſt, one thouſand ſeven hundred and ſeventy four, and that I will not, contrary to the ſpirit of an agreement entering into through this province import or purchaſe of any perſon ſo importing any goods as aforeſaid, until the port or harbour of Boſton, ſhall be opened, and we are fully reſtored to the free uſe of our conſtitutional and charter rights. And,

Laſtly, we agree, that after this, or a ſimilar covenant has been offered to any perſon and they refuſe to ſign it, or produce the oath, aboveſaid, we will conſider them as contumacious importers, and withdraw all commercial connexions with them, ſo far as not to purchaſe of them, any article whatever, and publiſh their names to the world.

Witneſs our hands, June, 1774.

| | |
|---|---|
| Revd Caleb Curtis | Daniel williams |
| mrs Charity his wife | Benjamin alton |
| Jonas Hammond | David rich |
| Ebenezer foskett | thomas haward |
| Ebenezer Hammond | Daniel Duggen |
| | [illegible] |

## 14. Thomas's Boston Almanack for 1775
[Boston: Isaiah Thomas, 1774]

THE production of almanacs was an old European tradition which was continued in the colonies from as early as 1639. Isaiah Thomas, the revolutionary patriot, annually published almanacs in addition to his well-known newspaper, *The Massachusetts Spy*.

This broadside version of an almanac is a condensed pamphlet-length document, a popular form which appeared often with other broadside announcements in taverns and public meeting houses. Though it did not offer the gleanings of wisdom usually found in the longer almanac books, the broadside almanac was easy to use and provided astrological information, some cursory astronomical data, and a quick glance at the year in advance.

NATIONAL INDEX 42711
BRISTOL 3865
FORD 1777
MILTON DRAKE ALMANACS OF THE UNITED STATES
(NEW YORK: SCARECROW PRESS, 1962) 3249
AMERICAN ANTIQUARIAN SOCIETY
50 x 38.7 cm.

# Thomas's Boston Almanack,

## For the Year of Our LORD GOD, 1775.

### JANUARY.

THIS month being cold, and seeing wood cannot be had without money, old batchelors and decayed widowers will do well to match with rich maids and wealthy widows, if either they can find. It appears that the kitchen will be more employed than the dairy, and a seat by the fire side more proper than a walk in the fields to look for primroses.

● New Moon, 1 Day, 8 After. ☽ First Quart. 8 Day, 1 After. ● Full Moon, 16 Day, 3 After. ☾ Last Quar. 24 Day, 2 After. ● New Moon, 31 Day, 6 Mor.

| Days M. | W | Calendar, Courts, Judgment of the Weather &c. | Sun rise and sets | Full Sea. | Moons place | Moon rs. & ss. |
|---|---|---|---|---|---|---|
| 1 | A | Circumcision. New-Year's Day | 7 28 5 | 11 1 | knees | ● sets |
| 2 | 2 | I. Court Bristol. ● Perigee. | 7 28 5 | 11 53 | 22 | 5 41 |
| 3 | 3 | I. Court, Boston, Amherst & York. | 7 27 5 | 12 48 | legs | 6 50 |
| 4 | 4 | Expect about this The greatest | 7 27 5 | 1 41 | 22 | 8 0 |
| 5 | 5 | Time Snow Comfort | 7 26 5 | 2 33 | feet | 9 10 |
| 6 | 6 | EPIPHANY. in time of | 7 26 5 | 3 25 | 21 | 10 23 |
| 7 | 7 | and Wind. Need | 7 25 5 | 4 18 | head | 11 27 |
| 8 | A | 1st Sunday past Epiphany. is | 7 24 5 | 5 11 | 16 | Morn. |
| 9 | 2 | ☌☽♃ Money, which | 7 23 5 | 5 57 | neck | 0 28 |
| 10 | 3 | I. Court, Charlestown, N. Hampsh. | 7 23 5 | 6 41 | 13 | 1 29 |
| 11 | 4 | A few Days, is greatly | 7 22 5 | 7 25 | 25 | 2 30 |
| 12 | 5 | △♃☿ of pleasant wanted in | 7 21 5 | 8 10 | arms | 3 30 |
| 13 | 6 | Weather, these very | 7 21 5 | 8 53 | 19 | 4 28 |
| 14 | 7 | Hard Times! | 7 20 5 | 9 37 | breast | 5 11 |
| 15 | A | 2d Sunday past Epiph. | 7 19 5 | 10 22 | 13 | 6 9 |
| 16 | 2 | I. Court, E. Greenwich, ● Apogee | 7 18 5 | 11 10 | 25 | ● rises |
| 17 | 3 | A change of Weather may | 7 17 5 | 11 54 | heart | 5 47 |
| 18 | 4 | now be looked for. He | 7 16 5 | 12 41 | 19 | 6 45 |
| 19 | 5 | that standeth let him take heed | 7 15 5 | 1 26 | belly | 7 47 |
| 20 | 6 | CHARLES, I. brought to trial. | 7 14 5 | 2 11 | 13 | 8 50 |
| 21 | 7 | The planets flatter lest he fall. | 7 13 5 | 2 55 | 25 | 9 51 |
| 22 | A | 3d Sunday past Epiph. | 7 12 5 | 3 31 | reins | 10 55 |
| 23 | 2 | us with pleasant weather | 7 11 5 | 4 25 | 20 | 11 54 |
| 24 | 3 | King of Prussia born 1712. Save | 7 10 5 | 5 9 | secrets | Morn. |
| 25 | 4 | Conversion of St. Paul. your | 7 9 5 | 6 4 | 17 | 0 54 |
| 26 | 5 | for some Time. □☉♃ | 7 8 5 | 6 57 | thighs | 1 55 |
| 27 | 6 | Expect more Money, and | 7 7 5 | 7 51 | 15 | 2 56 |
| 28 | 7 | Snow, and then save | 7 6 5 | 8 45 | knees | 3 57 |
| 29 | A | 4th Sunday past Epiph. your | 7 5 5 | 9 39 | 15 | 4 56 |
| 30 | 2 | K. CHARLES I. Martyr. ● Perigee. | 7 4 5 | 10 33 | legs | 5 55 |
| 31 | 3 | perhaps Rain. Country. | 7 3 5 | 11 27 | 15 | ● sets |

### FEBRUARY.

THIS being but a short month, our observation on it shall be as short, namely, that a good morning's draught to those that like it, will be thought very seasonable all the month long, as the mornings very likely will prove raw; and though a draught of Malaga with a toast, be in great vogue, great alterations will take place before 1776, or I am no conjuror.

☽ First Quart. 7 Day, 5 Morn. ● Full Moon 15 Day, 10 Mor. ☾ Last Quart. 23 Day, 1 Mor.

| Days M. | W | Calendar, Courts, Judgment of the Weather, &c. | Sun rise and sets. | Full Sea. | Moons place. | Moon rs. & ss. |
|---|---|---|---|---|---|---|
| 1 | 4 | Cold Winds do from the N.W. blow, | 7 2 5 | 12 19 | feet | 6 39 |
| 2 | 5 | Candlemas. Sharp Cold. | 7 1 5 | 1 11 | 15 | 7 49 |
| 3 | 6 | The World is finely cloth'd in Snow. | 6 59 6 | 2 3 | 29 | 8 55 |
| 4 | 7 | Cloudy, then Fair. | 6 58 6 | 2 55 | head | 10 0 |
| 5 | A | 5th Sunday past Epiph. | 6 57 6 | 3 45 | 26 | 11 7 |
| 6 | 2 | ☌☉☿. Winter never rots in the | 6 56 6 | 4 38 | neck | Morn. |
| 7 | 3 | I. C. Portsmouth. Sky. | 6 54 6 | 5 29 | 22 | 0 21 |
| 8 | 4 | Windy, and very The irreso- | 6 53 6 | 6 13 | arms | 1 15 |
| 9 | 5 | likely for a lute never prose- | 6 52 6 | 6 57 | 16 | 2 13 |
| 10 | 6 | Snow. cute their views, so long | 6 50 6 | 7 41 | 28 | 3 7 |
| 11 | 7 | Storm. as they have any excuse | 6 49 6 | 8 25 | breast | 4 0 |
| 12 | A | SEPTUAGESSIMA. ● Apogee. | 6 48 6 | 9 8 | 22 | 4 48 |
| 13 | 2 | I guess we may begin to look left | 6 46 6 | 9 51 | heart | 5 34 |
| 14 | 3 | VALENTINE. I.C. Northampton. | 6 45 6 | 10 34 | 16 | 6 14 |
| 15 | 4 | for good for defraying. As the | 6 44 6 | 11 17 | 27 | ● rise |
| 16 | 5 | ☍☽♀ Weather, climbing up of | 6 42 6 | 12 4 | belly | 6 33 |
| 17 | 6 | in these a Sandy Hill is to the | 6 41 6 | 12 51 | 22 | 7 32 |
| 18 | 7 | Days. aged, so is a Wife full of | 6 39 6 | 1 39 | reins | 8 30 |
| 19 | A | SEXAGESSIMA. words to a quiet | 6 38 6 | 2 26 | 17 | 9 33 |
| 20 | 2 | I. C. South-Kingston. Man. | 6 36 6 | 3 13 | secrets | 10 36 |
| 21 | 3 | S. C. Boston & Fairfield. That | 6 35 6 | 4 2 | 13 | 11 39 |
| 22 | 4 | Perhaps Rain, and man is | 6 34 6 | 4 48 | 27 | Morn. |
| 23 | 5 | ☍☉♂ then clears of most happy | 6 32 6 | 5 36 | thighs | 0 50 |
| 24 | 6 | St. MATTHIAS. who believes | 6 31 6 | 6 30 | 25 | 2 0 |
| 25 | 7 | Cold. himself to be really so. | 6 29 6 | 7 24 | knees | 3 2 |
| 26 | A | SHROVE SUNDAY. | 6 28 6 | 8 19 | 24 | 3 58 |
| 27 | 2 | ● Perigee. High Tides. | 6 26 6 | 9 14 | legs | 4 49 |
| 28 | 3 | S.C. New-Haven. I.C Pittsfield. | 6 25 6 | 10 10 | 23 | 5 36 |

The glorious Planet ♀ VENUS is morning Star to the 7th of January, then becomes an Evening Star to the 24th of October, then again Oriental, or Morning Star to the end of the year.

### MARCH.

THE wind blows hard in this month, yet if though canst walk five miles on thy own ground, thou wilt find it not only healthful to thy body, but comfortable to thy purse. Physicians have in some places much work where the scurvy is epidemical, but I would strongly recommend good wholesome exercise to keep thy body in order.

● New Moon, 1 Day, 5 After. ☽ First Quart. 8 Day, 12 Afte. ● Full Moon, 17 Day, 3 Mor. ☾ Last Quart. 24 Day, 9 Mor. ● New Moon, 31 Day, 4 Mor.

| Days M. | W | Calendar, Courts, Judgment of the Weather, &c. | Sun rise and sets | Full Sea. | Moons place. | Moon rs. & ss. |
|---|---|---|---|---|---|---|
| 1 | 4 | Ash-Wednesday. St. David. (beer, | 6 24 6 | 11 5 | feet | ● sets |
| 2 | 5 | If you would brew good napping | 6 23 6 | 11 5[illegible] | 23 | 6 35 |
| 3 | 6 | This time's the best of all the year. | 6 21 6 | 12 43 | head | 7 40 |
| 4 | 7 | Expect very high winds. | 6 20 6 | 1 35 | 21 | 8 47 |
| 5 | A | BOSTON MAS. Prince of Hesse | 6 18 6 | 2 26 | neck | 9 56 |
| 6 | 2 | S. C. Newport. (born. | 6 17 6 | 3 16 | 17 | 11 6 |
| 7 | 3 | LENT. S.C. Hart. Portf. I.C. Edgar. | 6 15 6 | 4 5 | arms | Morn. |
| 8 | 4 | If I guess right we shall have | 6 13 6 | 4 53 | 13 | 0 6 |
| 9 | 5 | plenty of Snow, or Take | 6 12 6 | 5 38 | 25 | 1 5 |
| 10 | 6 | Rain, great care of your Fires. | 6 11 6 | 6 23 | breast | 1 56 |
| 11 | 7 | ● Apogee. Dainty Food, and | 6 10 6 | 7 8 | 18 | 2 48 |
| 12 | A | 1st Sunday in Lent. Gregory. | 6 8 6 | 7 55 | heart | 3 34 |
| 13 | 2 | about this sumptious Fare, | 6 9 6 | 8 39 | 12 | 4 15 |
| 14 | 3 | I. C. Charlestown, & Taunton. | 6 7 6 | 9 23 | 24 | 4 51 |
| 15 | 4 | Time. causes innumerable diseases. | 6 6 6 | 10 17 | belly | 5 25 |
| 16 | 5 | Ever be watchful of thy Country's | 6 5 6 | 10 51 | 19 | 5 52 |
| 17 | 6 | St. PATRICK. ☌☽♄ good. | 6 3 6 | 11 35 | reins | ● rise |
| 18 | 7 | Stamp-Act repealed. He who is | 6 2 6 | 12 26 | 14 | 7 27 |
| 19 | A | 2d. Sunday in Lent. insolent in | 6 1 6 | 1 15 | 27 | 8 29 |
| 20 | 2 | S.C. Providence. Prosperity will | 6 0 6 | 2 5 | secrets | 9 40 |
| 21 | 3 | S.C. Windham. be faint-hearted | 5 59 7 | 2 54 | 24 | 10 48 |
| 22 | 4 | We may now in adversity. | 5 57 7 | 3 42 | thighs | 11 54 |
| 23 | 5 | look for a spell All we | 5 56 7 | 4 30 | 21 | Morn. |
| 24 | 6 | of pleasant weather. have to do | 5 54 7 | 5 19 | knees | 0 56 |
| 25 | 7 | Lady-Day, or Annunciation. | 5 53 7 | 6 13 | 19 | 1 57 |
| 26 | A | 3d Sunday in Lent. ● Perigee. | 5 51 7 | 7 8 | legs | 2 49 |
| 27 | 2 | for the Season. ☍☉♄ in life, | 5 49 7 | 8 2 | 18 | 3 37 |
| 28 | 3 | S.C. Norwich. I. C. Ipswich, Nan- | 5 48 7 | 8 54 | feet | 4 15 |
| 29 | 4 | [tucket, Worcester, & Falmouth. | 5 46 7 | 9 46 | 17 | 4 50 |
| 30 | 5 | Flying Clouds, is to prepare | 5 45 7 | 10 38 | head | 5 20 |
| 31 | 6 | with wind. for Death. | 5 44 7 | 11 32 | 15 | ● sets |

### APRIL.

IF thy purse be troubled this month with gross humours, thou mayest have it purged by the lawyer, doctor or merchant, but, I say, deliver thee and all of us from the three in conjunction. Some will think it most wholesome in the evening to take a pipe of tobacco, with a cheer-uping cup, in a company of jolly fellows, and to get up betimes in the morning. For my own part, instead of Galen, Hippocrates or Parcelsus, I take your Rare Ben, Aristippus, and Rabelais.

☽ First Quart. 7 Day, 7 After. ● Full Moon, 15 Day, 5 Afte. ☾ Last Quart. 22 Day, 4 Afte. ● New Moon, 29 Day, 3 Afte.

| Days M. | W | Calendar, Courts, Judgment of the Weather, &c. | Sun rise and sets | Full Sea. | Moons place. | Moon rs. & ss. |
|---|---|---|---|---|---|---|
| 1 | 7 | All Fools Day. | 5 43 7 | 12 21 | 29 | 7 44 |
| 2 | A | 4th Sunday in Lent. Fair | 5 41 7 | 1 10 | neck | 8 55 |
| 3 | 2 | S. C. South-Kingston. Weather. | 5 40 7 | 1 57 | 25 | 9 56 |
| 4 | 3 | St. Ambrose. I.C. Barnst. N. Haven. | 5 38 7 | 2 44 | arms | 10 56 |
| 5 | 4 | Cloudy, and likely (and Amherst. | 5 37 7 | 3 31 | 20 | 11 53 |
| 6 | 5 | New Birds on hedges sit and sing. | 5 35 7 | 4 18 | breast | Morn. |
| 7 | 6 | And leaves on Trees are flourishing. | 5 34 7 | 5 5 | 14 | 0 45 |
| 8 | 7 | ● Apogee. for Rain. | 5 32 7 | 5 51 | 26 | 1 36 |
| 9 | A | 5th Sunday in Lent. Palm Sunday. | 5 31 7 | 6 37 | heart | 2 20 |
| 10 | 2 | S. C. Bristol. Stormy. | 5 29 7 | 7 25 | 20 | 2 57 |
| 11 | 3 | S. C. Charlestown. I. C. Plymouth, | 5 28 7 | 8 8 | belly | 3 30 |
| 12 | 4 | (York, Hart. & N. Haven. | 5 27 7 | 8 53 | 14 | 4 2 |
| 13 | 5 | Cloudy and perhaps Rain. | 5 25 7 | 9 37 | 27 | 4 32 |
| 14 | 6 | GOOD FRIDAY. | 5 24 7 | 10 21 | reins | 5 2 |
| 15 | 7 | △☉♂ Sun and Clock together. | 5 23 7 | 11 7 | 22 | ● rise |
| 16 | A | EASTER SUNDAY. | 5 22 7 | 11 58 | secrets | 7 48 |
| 17 | 2 | (Fairfield. | 5 20 7 | 12 51 | 20 | 8 40 |
| 18 | 3 | S.C. Worcester. I.C. Boston and | 5 19 7 | 1 43 | thighs | 9 46 |
| 19 | 4 | Welcome my friends unto a glorious | 5 18 7 | 2 36 | 18 | 10 55 |
| 20 | 5 | spring, (thing. | 5 17 7 | 3 28 | knees | 11 59 |
| 21 | 6 | Which comforts and reviveth ev'ry | 5 16 7 | 4 21 | 16 | Morn. |
| 22 | 7 | ● Perigee. Expect a few Days | 5 15 7 | 5 14 | legs | 0 42 |
| 23 | A | 1st. Sunday past East. St. GEORGE. | 5 14 7 | 6 6 | 14 | 1 35 |
| 24 | 2 | S. C. East-Greenwich. of | 5 13 7 | 6 54 | 29 | 2 20 |
| 25 | 3 | St. MARK. S. C. Northam. I. C. | 5 11 7 | 7 46 | feet | 2 50 |
| 26 | 4 | pleasant weather. (Litchfield. | 5 10 7 | 8 38 | 26 | 3 23 |
| 27 | 5 | ☍☽♄ In the midst of life, | 5 9 7 | 9 30 | head | 3 55 |
| 28 | 6 | Cloudy, we are in death. | 5 7 7 | 10 22 | 24 | 4 27 |
| 29 | 7 | agreeable showers. | 5 6 7 | 11 12 | neck | ● sets |
| 30 | A | 2d Sunday past Easter. | 5 4 7 | 11 57 | 20 | 7 47 |

### MAY.

THIS has ever been accounted the merriest month in all the year trees now in blossom will hardly be bitten with the frost. Matrimony will begin to vegitate, and some women will be penny-wise and pound foolish. Tho' oysters will be out of season, turtle will be much eaten by those that like and can get it, wild fowls and bacon will equally please others.

☽ First Quart. 7 Day, 2 After. ● Full Moon, 15 Day 4 Mor. ☾ Last Quart. 21 Day, 9 Afte. ● New Moon, 29 Day, 4 Mor.

| Days M. | W | Calendar Courts, Judgment of the Weather, &c. | Sun rise and sets | Full Sea. | Moons place. | Moon rs. & ss. |
|---|---|---|---|---|---|---|
| 1 | 2 | St. Philip and St. James. | 5 2 7 | 12 43 | arms | 8 47 |
| 2 | 3 | I. C. Portsmouth. | 5 0 7 | 1 29 | 16 | 9 46 |
| 3 | 4 | General Election Newport. | 4 59 8 | 2 13 | 28 | 10 42 |
| 4 | 5 | Now early walk in Fields so gay, | 4 58 8 | 2 58 | breast | 11 35 |
| 5 | 6 | As they appear this month of May. | 4 57 8 | 3 42 | 22 | Morn. |
| 6 | 7 | ● Apogee. | 4 56 8 | 4 29 | heart | 0 20 |
| 7 | A | 3d Sunday past Easter. | 4 55 8 | 5 15 | 16 | 0 58 |
| 8 | 2 | Expect plenty of showers, | 4 54 8 | 5 57 | 28 | 1 37 |
| 9 | 3 | about this time. | 4 53 8 | 6 57 | belly | 2 8 |
| 10 | 4 | S.C. Barnstable, G. Elect. Hartford. | 4 52 8 | 7 35 | 22 | 2 34 |
| 11 | 5 | Flying Clouds with wind. | 4 51 8 | 8 23 | reins | 2 55 |
| 12 | 6 | ☌☽♄ If I am not wrong in | 4 50 8 | 9 7 | 18 | 3 33 |
| 13 | 7 | my guess we shall have | 4 49 8 | 9 57 | secrets | 4 2 |
| 14 | A | 4th Sunday past Easter. | 4 48 8 | 10 45 | 15 | 4 30 |
| 15 | 2 | a spell of very pleasant | 4 47 8 | 11 29 | 29 | ● rise |
| 16 | 3 | S. C. Plymouth, I. C. Cambridge. | 4 46 8 | 12 25 | thighs | 8 49 |
| 17 | 4 | Weather. (G. Barrington & Spring. | 4 45 8 | 1 21 | 28 | 9 52 |
| 18 | 5 | Thunder in That evil that a | 4 44 8 | 2 16 | knees | 10 54 |
| 19 | 6 | these days person brings | 4 43 8 | 3 10 | 27 | 11 44 |
| 20 | 7 | ● Perigee. upon themselves | 4 42 8 | 4 4 | legs | Morn. |
| 21 | A | Rogation Sunday. is hardest to bear. | 4 41 8 | 4 59 | 25 | 0 20 |
| 22 | 2 | Showery. He that says all be | 4 40 8 | 5 49 | feet | 0 57 |
| 23 | 3 | Pleasant. knows, will readily | 4 39 8 | 6 49 | 23 | 1 33 |
| 24 | 4 | ☍☽♄ say what he doth not know. | 4 38 8 | 7 26 | head | 2 4 |
| 25 | 5 | Ascention. Pain affects us more | 4 37 8 | 8 18 | 20 | 2 35 |
| 26 | 6 | ☌♃☿ Augustine. than | 4 37 8 | 9 7 | neck | 3 6 |
| 27 | 7 | pleasant weather. pleasure. | 4 36 8 | 9 53 | 16 | 3 40 |
| 28 | A | Sunday past Ascention. | 4 35 8 | 10 45 | 29 | 4 13 |
| 29 | 2 | I.C. Newport. K. Cha. II. Nativity | 4 34 8 | 11 36 | arms | ● sets |
| 30 | 3 | S. C. Dover. (and Restoration. | 4 33 8 | 12 17 | 24 | 8 35 |
| 31 | 4 | GENERAL ELECTION, Boston. | 4 32 8 | 1 2 | breast | 9 29 |

### JUNE.

NOW Cancer and Leo being hot signs many shall spend as much in one day as they can get in three, and never think of the fevers and pains they are laying in fodder for, nor of the twitches in the toes, many of them will receive before the year is out. By the position of the stars in regard to matrimony it appears, that a man had better marry a wife of ginger-bread than a scold, for if he is hungry he may eat up the one, but shall hardly lick his lips at the other.

☽ First Quart, 6 Day, 7 Morn. ● Full Moon, 13 Day, Noon. ☾ Last Quart. 20 Day 3 Morn. ● New Moon, 27 Day, 5 Afte.

| Days M. | W | Calendar, Courts, Judgment of the Weather, &c. | Sun rise and sets | Full Sea. | Moons place. | Moon rs. & ss. |
|---|---|---|---|---|---|---|
| 1 | 5 | ● Apogee. Boston [illegible] | 4 32 8 | 1 45 | 17 | 10 12 |
| 2 | 6 | This month produces [illegible] | 4 32 8 | 2 33 | heart | 10 54 |
| 3 | 7 | Which Old and Young hold to their | 4 31 8 | 3 16 | 12 | 11 31 |
| 4 | A | WHIT. K. GEO. III. born. (Noses. | 4 31 8 | 3 55 | 24 | Morn. |
| 5 | 2 | ARTILLERY ELECTION Bost. | 4 30 8 | 4 43 | belly | 0 6 |
| 6 | 3 | I. C. Pownalborough. | 4 30 8 | 5 28 | 18 | 0 36 |
| 7 | 4 | ☌☽♄ The Stars, as the saying | 4 30 8 | 6 17 | reins | 1 5 |
| 8 | 5 | is, prognosticate some alteration | 4 29 8 | 7 4 | 13 | 1 30 |
| 9 | 6 | in the weather, I guess we shall | 4 29 8 | 7 53 | 26 | 1 59 |
| 10 | 7 | have rain, and then it will | 4 29 8 | 8 47 | secrets | 2 29 |
| 11 | A | St. BARNABAS. TRINITY Sun. | 4 28 8 | 9 38 | 23 | 2 49 |
| 12 | 2 | clear off very pleasant. | 4 28 8 | 10 27 | thighs | 3 40 |
| 13 | 3 | I.C. Taunton, Worcester & N. Lon. | 4 28 8 | 11 17 | 22 | ● rise |
| 14 | 4 | Cloudy. (S.C. Plym. N. Ham. | 4 28 8 | 12 11 | knees | 8 32 |
| 15 | 5 | ● Perigee. Cowards die many times. | 4 28 8 | 1 4 | 22 | 9 29 |
| 16 | 6 | ☍☽♀ the valiant never taste of | 4 27 8 | 1 59 | legs | 10 20 |
| 17 | 7 | St. ALBAN. death but once. | 4 27 8 | 2 50 | 21 | 10 59 |
| 18 | A | 1st. Sunday past Trinity. | 4 27 8 | 2 40 | feet | 11 30 |
| 19 | 2 | I. C. Providence. Ignorance is the | 4 27 8 | 3 35 | 20 | Morn. |
| 20 | 3 | S. C. Ipswich. mother of fear, | 4 27 8 | 5 32 | head | 0 3 |
| 21 | 4 | Expect as well as of ad- | 4 27 8 | 6 20 | 16 | 0 35 |
| 22 | 5 | Thunder. miration. | 4 26 8 | 7 9 | neck | 1 5 |
| 23 | 6 | Pleasant weather about this time. | 4 26 8 | 7 57 | 13 | 1 36 |
| 24 | 7 | St. JOHN, baptist born. | 4 26 8 | 8 40 | 26 | 2 12 |
| 25 | A | 2d. Sunday past Trinity. | 4 27 8 | 9 29 | arms | 2 49 |
| 26 | 2 | ☌☽♃ (ham. | 4 27 8 | 10 17 | 21 | 3 30 |
| 27 | 3 | S.C. York. I.C Barnstable & Wind- | 4 27 8 | 11 7 | breast | ● sets |
| 28 | 4 | ● Apogee. A chearful countenance, | 4 27 8 | 12 51 | 15 | 8 6 |
| 29 | 5 | St. PETER. betokens a good heart. | 4 27 8 | 12 35 | 27 | 8 44 |
| 30 | 6 | Showery, perhaps Thunder. | 4 28 8 | 1 19 | heart | 9 23 |

### JULY.

THE tavern will be more frequented than the church. Those who live in low lands or swamps would do well to change their places of abode, otherwise the doctor will cost them more than the butcher. Few minced pyes will be eaten this month, but limes and lemmons will be in great demand. Adam's ale will not do in this month, unless well qualified with good spirit.

☽ First Quart. 5 Day, 9 After. ● Full Moon, 12 Day, 7 Afte. ☾ Last Quar. 19 Day, 11 Mor. ● New Moon, 27 Day, 8 Mor.

| Days M. | W | Calendar, Courts, Judgment of the Weather, &c. | Sun rise and sets | Full Sea. | Moons place. | Moon rs. & ss. |
|---|---|---|---|---|---|---|
| 1 | 7 | A King by judgment establisheth | 4 28 8 | 2 4 | 20 | 9 57 |
| 2 | A | 3d Sunday past Trinity. the land. | 4 28 8 | 2 48 | belly | 10 25 |
| 3 | 2 | I. C. Bristol. Cloudy. | 4 29 8 | 3 35 | 14 | 10 53 |
| 4 | 3 | S.C. Falm. I.C. Plymo. & Amherst. | 4 29 8 | 4 17 | 26 | 11 25 |
| 5 | 4 | ☌☽♄ Thunder, & showers. | 4 29 8 | 4 57 | reins | 11 56 |
| 6 | 5 | Let not thy business wholly be forgot, | 4 30 8 | 5 51 | 21 | Morn. |
| 7 | 6 | Altho' the weather now be very hot. | 4 30 8 | 6 43 | secrets | 0 20 |
| 8 | 7 | South The majesty of the people | 4 30 8 | 7 35 | 18 | 0 41 |
| 9 | A | 4th Sunday past Trinity. terrifieth | 4 31 8 | 8 36 | thighs | 1 26 |
| 10 | 2 | Winds and Tyrants. | 4 32 8 | 9 18 | 16 | 2 12 |
| 11 | 3 | I.C. Boston, Salem, York & Kenne. | 4 33 8 | 10 11 | knees | 2 57 |
| 12 | 4 | very warm, and perhaps Thunder. | 4 33 8 | 11 2 | 16 | ● rise |
| 13 | 5 | I.C. Dover, N. Hampsh. ● Perigee. | 4 34 8 | 11 55 | legs | 8 1 |
| 14 | 6 | When the righteous are in authority, | 4 35 8 | 12 50 | 16 | 8 48 |
| 15 | 7 | the people rejoice, but when the wick- | 4 35 8 | 1 45 | feet | 9 30 |
| 16 | A | 5th Sunday past Trinity. ed beareth | 4 36 8 | 2 40 | 15 | 10 2 |
| 17 | 2 | I.C. E. Greenwich. rule, the peo- | 4 36 8 | 3 33 | head | 10 31 |
| 18 | 3 | □♃♀ Sun-shine. ple mourn. | 4 37 8 | 4 26 | 14 | 11 7 |
| 19 | 4 | COMMENCEMENT Cambridge. | 4 38 8 | 5 19 | 27 | 11 30 |
| 20 | 5 | I.C. Plymouth, N. Hamp. Drink | 4 39 8 | 6 5 | neck | Morn. |
| 21 | 6 | not freely of cold water, the song | 4 40 8 | 6 52 | 23 | 0 9 |
| 22 | 7 | M. Magdalen. Q. of Denm. born. | 4 41 8 | 7 40 | arms | 0 49 |
| 23 | A | 6th Sunday past Trinity. says | 4 42 8 | 8 25 | 18 | 1 26 |
| 24 | 2 | ✶♃☿ "Grog is the liquor of life." | 4 43 8 | 9 10 | breast | 2 13 |
| 25 | 3 | St. JAMES. Dog-Days begin. I.C. | 4 44 8 | 9 58 | 12 | 2 59 |
| 26 | 4 | St. ANNE. Expect (Falm. Exeter. | 4 45 8 | 10 40 | 24 | 3 56 |
| 27 | 5 | ● Apogee. rain and ☉♄ | 4 46 8 | 11 29 | heart | ● sets |
| 28 | 6 | Take away the wicked from before | 4 47 8 | 12 9 | 18 | 8 0 |
| 29 | 7 | the King, and his throne shall be est- | 4 48 8 | 12 53 | 29 | 8 36 |
| 30 | A | 7th Sunday past Trinity. ablished | 4 49 8 | 1 38 | belly | 8 59 |
| 31 | 2 | wet weather. in Righteousness. | 4 50 8 | 2 25 | 23 | 9 27 |

### AUGUST.

IF it should rain maids and featherbeds this month, catch the featherbeds first, and the maids you may catch afterwards. About the middle and end good wine, (if red so much the better) will be very proper, and if you are in health you will find good butchers-meat and poultry agree with your stomach, and a dose of bark by way of bitters to your wine will not be amiss.

☽ First Quart. 4 Day, 10 Mor. ● Full Moon, 11 Day, 3 Mor. ☾ Last Quart. 17 Day 9 After. ● N. Moon, 26 Day, 12 Afte.

| Days M. | W | Calendar, Courts, Judgment of the Weather, &c. | Sun rise and sets | Full Sea. | Moons place. | Moon rs. & ss. |
|---|---|---|---|---|---|---|
| 1 | 3 | LAMMAS. Cloudy. ☊ 25 ♌ | 4 51 8 | 3 7 | reins | 9 55 |
| 2 | 4 | Your cattle will want food in win- | 4 52 8 | 3 51 | 18 | 10 27 |
| 3 | 5 | ter's day, (your hay. | 4 53 8 | 4 36 | secrets | 10 55 |
| 4 | 6 | Therefore this month before to mind | 4 54 8 | 5 2[illegible] | 13 | 11 20 |
| 5 | 7 | The planets prognosticate Rain, | 4 56 8 | 6 15 | 26 | Morn. |
| 6 | A | 8th Sunday past Trinity. Reflect | 4 57 8 | 7 8 | thighs | 0 4 |
| 7 | 2 | Name of JESUS. and then | 4 58 8 | 8 0 | 24 | 0 47 |
| 8 | 3 | a spell of but on the common lot | 5 0 7 | 8 55 | knees | 1 40 |
| 9 | 4 | pleasant of Humanity, and the | 5 1 7 | 9 49 | 24 | 2 46 |
| 10 | 5 | ● Perigee misfortunes that have | 5 2 7 | 10 45 | legs | 3 50 |
| 11 | 6 | ✶☉♂ weather. befallen others | 5 3 7 | 11 37 | 24 | ● rises |
| 12 | 7 | P. of WALES born, 1762. and you | 5 5 7 | 12 32 | feet | 7 48 |
| 13 | A | 9th Sunday past Trinity. will find | 5 6 7 | 1 26 | 24 | 8 40 |
| 14 | 2 | I.C. S. Kingston. your own not of | 5 7 7 | 2 20 | head | 9 8 |
| 15 | 3 | S. C. Litchfield. I. C. G. Barring. | 5 8 7 | 3 15 | 23 | 9 36 |
| 16 | 4 | Windy the first magnitude. | 5 9 7 | 4 7 | neck | 10 13 |
| 17 | 5 | about Shun the proud and | 5 10 7 | 5 0 | 20 | 10 50 |
| 18 | 6 | this arrogant; but without | 5 12 7 | 5 45 | arms | 11 26 |
| 19 | 7 | ☌☽♃ Time. letting them per- | 5 13 7 | 6 30 | 15 | Morn. |
| 20 | A | 10th Sunday past Trinity. ceive it; | 5 14 7 | 7 15 | 27 | 0 15 |
| 21 | 2 | Sun-shine. otherwise you provoke | 5 15 7 | 8 0 | breast | 1 8 |
| 22 | 3 | S. C. Fairfield. dangerous enemies. | 5 17 7 | 8 42 | 21 | 1 54 |
| 23 | 4 | Rather cool. Chuse what is most | 5 18 7 | 9 25 | heart | 2 49 |
| 24 | 5 | St. BATHOLOMEW. ● Apog. fit, | 5 19 7 | 10 9 | 15 | 3 40 |
| 25 | 6 | Cloudy and and custom will make | 5 20 7 | 10 56 | 27 | ● sets |
| 26 | 7 | likely for rain. it most agreable. | 5 22 7 | 11 40 | belly | 7 10 |
| 27 | A | 11th Sunday past Trinity. | 5 23 7 | 12 46 | 20 | 7 40 |
| 28 | 2 | St. AUSTIN. The rich are gene- | 5 24 7 | 1 12 | reins | 8 4 |
| 29 | 3 | John Baptist beheaded. ☌☽♄ | 5 25 7 | 1 59 | 15 | 8 31 |
| 30 | 4 | Commence. Dartmouth-College. | 5 26 7 | 2 44 | 27 | 8 59 |
| 31 | 5 | Windy. rally the most necessituous. | 5 28 7 | 3 30 | secrets | 9 31 |

### SEPTEMBER.

THOSE light-heeled, light-fingered blades, who during the warm months, made free with other men's horses and cattle will be afraid of their staring them in the face before winter sets in. Those who have had no fevers during the last two months, will find it unwholsome to get drunk and lie out in the dew, but be that as it may, I will hold any of you fifty pounds to a hickory-nut that the days and nights will be equal about the 23d.

☽ First Quart. 2 Day, 7 After. ● Full Moon, 9 Day. 10 Mor. ☾ Last Quart. 16 Day, Noon. ● New Moon, 24 Day, 4 Aft.

| Days M. | W | Calendar, Courts, Judgment of the Weather, &c. | Sun rise and sets | Full Sea. | Moons place. | Moon rs. & ss. |
|---|---|---|---|---|---|---|
| 1 | 6 | This month it is fit more clothes to | 5 30 7 | 4 17 | 23 | 10 8 |
| 2 | 7 | put on, [ing & Summer is gone. | 5 31 7 | 5 6 | thighs | 10 49 |
| 3 | A | 12th. S. p. Tri. For Autumn is com- | 5 33 7 | 5 54 | 20 | 11 37 |
| 4 | 2 | S. C. Providence. Dog-Days end. | 5 34 7 | 6 48 | knees | Morn. |
| 5 | 3 | I. C. Worcest. S.C. Hartf. & Exet. | 5 36 7 | 7 41 | 18 | 0 33 |
| 6 | 4 | Commencement Providence. | 5 37 7 | 8 40 | legs | 1 37 |
| 7 | 5 | ● Perigee. Cold Mornings & Even. | 5 39 7 | 9 35 | 18 | 2 45 |
| 8 | 6 | Nativity blessed Virgin Mary. | 5 40 7 | 10 27 | feet | 3 59 |
| 9 | 7 | If I guess right we shall have | 5 41 7 | 11 20 | 18 | ● rises |
| 10 | A | 13th. Sunday past Trinity. | 5 42 7 | 12 11 | head | 7 14 |
| 11 | 2 | ☍☽♄ plenty of | 5 44 7 | 1 5 | 17 | 7 48 |
| 12 | 3 | S.C. Amherst. I.C. Taunt. Con. | 5 45 7 | 1 55 | neck | 8 20 |
| 13 | 4 | Commencement New-Haven. | 5 47 7 | 2 46 | 15 | 8 59 |
| 14 | 5 | Rain, about The husbandman re- | 5 48 7 | 3 37 | 28 | 9 45 |
| 15 | 6 | this time. joices at the gathering | 5 49 7 | 4 30 | arms | 10 15 |
| 16 | 7 | ☌☽♃ in the fruits of his | 5 51 7 | 5 18 | 24 | 11 6 |
| 17 | A | 14th. Sunday past Trinity. Labour. | 5 52 7 | 6 0 | breast | 11 55 |
| 18 | 2 | I.C. Newp. Few men have their | 5 54 7 | 6 45 | 18 | Morn. |
| 19 | 3 | S.C. Worces. Windham, & Keene. | 5 55 7 | 7 28 | heart | 0 49 |
| 20 | 4 | Cloudy with Happiness without | 5 57 7 | 8 15 | 12 | 1 40 |
| 21 | 5 | St. MATTHEW. ● Apogee. | 5 58 7 | 8 58 | 23 | 2 37 |
| 22 | 6 | K. GEORGE. III. crowned 1761. | 5 59 7 | 9 39 | belly | 3 33 |
| 23 | 7 | Wind. Clouds, or their virtues | 6 1 6 | 10 25 | 17 | 4 35 |
| 24 | A | 15th. S. past Trin. without stain. | 6 2 6 | 11 9 | 29 | ● sets |
| 25 | 2 | ☌♄☿ Likely for a Storm. | 6 4 6 | 11 57 | reins | 6 45 |
| 26 | 3 | S.C. Spring. N. Lon. I.C. Newb. P. | 6 5 6 | 12 45 | 24 | 7 15 |
| 27 | 4 | Commenc. N. Jers. (Barnsta. Pow- | 6 7 6 | 1 32 | secrets | 7 40 |
| 28 | 5 | Expect blustering (nalbor. Litchfi. | 6 8 6 | 2 20 | 20 | 8 18 |
| 29 | 6 | St. MICHAEL. weather. | 6 10 6 | 3 10 | thighs | 8 59 |
| 30 | 7 | St. JEROM. | 6 11 6 | 3 58 | 16 | 9 42 |

### OCTOBER.

A MAN may take his female bed-fellow in his arms without danger of over-heating his reins, and of which a good account may be given some nine months after. We find by the planets that the length of the days, and money with many poor men, will begin to grow shorter.

☽ First Quart. 2 Day, 4 Morn. ● Full Moon, 8 Day, 8 After. ☾ Last Quart. 16 Day, 6 Mor. ● New Moon, 24 Day, 8 Mo. ☾ First Quarter 31 Day, 11 Morning.

| Days M. | W | Calendar, Courts, Judgment of the Weather, &c. | Sun rise and sets | Full Sea. | Moons place. | Moon rs. & ss. |
|---|---|---|---|---|---|---|
| 1 | A | 16th. Sunday past Trin. The be- | 6 13 6 | 4 47 | knees | 10 37 |
| 2 | 2 | S.C. South-Kingston. gining of | 6 14 6 | 5 36 | 14 | 11 36 |
| 3 | 3 | I.C. Bost. Plym. Nantu. & Amher. | 6 15 6 | 6 33 | 28 | Morn. |
| 4 | 4 | ● Perigee. love is in the power | 6 17 6 | 7 28 | legs | 0 39 |
| 5 | 5 | Pinching cold comes on a new apace, | 6 18 6 | 8 25 | 27 | 1 45 |
| 6 | 6 | Provide for winter now in ev'ry | 6 20 6 | 9 20 | feet | 3 0 |
| 7 | 7 | Middling high tides. (case. | 6 21 6 | 10 17 | 26 | 4 12 |
| 8 | A | 17th. Sun. p. Trin. of every one; | 6 23 6 | 11 13 | head | ● rise. |
| 9 | 2 | S.C. Bristol. St. DENNIS. To put | 6 24 6 | 12 0 | 25 | 6 22 |
| 10 | 3 | S.C. Taunton. I.C. Biddif. & Keen. | 6 26 6 | 12 47 | neck | 6 59 |
| 11 | 4 | Expect an end to it, is not in | 6 27 6 | 1 30 | 23 | 7 39 |
| 12 | 5 | Gen. Court N. Haven. I.C. Dover. | 6 29 6 | 2 21 | arms | 8 19 |
| 13 | 6 | wind and ☌♀☿ the power | 6 30 6 | 3 9 | 19 | 9 18 |
| 14 | 7 | Rain. △☉♃ of any one. | 6 31 6 | 3 56 | breast | 9 55 |
| 15 | A | 18th. Sunday past Trinity. | 6 33 6 | 4 43 | 14 | 10 49 |
| 16 | 2 | S.C. E. Greenwich. Absence cools | 6 34 6 | 5 30 | 27 | 11 18 |
| 17 | 3 | A spell moderate love, but | 6 36 6 | 6 17 | heart | Morn. |
| 18 | 4 | St. LUKE. Hardwick Fair. in- | 6 37 6 | 6 59 | 20 | 0 30 |
| 19 | 5 | ● Apogee. I.C. Haverhill. flames, | 6 38 6 | 7 45 | belly | 1 30 |
| 20 | 6 | of pleasant that which is violent | 6 40 6 | 8 28 | 14 | 2 29 |
| 21 | 7 | weather about just as the wind | 6 41 6 | 9 10 | 26 | 3 25 |
| 22 | A | 19th. Sunday past Trinity. blows | 6 42 6 | 9 57 | reins | 4 21 |
| 23 | 2 | this time. out a candle, but | 6 44 6 | 10 42 | 21 | 5 23 |
| 24 | 3 | S.C. Cambrid. I.C. Falm. & Tisb. | 6 45 6 | 11 27 | secrets | ● sets. |
| 25 | 4 | K. GEO. III. b. to reig. Derry Fair. | 6 46 6 | 12 16 | 16 | 6 24 |
| 26 | 5 | K. GEO. III. proclaimed 1760. | 6 48 6 | 1 0 | 29 | 7 2 |
| 27 | 6 | Windy and cold. kindles a fire. | 6 49 6 | 1 53 | thighs | 7 46 |
| 28 | 7 | St. SIMON & St. JUDE. Man is | 6 50 6 | 2 47 | 27 | 8 37 |
| 29 | A | 20th. Sunday past Trin. always | 6 52 6 | 3 38 | knees | 9 36 |
| 30 | 2 | A change in a hurry to defend | 6 53 6 | 4 30 | 25 | 10 39 |
| 31 | 3 | of weather. his weak side. | 6 54 6 | 5 20 | legs. | 11 34 |

### NOVEMBER.

THE old proverb for this month, "Let the thresher take his flail and the ship no more sail," will but in part hold good in the country these calculations are made for; yet him that then goes with his gloves in his pocket, the weather may invite, to put them on; and him that is in bed with another man's wife, her husband may invite to come out. If the weather proves as it sometimes does, you will find boots a good preservative against the wet.

● Full Moon, 7 Day, 8 Morn. ☾ Last Quart. 15 Day, 3 Mor. ● New Moon, 22 Day, 10 Af. ☽ First Quart. 29 Day, 7 Aft.

| Days M. | W | Calendar, Courts, Judgment of the Weather, &c. | Sun rise and set. | Full Sea. | Moons place. | Moon rs. & ss. |
|---|---|---|---|---|---|---|
| 1 | 4 | All Saints. ● Perigee. It is a | 6 55 6 | 6 12 | 22 | Morn. |
| 2 | 5 | All Souls. showy thing, to | 6 57 6 | 7 0 | feet | 0 50 |
| 3 | 6 | If thou thy feet this month keep dry | 6 58 6 | 7 56 | 21 | 2 3 |
| 4 | 7 | Thou may'st thy health preserve | 6 59 6 | 8 52 | head | 3 14 |
| 5 | A | P. PLOT. 21st past Trin. (thereby. | 7 0 5 | 9 43 | 20 | 4 21 |
| 6 | 2 | ☍☽♀ build a palace, lay out | 7 2 5 | 10 37 | neck | 5 29 |
| 7 | 3 | S.C. Salem. I.C. Hartf. and Ports. | 7 3 5 | 11 28 | 18 | ● rises |
| 8 | 4 | Likely for a garden, or appoint | 7 4 5 | 12 14 | arms | 6 15 |
| 9 | 5 | Snow or an equipage: This the | 7 6 5 | 12 59 | 14 | 7 0 |
| 10 | 6 | Rain. great understanding, this | 7 7 5 | 1 45 | 27 | 7 45 |
| 11 | 7 | St. MAR. they pique themselves | 7 8 5 | 2 33 | breast | 8 37 |
| 12 | A | 22d. Sunday past Trinity. upon: | 7 9 5 | 3 18 | 22 | 9 30 |
| 13 | 2 | Windy & cloudy. But to fill a heart | 7 10 5 | 4 0 | heart | 10 24 |
| 14 | 3 | S. C. Ports. I.C. Northa. N. Hav. | 7 11 5 | 4 47 | 16 | 11 18 |
| 15 | 4 | ● Apogee. with joy, restore content | 7 12 5 | 5 35 | 28 | Morn. |
| 16 | 5 | If I am not wrong to the afflicted, | 7 13 5 | 6 21 | belly | 0 22 |
| 17 | 6 | in my guess, or relieve the necessit- | 7 14 5 | 7 5 | 21 | 1 18 |
| 18 | 7 | we shall have cus; these fall not in | 7 15 5 | 7 53 | reins | 2 13 |
| 19 | A | 23d. Sund. past Trin. the reach | 7 16 5 | 8 40 | 16 | 3 11 |
| 20 | 2 | I. C. Newport. of their five | 7 17 5 | 9 35 | 29 | 4 15 |
| 21 | 3 | I. C. Fairfield. senses; they | 7 18 5 | 10 10 | secrets | 5 17 |
| 22 | 4 | St. CÆCILIA. do not compre- | 7 19 5 | 11 0 | 25 | ● sets |
| 23 | 5 | St. CLEMENT. ☍☽♃ hend, | 7 20 5 | 11 51 | thighs | 5 42 |
| 24 | 6 | a few days they have no relish | 7 21 5 | 12 40 | 23 | 6 28 |
| 25 | 7 | of pleasant for such | 7 22 5 | 1 36 | knees | 7 23 |
| 26 | A | 24th Sund. past Trinity. actions. | 7 23 5 | 2 28 | 21 | 8 24 |
| 27 | 2 | weather; then cold. Money creates | 7 24 5 | 3 20 | legs | 9 31 |
| 28 | 3 | I. C. Charlest. Pittsfi. & Norw. | 7 25 5 | 4 12 | 20 | 10 38 |
| 29 | 4 | ● Perigee. avarice, but does not | 7 26 5 | 5 0 | feet | 11 47 |
| 30 | 5 | St. ANDREW. satisfy it. | 7 26 5 | 5 54 | 18 | Morn. |

### DECEMBER.

NOW enters the old champion CHRISTMAS, armed with spit and dripping-pan, bidding defiance to all hungry stomachs. Beasts, fowls and fish come to general execution. Cooks will be more in request than hay-makers, and there shall be more resort to the shops for plumbs, than to the garden for green pease. A purse of gold will joy the heart, and a belly-full of roast beef appease hunger.

● Full Moon, 6 Day, 10 Aft. ☽ Last Quart. 14 Day, 12 Aft. ● N. Moon, 22 Day, 10 Mor. ☾ First Quar. 29 Day, 3 Mor.

| Days M. | W | Calendar, Courts, Judgment of the Weather, &c. | Sun rise and set. | Full Sea. | Moons place. | Moon rs. & ss. |
|---|---|---|---|---|---|---|
| 1 | 6 | ☋ 18 ♌ Looks and Fine weather to | 7 27 5 | 6 46 | head | 0 56 |
| 2 | 7 | ☍☽♄ feels like marry; a good | 7 27 5 | 7 37 | 16 | 2 6 |
| 3 | A | Advent Sunday. bed & bed-fellow | 7 28 5 | 8 27 | 29 | 3 10 |
| 4 | 2 | Snow. are very comfortable | 7 28 5 | 9 17 | neck | 4 17 |
| 5 | 3 | I.C. Barnst. & Worcest. things. | 7 29 5 | 0 8 | 26 | 5 22 |
| 6 | 4 | Clear and The shortest way to be- | 7 30 5 | 10 56 | arms | ● rises |
| 7 | 5 | Cold. rich, is not by en- | 7 30 5 | 11 43 | 22 | 5 29 |
| 8 | 6 | Conception blessed Virgin Mary. | 7 31 5 | 12 29 | breast | 6 19 |
| 9 | 7 | ☍☉♃ larging our estates, but by | 7 31 5 | 1 10 | 17 | 7 13 |
| 10 | A | 2d. Sun. in Advent. contracting | 7 32 5 | 1 59 | heart | 8 6 |
| 11 | 2 | ● Apogee. our desires; and to | 7 32 5 | 2 43 | 12 | 9 0 |
| 12 | 3 | I.C. Plymouth & Windham. be | 7 32 5 | 3 27 | 24 | 9 51 |
| 13 | 4 | Windy. contented with a little | 7 32 5 | 4 0 | belly | 10 47 |
| 14 | 5 | Cloudy, & takes from our pain | 7 32 5 | 4 57 | 17 | 11 45 |
| 15 | 6 | perhaps Snow, rather than | 7 33 5 | 5 47 | 29 | Morn. |
| 16 | 7 | after which our plea- | 7 33 5 | 6 30 | reins | 0 46 |
| 17 | A | 3d. Sunday in Advent. sure. | 7 33 5 | 7 20 | 24 | 1 45 |
| 18 | 2 | I. C. Providence. The difficulty | 7 33 5 | 8 0 | secrets | 2 47 |
| 19 | 3 | I.C. Taunton. is not so great | 7 34 5 | 8 50 | 20 | 3 51 |
| 20 | 4 | expect it fair and to die for a | 7 34 5 | 9 43 | thighs | 4 59 |
| 21 | 5 | St. THOMAS. friend, as to find | 7 34 5 | 10 30 | 17 | 6 4 |
| 22 | 6 | clear & cold. a friend | 7 34 5 | 11 20 | knees | ● sets |
| 23 | 7 | ☍♃☿ w[illegible] dying for. | 7 34 5 | 12 12 | 16 | 5 56 |
| 24 | A | 4th Sun. in Adven[illegible] be coward | 7 34 5 | 1 0 | legs | 7 3 |
| 25 | 2 | CHRISTMAS. [illegible] hunt himself | 7 34 5 | 2 0 | 15 | 8 11 |
| 26 | 3 | St. STEPH. I.C.S[illegible] ● Perigee. | 7 33 5 | 2 54 | feet | 9 23 |
| 27 | 4 | St. JOHN, Evan. cautious, the | 7 33 5 | 3 50 | 14 | 10 34 |
| 28 | 5 | Holy Innocents. miser frugal. | 7 33 5 | 4 43 | 29 | 11 42 |
| 29 | 6 | Vain are all things under the Sun, | 7 33 5 | 5 34 | head | Morn. |
| 30 | 7 | Time flies away the year is done. | 7 32 5 | 6 28 | 26 | 0 47 |
| 31 | A | Sund. past Christ. Reader, Adieu. | 7 32 5 | 7 5 | neck | 1 54 |

### ECLIPSES, for the Year 1775.

THERE will be FOUR Eclipses this year, two of the Sun, and two of the Moon.

The first will be of the Moon, on the 15th day of February, at 9 minutes after 10 o'clock in the morning, invisible.

The second will be of the Sun, on the 1st day of March, at 30 minutes after 4 o'clock, in the afternoon, invisible.

The third will be of the Moon, on the 11th day of August, beginning at 7 minutes after 1 o'clock in the morning, and ending at 5 minutes past 4, visible.

The fourth will be of the Sun, on the 25th day of August, at 46 min. past 11 o'clock, afternoon, invisible.

*Names of the Twelve Sings, and the Parts they govern.*

♈ Aries governs the Head and Breast. ♉ Taurus the Neck. ♊ Gemini the Arms. ♋ Cancer the Breast. ♌ Leo the Heart. ♍ Virgo the Belly. ♎ Libra the Reins. ♏ Scorpio the Secrets. ♐ Sagittarius the Thighs. ♑ Capricornus the Knees. ♒ Aquarius the Legs. ♓ Pisces the Feet.

*The Names of the Seven Planets and Five Aspects.*

Sol ☉. Saturn ♄, Jupiter ♃, Mars ♂, Venus ♀, Earth ⊕, Mercury ☿, Luna ☽. Conjunction ☌, Opposition ☍, Sextile ✶, Trine △, Quartile □, Dragon's Head ☊ and ☋ Tail.

*VULGAR NOTES for the Year 1775.*

| | | | |
|---|---|---|---|
| Golden Number | 9 | Epact | 28 |
| Cycle of the Sun | 20 | Dominical Letter | A |

*FRIENDS Yearly Meetings in New-England.*

AT Sandwich, the 6th Day before the last 1st Day of the 3d Month.
At Greenwich, the last First Day of the 5th Month.
At Rhode-Island, the 2d Sixth Day of the 6th Month.
At Nantucket, the 4th Sixth Day of the 6th Month.
At Kingston, the 2d First Day of the 8th Month.
At Providence, the 4th First Day of the 8th Month.
At Salem, the 4th First Day of the 9th Month.
At Scituate, the 1st Sixth Day of the 10th Month.
At Dartmouth, the 4th Sixth Day of the 10th Month.
At Swanzey, the 2d Seventh Day of the 11th Month.

BOSTON: Printed and sold by ISAIAH THOMAS, at the South Corner of MARSHALL'S-LANE, near the MILL-BRIDGE.

## 15. In Provincial Congress, April 15, 1775
[Boston: Edes and Gill]

As the colonists grew increasingly weary of British interference in their affairs, and as the coercive measures adopted by England to strangle colonial resistance were increasingly enforced, the pressure for confrontation intensified, and declarations on both sides reflected the developing crisis. This declaration, which appeared four days before the battle of Lexington and Concord, clearly shows how strongly the colonists felt about their independence.

NATIONAL INDEX 14220
FORD 1845
AMERICAN ANTIQUARIAN SOCIETY
37.3 x 29.8 cm.

# In *Provincial Congress*,

## Concord, *April* 15, 1775.

*WHEREAS it has pleased the righteous Sovereign of the Universe, in just Indignation against the Sins of a People long blessed with inestimable Privileges, civil and religious, to suffer the Plots of wicked Men on both Sides of the Atlantcik, who for many Years have incessantly laboured to sap the Foundation of our public Liberties, so far to succeed; that we see the* New-England *Colonies reduced to the ungrateful Alternative of a tame Submission to a State of absolute Vassalage to the Will of a despotic Minister—or of preparing themselves speedily to defend, at the Hazard of Life, the unalienable Rights of themselves and Posterity, against the avowed Hostilities of their Parent State, who openly threatens to wrest them from their Hands by Fire and Sword.*

*In Circumstances dark as these, it becomes us, as Men and Christians, to reflect that, whilst every prudent Measure should be taken to ward off the impending Judgments, or prepare to act a proper Part under them when they come; at the same Time, all Confidence must be with-held from the Means we use; and reposed only on that* GOD *who rules in the Armies of Heaven, and without whose Blessing the best human Counsels are but Foolishness—and all created Power Vanity;*

*It is the Happiness of his Church that, when the Powers of Earth and Hell combine against it, and those who should be Nursing Fathers become its Persecutors—then the Throne of Grace is of the easiest Access—and its Appeal thither is graciously invited by the Father of Mercies, who has assured it, that* when his Children ask Bread he will not give them a Stone:

THEREFORE, in Compliance with the laudable Practice of the People of GOD in all Ages, with humble Regard to the Steps of Divine Providence towards this oppressed, threatened and endangered People, and especially in Obedience to the Command of Heaven, that binds us *to call on him in the Day of Trouble*,——

*RESOLVED*, That it be, and hereby is recommended to the good People of this Colony, of all Denominations, That THURSDAY the Eleventh Day of *May* next be set apart as a Day of Public Humiliation, Fasting and Prayer; that a total Abstinence from servile Labor and Recreation be observed, and all their religious Assemblies solemnly convened, to humble themselves before GOD under the heavy Judgments felt and feared, to confess the Sins that have deserved them, to implore the Forgiveness of all our Transgressions, and a Spirit of Repentance and Reformation—and a Blessing on the Husbandry, Manufactures, and other lawful Employments of this People; and especially that the Union of the American Colonies in Defence of their Rights (for which hitherto we desire to thank Almighty GOD) may be preserved and confirmed,—that the Provincial and especially the Continental CONGRESSES, may be directed to such Measures as GOD will countenance.—That the People of *Great-Britain*, and their Rulers, may have their Eyes open'd to discern the Things that shall make for the Peace of the Nation and all its Connexions——And that AMERICA may soon behold a gracious Interposition of Heaven, for the Redress of her many Grievances, the Restoration of all her invaded Liberties, and their Security to the latest Generations.

*By Order of the Provincial Congress,*

JOHN HANCOCK, President.

## 16. Bloody Butchery, by the British Troops
[Boston?, 1775]

THE colonial point of view is expressed in this broadside account of the Lexington-Concord conflict. The symbolic use of coffins was common to published funeral elegies, and the designers of this broadside chose the funeral motif to give visual emphasis to their assessment of Lexington and Concord as further examples of British atrocity. However, as Ola Winslow affirms, this broadside is more interesting as a contemporary news account of the battles of Lexington and Concord, than as a funeral elegy for the slain. "The battle, characterized in the heading as an event 'on which, perhaps, may depend the future *Freedom,* and *Greatness,* of the *Commonwealth* of *America,'* took place on April 19, 1775, and marked the outbreak of actual hostilities in the War of the Revolution. The news account here reprinted had appeared in Russell's *Salem Gazette* on April 21; the elegy, in the *Essex Journal and Merrimack Packet* on April 26. This broadside was probably issued soon after May 5, the date of the Salem item included." Interestingly, there are a number of variant issues of this broadside, including two separate editions by Ezekiel Russell, the Salem printer, which are distinguished by the changes of accidentals in the poem.

NATIONAL INDEX 13839
FORD 1792
JOHN CARTER BROWN LIBRARY, BROWN UNIVERSITY
51 x 39 cm.

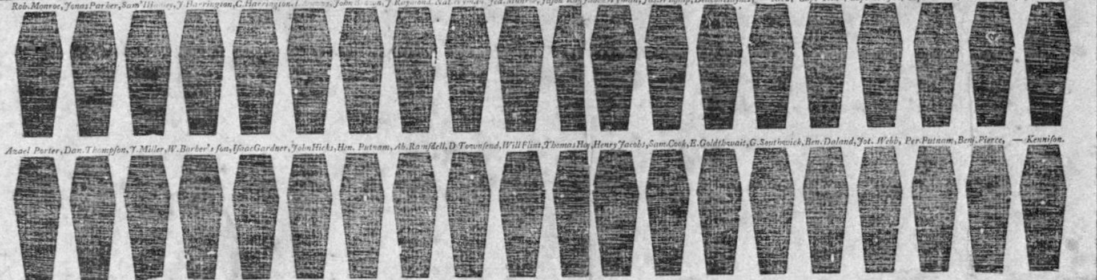


# BLOODY BUTCHERY,

BY TH[E]

# BRITISH TROOPS;

OR THE

## RUNAWAY FIGHT OF THE REGULARS.

Being the PARTICULARS of the VICTORIOUS BATTLE fought at and near CONCORD, ſituated Twenty Miles from Boſton, in the Province of the Maſſachuſetts-Bay, in New-England, between Two Thouſand Regular Troops, belonging to his Britannic Majeſty, and a few Hundred Provincial Troops, belonging to the Province of Maſſachuſetts-B[ay], which laſted from ſunriſe to ſunſet, on the 19th of April, 1775, when it was decided greatly in favor of the latter. Theſe particulars [are] now publiſhed in this cheap form, at the requeſt of the friends of the deceaſed WORTHIES, who died glorioully fighting in the CAUSE OF LIBERTY and their COUNTRY, and it is their ſincere deſire that every Houſeholder in the country, who are ſincere well-wiſhers to America, may [be] poſſeſſed of the ſame, either to frame and glaſs, or otherwiſe to preſerve in their houſes, not only as a Token of Gratitude to the memory of the Deceaſed Forty Perſons, but as a perpetual memorial of that important event, on which, perhaps, may depend the future Freedom and G[re]atneſs of the Commonwealth of America. To which is annexed, a Funeral Elegy on thoſe who were ſlain in the Battle.

From E. RUSSELL's *Salem Gazette*, or *Newbury* and *Marblehead Advertiſer*, publiſhed on Friday, April 21, 1775.

ON Tueſday evening the eighteenth inſtant, a body of ſoldiers under the command of Lieutenant-Colonel *Smith*, to the amount of about eight hundred men, embarked from *Barton's*-Point in *Boſton*, about eleven o'clock, croſſed *Charles*-River, landed at *Phips's*-Farm, in *Cambridge*, and marched immediately up to *Lexington*, near twelve miles from *Boſton*; at ſunriſe they obſerving between thirty and forty inhabitants exerciſing near the meeting-houſe, the Commanding-Officer ordered them to lay down their arms and diſperſe, which not being directly complied with, he "*demanded them for a pack of rebels*," ordered his men to fire upon them, and killed eight men on the ſpot, beſides wounding ſeveral more. The army then proceeded to *Concord*, drew up on the parade, near the meeting-houſe, during which time the inhabitants from the neighboring towns collected and took poſſeſſion of the adjacent hills; about eleven o'clock the firing began on both ſides, which laſted near an hour, when the regular troops began to retreat, the provincials cloſely purſuing them to a bridge at a ſmall diſtance, which the regulars took up as they paſſed; they then renewed the fire, and ſome were ſlain on both ſides; but the regulars ſtill retreated, and the provincials purſued them down to *Lexington*, where the regulars, about three o'clock in the afternoon, met with a reinforcement of about twelve hundred men commanded by Earl *Percy*, with two braſs field pieces; they again renewed the attack upon the provincials, but ſoon thought proper further to retreat towards their head-quarters, the provincials purſued them into *Charleſtown*, where they arrived at 6 o'clock; taking immediately, an advantageous poſt on *Bunker's*-Hill, about a mile from the ferry; the provincials now diſcontinued the purſuit. The loſs on either ſide we have not yet been able to aſcertain, but it is ſaid about one hundred regulars were killed and fifty wounded, among which were ſeveral officers: Two officers and a number of ſoldiers were taken priſoners. On the part of the province, we hear that thirty-five were ſlain, and ſeveral wounded. The above is as particular an account of the engagement, as can at this time be collected, in the preſent confuſed ſtate of the province.

We hear an officer and his ſervant, with two pair of piſtols, were yeſterday taken and ſecured by our people, at *Roxbury*, on their way to Caſtle-*William*.

S A L E M, April 25.

LAST Wedneſday, the nineteenth of April, the troops of his *Britannic* Majeſty commenced hoſtilities upon the people of this province, attended with circumſtances of cruelty not leſs brutal than what our venerable Anceſtors received from the vileſt ſavages of the wilderneſs. The particulars relative to this intereſting event, by which we are involved in all the horrors of a civil war, we have endeavored to collect as well as the preſent confuſed ſtate of affairs will admit.

On Thurſday evening a detachment from the army, conſiſting, it is ſaid, of eight or nine hundred men, commanded by Lieutenant-Colonel *Smith*, embarked at the bottom of the common in *Boſton*, on board a number of boats, and landed at *Phillips's*-farm, a little way up *Charles*-River, from whence they proceeded with ſilence and expedition, on their way to *Concord*, about twenty miles from *Boſton*. The people were ſoon alarmed, and began to aſſemble, in ſeveral towns, before day-light, in order to watch the motion of the troops.— At *Lexington*, ſix miles below *Concord*, a company of militia, of about one hundred men, muſtered near the meeting-houſe; the troops came in ſight of them juſt before ſun-riſe; and running within a few rods of them, the Commanding-Officer accoſted the militia in words to this effect:—"*Diſperſe you rebels—Damn you, throw down your arms and diſperſe*;" Upon which the troops huzza'd, and immediately one or two officers diſcharged their piſtols, which were inſtantaneouſly followed by the firing of four or five of the ſoldiers, and then there ſeemed to be a general diſcharge from the whole body; Eight of our men were killed, and nine wounded. In a few minutes after this action the enemy renewed their march for *Concord*; at which place they deſtroyed ſeveral carriages, carriage-wheels, and about twenty barrels of flour, all belonging to the province. Here about one hundred men, going towards a bridge, of which the enemy were in poſſeſſion, the latter fired, and killed two of our men, who then returned the fire, and obliged the enemy to retreat back to *Lexington*, where they met Lord *Percy*, with a large reinforcement, with two pieces of cannon. The enemy now having a body of about eighteen-hundred men made a halt, picked up many of their dead, and took care of their wounded. At *Menotomy*, a few of the men, belonging to the detachment from *Lynn-End*, attacked a party of twelve of the enemy (carrying ſtores and proviſions to the troops) killed two of them, wounded ſeveral, took ſix priſoners, ſhot five horſes, and took poſſeſſion of all their arms, ſtores, proviſions, &c. without any loſs on our ſide; among thoſe who were killed was a Lieutenant, who went with the proviſions for his recreation, and to view the country, the officer of the guard who generally attends on ſuch occaſions being only a ſerjant.—The enemy having halted one or two hours at *Lexington*, found it neceſſary to make a ſecond retreat, carrying with them many of their dead and wounded, who they put into chaiſes and on horſes that they found ſtanding in the road. They continued their retreat from *Lexington* to *Charleſtown* with great precipitation; and notwithſtanding their field pieces, our people continued the purſuit, firing at them until they got to *Charleſtown* neck, (which they reached a little after ſunſet) over which the enemy paſſed, proceeded up *Bunker's* Hill, and ſoon afterwards went into the town, under the protection of the *Somerſet* man of war of ſeventy-four guns.

In *Lexington* the enemy ſet fire to Deacon *Joſeph Loring's* houſe and barn, Mrs. *Mulliken's* houſe and ſhop, and Mr. *Joſhua Bond's* houſe and ſhop, which were all conſumed. They alſo ſet fire to ſeveral other houſes, but our people extinguiſhed the flames. They pillaged almoſt every houſe they paſſed by, breaking and deſtroying doors, windows, glaſſes, &c. and carrying off cloathing and other valuable effects. It appeared to be their deſign to burn and deſtroy all before them; and nothing but our vigorous purſuit prevented their infernal purpoſes from being put in execution. But the ſavage barbarity exerciſed upon the bodies of our unfortunate brethren who fell, is almoſt incredible. Not content with ſhooting down the unarmed, aged, and infirm, they diſregarded the [illegible] of the wounded, killed them without mercy, and mangling their bodies in the moſt [illegible] manner.

We have the pleaſure to ſay, that notwithſtanding the higheſt provocations given by the enemy, not one inſtance of cruelty, that we have heard was committed by our victorious militia; but, liſtned to the merciful dictates of the chriſtian religion, they "breathed higher ſentiments of humanity."

By an account of the loſs of the enemy, ſaid to have come from an officer of one of the men of war, it appears that ſixty-three of the regulars, forty-nine marines were killed and one hundred and three of both wounded: In all two hundred and fifteen. Lieut. *Gould*, of the fourth regiment, who is wounded, and [illegible], of the marines, and about twelve ſoldiers, are priſoners.

Mr. *James Howard* and one of the regulars diſcharged their pieces at the ſame inſtant, and each killed the other.

The public moſt ſincerely ſympathize with the friends, and relations of our deceaſed brethren, who glorioully ſacrificed their lives in fighting for the liberties of their country.—By their noble, intrepid conduct, in helping to defeat the forces of an ungrateful Tyrant, they have endeared their memories to the preſent generation, who will tranſmit their virtues down to the lateſt poſterity.

The above account is the beſt we have been able to obtain. We can only add, that the town of *Boſton* is now inveſted by a vaſt army of our brave countrymen, who have flown to our aſſiſtance from all quarters. GOD grant them aſſiſtance in the extirpation of our cruel and unnatural enemies.

S A L E M, May [illegible].

ON the nineteenth of April was killed, among others, by the *Britiſh* troops, at *Menotomy*, as he was courageouſly defending his country's rights, the good, the pious, and friendly Mr. DANIEL TOWNSEND, of *Lynd*. He was a conſtant and ready friend to the poor and afflicted; a good adviſer in caſe of difficulty, and an able, mild, and ſincere reprover of thoſe who were out of the way. In ſhort, he was a friend to his country, a bleſſing to ſociety, and an ornament to the church of which he was a member. He has left an amiable conſort, and five young children, to bewail the loſs.

Lie, valiant *Townſend*, in the peaceful ſhades.—We truſt
Immortal honors mingle with thy duſt.
What! tho' thy body ſtruggled in the gore;
So did thy Saviour's body long before!
And as he rais'd his own, by power divine;
So the ſame power ſhall alſo quicken thine,
And in eternal glory, mayſt thou ſhine.

On Thurſday the twentieth paſt, the bodies of eleven of the unfortunate perſons who fell in the battle, were collected together and buried at *Medford*.

And on Friday the bodies of Meſſrs. Henry Jacobs, Samuel Cook, Ebenezer Goldthwait, George Southwick, Benjamin Daland, jun. Jotham Webb, and Perley Putnam, of *Danvers*, who were likewiſe ſlain fighting in the GLORIOUS CAUSE OF LIBERTY AND THEIR COUNTRY, on the nineteenth of April, were reſpectfully interred among their friends in the different pariſhes belonging to that town, their corpſe being attended to the place of interment by two companies of minute-men from this place, and a large concourſe of people from this and the neighboring towns; previous to that interment, an excellent and well adapted prayer was delivered by the Rev. Mr. Holt, of that place.

Same day, the remains of Meſſrs. Azel Porter and Daniel Thompſon, of *Woburn*; who alſo fell victims to tyranny, were decently interred at that place, attended to the grave by a multitude of perſons who aſſembled on the occaſion from that and the neighboring towns: Before they were interred, a very ſuitable ſermon and prayer was delivered by the Rev. Mr. Sherman.

Captain Thomas Knights, of the fifth regiment, died at *Boſton* the next day after the engagement, of his wounds he received in the ſame. He was greatly regretted, being eſteemed one of the beſt officers among the King's troops.

Lieut. Hull, of the regulars, died of his wounds on Wedneſday laſt at the provincial hoſpital: His remains were next day conveyed to *Charleſtown*, attended by a company of provincials, and ſeveral officers of diſtinction, and then delivered to the order of General Gage. Twenty-three wounded ſoldiers lately died at the Caſtle.

Lieutenant Hawkſhaw was wounded in the cheek, and it is tho't will not recover.

Lieutenant Gore was wounded in the arm: About [illegible] other officers are wounded.

We can aſſure the public, from the beſt authority, that our brethren, of all the colonies which we can yet have heard from, are firm and unſhaken in their attachment to the common cauſe of *America*; and that they are now ready, with their lives and fortunes, to aſſiſt us in defeating the cruel deſigns of our implacable enemies.

We have received no particulars of the tranſactions between General Gage and the inhabitants of *Boſton*. It is certain that the people have delivered up their arms; very few of them have, however been permitted to leave the town, notwithſtanding the promiſe of the General.

The following is a liſt of the Provincials who were KILLED and WOUNDED.

Belonging to L E X I N G T O N.

K I L L E D.

1 * Mr. Robert Monroe,
2 * Mr. Jonas Parker,
3 * Mr. Samuel Hadley,
4 * Mr. Jonathan Harrington,
5 * Mr. Caleb Harrington,
6 * Mr. Iſaac Muzzy,
7 * Mr. John Brown,
8 Mr. John Raymond,
9 Mr. Nathaniel Wyman,
10 Mr. Jedediah Munroe.

W O U N D E D.

1 Mr John Robbins
2 Mr John Tidd
3 Mr Solomon Pierce
4 Mr Thomas Winſhip
5 Mr Nathan Farmer
6 Mr Joſeph Comee
7 Mr Ebenezer Munroe
8 Mr Francis Brown
9 Prince Eaſterbrooks (a Negro Man)

*M E N O T O M Y.*

K I L L E D

11 Mr Jaſon Ruſſell*
12 Mr Jabez Wyman
13 Jaſon Winſhip

M I S S I N G, (ſuppoſed to be on board one of the men of war)

Mr Samuel Froſt
Mr Seth Ruſſell

*S U D B U R Y.*

K I L L E D

14 Deacon Haynes,
15 Mr — Reed

*C O N C O R D.*

K I L L E D

16 Captain Miles

*B E D F O R D.*

K I L L E D

17 Captain Jonathan Willſon

*A C T O N.*

K I L L E D

18 Captain Davis
19 Mr ——— Hoſmer
20 Mr James Howard

*W O B U R N.*

K I L L E D

21 * Mr Azel Porter
22 Mr. Daniel Thompſon

W O U N D E D

10 Mr George Reed
11 Mr Jacob Bacon

*C H A R L E S T O W N.*

K I L L E D

23 Mr James Miller
24 Captain William Barber's Son, aged 14

*B R O O K L I N E.*

K I L L E D

25 Iſaac Gardiner, Eſquire

*C A M B R I D G E.*

K I L L E D

26 Mr John Hicks

*M E D F O R D.*

K I L L E D

27 Mr Henry Putnam

W O U N D E D

12 Mr William Polly

*L Y N N.*

K I L L E D

28 Mr Abednego Ramſdell
29 Daniel Townſend
30 William Flint
31 Thomas Hadley

W O U N D E D

13 Mr Joſhua Felt
14 Mr Timothy Munroe

*D A N V E R S.*

K I L L E D

32 Mr Henry Jacobs
33 Mr Samuel Cook
34 Mr Ebenezer Goldthwait
35 Mr George Southwick
36 Mr Benjamin Daland, jun.
37 Mr Jotham Webb
38 Perley Putnam

W O U N D E D

15 Mr Nathan Putnam
16 Mr Dennis Wallis

*S A L E M.*

K I L L E D

39 Mr Benjamin Pierce

*B E V E R L Y.*

K I L L E D

40 ——— Kenniſon

W O U N D E D

17 Mr Samuel Woodbury
18 Mr Nathaniel Cleaves

*F R A M I N G H A M.*

19 Mr ——— Hemmenway.

*B E D F O R D.*

20 Mr John Lane.

*Thoſe diſtinguiſhed with this mark [*] were killed by the firſt fire of the enemy.*

A FUNERAL

# ELEGY,

TO THE

## IMMORTAL MEMORY

*Of thoſe* WORTHIES *who were ſlain in the Battle of* Concord, *April* 19, 1775.

AID me ye nine! my muſe aſſiſt,
A ſad tale to relate,
When ſuch a number of brave men
Met their unhappy fate.
At *Lexington* they met their foe
Completely all equipp'd,
Their guns & ſwords made glit'ring ſhow,
But their baſe ſchemes were nipp'd.

*Americans*, go drop a tear
Where your ſlain brethren lay!
O! mourn and ſympathize for them!
O! weep this very day!
What ſhall we ſay to this loud call
From the Almighty ſent?
It ſurely bids both great and ſmall
Seek God's face and repent.
[illegible] perſons to view,
When forty of our brave countrymen
Sure bid their friends adieu.
Oh! think how awful it muſt ſeem,
To hear widows [illegible]
Their huſbands and their children
Who to their graves were ſent.

The tender babes, nay thoſe unborn,
O! diſmal cruel death!
To ſnatch their fondeſt parents dear
And leave them thus bereft.
O! *Lexington!* your loſs is great!
Alas! too great to tell;
Our juſtice bids me to relate
What to you has befell.
Ten of your hardy, braveſt ſons,
Some in their prime did fall;
They were by their noiſe of guns,
To terrify us all.
Let's not forget the *Danvers* race,
So late in battle ſlain,
Their valor and their courage ſhown,
Upon this crimſon'd plain.

Seven of your youthful ſprightly ſons
In the fierce fight were ſlain,
O! may your loſs be all made up,
And prove a laſting gain.
*Cambridge* and *Medford's* loſs is great,
Though not like *Acton's* town,
Where three brave military ſons
Met their untimely doom.
*Menotomy* and *Charleſtown* meet
A ſore and heavy ſtroke,
In loſing five of their townſmen
Who fell by a tyrant's yoke.
Unhappy *Lynn* and *Beverly*,
Your loſs I to bemoan,
Five your brave ſons in death that doth lie,
So late were in the bloom.

*Bedford*, *Woburn*, *Sudbury*, all,
Have ſuffer'd moſt ſevere,
You miſs five of your choiceſt chore,
On them let's drop a tear.
*Concord*, your Captain's fate rehearſe,
His loſs is felt ſevere,
Come, brethren, join with me in verſe,
His mem'ry hence revere.
O! 'Squire *Gardiner's* death we feel,
And ſympathizing mourn,
Let's drop a tear when it we tell,
And view his hapleſs urn.
We ſore regret poor *Pierce's* death,
A ſtroke to *Salem* known,
Where tears did flow from every brow
When the ſad tidings come.

The groans of wounded, dying men,
Would melt the ſtouteſt ſoul,
O! how it ſtrikes thro' every vein,
My fleſh and blood runs cold.
May all prepare to meet their fate
At God's tribunal bar,
And may war's terrible alarm,
For death us now prepare.
Your country calls you far and near,
*America's* ſons awake,
Your helmet, buckler, and your ſpear,
The LORD's own arm now make.
Be ſhield, will keep us from all harm,
Tho' thouſands 'gainſt us riſe,
No buckler we muſt fear put on,
If we would win the prize.

## 17. A Circumstantial Account of an Attack
[Boston, 1775]

THE British account of the Lexington-Concord incident is more detached and restrained than would be expected. In contrast to General Gage's authoritative "Proclamation," or to the summaries provided by colonial writers, this version has a tone of objectivity that disguises the bias in this recapitulation of the events. But throughout the broadside account, examples of colonial atrocities are cited, such as: "Captain Parsons returned with the three companies over the bridge, they observed three Soldiers on the Ground one of them scalped, his Head much mangled, and his Ears cut off, tho' not quite dead; a Sight which struck the Soldiers with Horror . . ." The broadside concludes with a mild indictment of the colonial insurgents, and assigns the responsibility for firing the first shot: "Thus this unfortunate Affair has happened through the Rashness and Imprudence of a few People, who began Firing on the Troops at Lexington."

NATIONAL INDEX 13869
FORD 1803
AMERICAN ANTIQUARIAN SOCIETY
35 x 21.9 cm.

# A CIRCUMSTANTIAL ACCOUNT

## Of an Attack that happened on the 19th of April 1775, on his MAJESTY's Troops,

## By a Number of the People of the Province of MASSACHUSETTS-BAY.

ON Tueſday the 18th of April, about half paſt 10 at Night, Lieutenant Colonel Smith of the 10th Regiment, embarked from the Common at Boſton, with the Grenadiers and Light Infantry of the Troops there, and landed on the oppoſite Side, from whence he began his March towards Concord, where he was ordered to deſtroy a Magazine of Military Stores, depoſited there for the Uſe of an Army to be aſſembled, in Order to act againſt his Majeſty, and his Government. The Colonel called his Officers together, and gave Orders, that the Troops ſhould not fire, unleſs fired upon; and after marching a few Miles, detached ſix Companies of Light Infantry, under the Command of Major Pitcairn, to take Poſſeſſion of two Bridges on the other Side of Concord: Soon after they heard many Signal Guns, and the ringing of Alarm Bells repea edly, which convinced them that the Country was riſing to oppoſe them, and that it was a preconcerted Scheme to oppoſe the King's Troops, whenever there ſhould be a favorable Opportunity for it. About 3 o'Clock the next Morning, the Troops being advanced within two Miles of Lexington, Intelligence was recei ed that about Five Hundred Men in Arms, were aſſembled, and determined to oppoſe the King's Troo s;* and on Major Pitcairn's gallo ping up to the Head of the advanced Companies, two Officers informed him that a Man advanced from thoſe that were aſſembled) had preſented his Muſquit and attempted to ſhoot them, but the Piece flaſhed in the Pan: On this the Major gave directions to the Troops to move forward, but on no Account to fire, nor even to attempt it without Orders. When they arrived at the End of the Village, they obſerved about 200 armed Men, drawn up on a Green, and when the Troops came within a Hundred Yards of them, they began to file off towards ſome Stone Walls, on their right Flank: The Light Infantry obſerving this, ran after them; the Major inſtantly called to the Soldiers not to fire, but to ſurround and diſarm them; ſome of them who had jumped over a Wall, then fired four or five Shot at the Troops, wounded a Man of the 10th Regiment, and the Major's Horſe in two Places, and at the ſame Time ſeveral Shots were fired from a Meeting-Houſe on the left: Upon this, without any Order or Regularity, the Light Infantry began a ſcattered Fire, and killed ſeveral of the Country People; but were ſilenced as ſoon as the Authority of their Officers could make them.

† After this, Colonel Smith marched up with the Remainder of the Detachment, and the whole Body proceeded to Concord, where they arrived about 9 o'Clock, without any Thing further happening; but vaſt numbers of armed People were ſeen Aſſembling on all the Heights: while Colonel Smith with the Grenadiers, and Part of the Light Infantry remained at Concord, to ſearch for Cannon, &c. there; he detached Captain Parſons with ſix Light Companies to ſecure a Bridge at ſome Diſtance from Concord, and to proceed from thence to certain Houſes, where it was ſuppoſed there was Cannon, and Ammunition; Captain Parſons in purſuance of theſe Orders, poſted three Companies at the Bridge, and on ſome Heights near it, under the Command of Captain Laurie of the 43d Regiment; and with the Remainder went and deſtroyed ſome Cannon Wheels, Powder, and Ball; the People ſtill continued encreaſing on the Heights; and in about an Hour after, a large Body of them began to move towards the Bridge, the Light Companies of the 4th and 10th then deſcended, and joined Captain Laurie, the People continued to advance in great Numbers; and fired upon the Kings Troops, killed three Men, wounded four Officers, one Serjeant, and four private Men, upon which (after returning the fire) Captain Laurie and his Officers, thought it prudent to retreat towards the Main Body at Concord, and were ſoon joined by two Companies of Grenadiers; when Captain Parſons returned with the three Companies over the Bridge, they obſerved three Soldiers on the Ground one of them ſcalped, his Head much mangled, and his Ears cut off, tho' not quite dead; a Sight which ſtruck the Soldiers with Horror; Captain Parſons marched on and joined the Main Body, who were only waiting for his coming up, to march back to Boſton; Colonel Smith had executed his Orders, without Oppoſition, by deſtroying all the Military Stores he could find; both the Colonel, and Major Pitcairn, having taken all poſſible Pains to convince the Inhabitants that no Injury was intended them, and that if they opened their Doors when required, to ſearch for ſaid Stores, not the ſlighteſt Miſchief ſhould be done; neither had any of the People the leaſt Occaſion to com lain, but they were ſulky, and one of them even ſtruck Major Pitcairn. Except upon Captain Laurie, at the Bridge, no Hoſtilities happened from the Affair at Lexington, until the Troops began their March back. As ſoon as the Troops had got out of the Town of Concord, they received a heavy Fire from all Sides, from Walls, Fences, Houſes, Trees, Barns, &c. which continued without Intermiſſion, till they met the firſt Brigade, with two Field Pieces, near Lexington, ordered out under the Command of Lord Percy to ſupport them; (advice having been received about 7 o'Clock next Morning, that Signals had been made, and Expreſſes gone out to alarm the Country, and that the People were riſing to attack the Troops under Colonel Smith.) Upon the Firing of the Field Pieces, the People's Fire was for a while ſilenced, but as they ſtill continued to encreaſe greatly in Numbers, they fired again as before, from all Places were they could find Cover, upon the whole Body, and continued ſo doing for the Space of Fifteen Miles: Notwithſtanding their Numbers they did not attack openly during the Whole Day, but kept under Cover on all Occaſions. The Troops were very much fatigued, the greater Part of them having been under Arms all Night, and made a March of upwards of Forty Miles before they arrived at Charleſtown, from whence they were ferryed over to Boſton.

The Troops had above Fifty killed, and many more wounded: Reports are various about the Loſs ſuſtained by the Country People, ſome make it very conſiderable, others not ſo much.

Thus this unfortunate Affair has happened through the Raſhneſs and Imprudence of [illegible] People, who began Firing on the Troops at Lexington.

* At this Time the advanc'd Light Companies loaded, but the Grenadiers were not loaded when they received their firſt Fire.

† Notwithſtanding the Fire from the Meeting-Houſe, Colonel Smith and Major Pitcairn, with the greateſt Difficulty, kept the Soldiers from forcing into the Meeting-Houſe and putting all thoſe in it to Death.

## 18. The Yankey's return from Camp
[Boston?, 1775]

"THE Yankey's return from Camp" is a version of "Yankee Doodle" which was sung by the colonial army following the battle of Lexington and Concord. The tune followed the then popular "Lexington March," which was sung by the British soldiers on their way to Lexington, and was modified and adopted by the patriots after the conflict. This reflects the kind of transformation that was also made by other Scottish and English ballads brought over during the colonial period. In "The Yankey's return from Camp," the tune pattern is clearly that of "Yankee Doodle, or, as now christened by the Saints of New England, *The Lexington March*," the latter being a parody of the American version, published in London in 1775. This well-known song, however, contains the modal tune pattern and rhythm of the American broadside reproduced here, suggesting the close association of "Yankey's return" to the more popular title "Yankee Doodle."

The actual tune to which "Yankey's return" would have been sung would probably have been close to the tune now recognized as "Yankee Doodle," which is a late eighteenth-century modification of "The Lexington March" circulated by Hewitt in New York and the Carrs of Philadelphia and Baltimore. An early version of the "Yankey's return" tune is that reproduced below, taken from a 1775 copy of "The Lexington March" which is housed in the Huntington Library.

Unlike some of the more difficult songs published on broadsides, "The Yankey's return" was clearly written to be adapted from a popular tune already widely sung. The earliest version probably dates from the French and Indian War, but the exact origins are not known. There is no extant copy of that original, according to Ola Winslow. The illustration on the "Yankey's return" broadside is identical to that appearing on "The Farmer and his Son's Return from a visit to the *Camp*," another contemporary version of "Yankee Doodle," modified to fit another occasion in the evolving conflict.

AMERICAN ANTIQUARIAN SOCIETY
26.4 x 21.9 cm.

# The YANKEY's return from CAMP.

FATHER and I went down to camp,
Along with Captain Gooding,
There we ſee the men and boys,
As thick as haſty pudding.
Yankey doodle keep it up,
Chorus. Yankey doodle, dandy,
Mind the muſic and the ſtep,
And with the girls be handy.

And there we ſee a thouſand men,
As rich as 'Squire David ;
And what they waſted every day,
I wiſh it could be ſaved.
Yankey dooole, &c.

The 'laſſes they eat every day,
Would keep a houſe a winter :
They have as much that I'll be bound
They eat it when they're a mind to.
Yankey doodle, &c.

And there we ſee a ſwamping gun,
Large as a log of maple,
Upon a ducid little cart,
A load for father's cattle.
Yankey doodle, &c.

And every time they ſhoot it off,
It takes a horn of powder—
It makes a noiſe like father's gun,
Only a nation louder.
Yankey doodle, &c.

I went as nigh to one myſelf,
As 'Siah's underpining ;
And father went as nigh again,
I tho't the deuce was in him.
Yankey doodle, &c.

Couſin Simon grew ſo bold,
I tho't he would have cock'd it :
It ſcar'd me ſo, I ſhrink'd it off,
And hung by father's pocket.
Yankey doodle, &c.

And captain Davis had a gun,
He kind of clapt his hand on't,
And ſtuck a crooked ſtabbing iron
Upon the little end on't.
Yankey doodle, &c.

And there I ſee a pumpkin ſhell
As big as mother's baſon,
And ev'ry time they touch'd it off,
They ſcamper'd like the nation.
Yankey doodle, &c.

I ſee a little barrel too,
The heads were made of leather,
They knock'd upon't with little clubs,
And call'd the folks together.
Yankey doodle, &c.

And there was captain Waſhington,
And gentlefolks about him,
They ſay he's grown ſo tarnal proud,
He will not ride without 'em.
Yankey doodle, &c.

He got him on his meeting clothes,
Upon a ſlapping ſtallion,
He ſet the world along in rows,
In hundreds and in millions.
Yankey doodle, &c.

The flaming ribbons in their hats,
They look'd ſo taring fine, ah,
wanted pockily to get,
To give to my Jemimah.
Yankey doodle, &c.

I ſee another ſnarl of men
A digging graves, they told me,
So tarnal long, ſo tarnal deep,
They 'tended they ſhould hold me.
Yankey doodle, &c.

It ſcar'd me ſo, I hook'd it off,
Nor ſtop'd, as I remember,
Nor turn'd about 'till I got home,
Lock'd up in mother's chamber.
Yankey doodle, &c.

## 19. The Recantations of Robert Hooper and Others
[Salem: Ezekiel Russell, 1775]

THE issues of allegiance and loyalty were complex during the pre-revolutionary era, but simple solutions were often sought in determining each citizen's position in relation to the colonial cause. As in most revolutionary uprisings, those not joining in directly were regarded as sympathetic toward the opposing group, and often "loyalty" was determined by public statements and declarations designed for signature. To this day, the "loyalty oath" concept persists in many states, as a condition of employment by the state government.

The recantations printed here are similar to loyalty oaths because they are public declarations of positions taken in the context of several alternative extremes. Conspiracy trials were common during the Revolution, and for their part, the insurgents accused and sought judgment against those suspected of opposing their revolutionary plans. Thus "trials," or appearances before town councils and Committees of Correspondence, would help establish an individual's position or could exonerate an accused conspirator. Frequently, these declarations were printed for circulation, so that those exonerated "might be protected from all Injuries and Insults whatsoever," as this broadside states. It must be remembered that ideological sympathy for the revolutionary cause was not overwhelming among the citizens of Massachusetts Bay Colony until after Lexington and Concord, so that a merchant whose livelihood depended on trade with Britain or any individual whose ties with England were unusually strong might have fallen suspect if open declarations of loyalty and public proclamations of position had not been available.

NATIONAL INDEX 42927
BRISTOL 4103
FORD 1920
AMERICAN ANTIQUARIAN SOCIETY
38 x 25.4 cm.

# THE RECANTATIONS OF

## ROBERT HOOPER, JOHN PEDRICK, ROBERT HOOPER, Jun. GEORGE M'CALL, RICHARD REED, and HENRY SANDERS.

In COMMITTEE OF SAFETY,
*Cambridge, May* 4, 1775.

THE Recantations of a Number of Persons of the Town of *Marblehead*, viz. *Robert Hooper, John Pedrick, Robert Hooper*, Jun. *George M'Call, Richard Reed*, and *Henry Sanders*, having been laid before this Committee for their Opinion as to the Propriety of accepting them;

VOTED, That it is the Opinion of this Committee, That the Recantations of these Persons be accepted, and that they be made acquainted with the Proclamation lately issued by the PROVINCIAL CONGRESS, respecting those who may incline to go into *Boston*; and that it be recommended to the Inhabitants of this Province, that they be protected from all Injuries or Insults whatsoever, so long as they adhere to their several Recantations, and continue to assist and abide by their Country and the Inhabitants of *Marblehead* in particular, in the important Dispute between *Great-Britain* and *America*.

WILLIAM COOPER, Sec'y.

---

To the Inhabitants of the Town of *Marblehead*.

WHEN Governor *Hutchinson* was about leaving the Province, I signed an Address to him with no other Motive, than the Hopes it would have a Tendency to serve the Province in general, and this Town in particular. I am now convinced it has not had the hoped for Success, and therefore renounce it in all its Parts, and am sorry for it; and stand ready with my Interest to defend the Rights of my injured Country.

ROBERT HOOPER.

*Marblehead*, May 3, 1775.

---

WHEREAS I the Subscriber did some Time since sign an Address to Governor *Hutchinson*, which has given just Cause of Resentment to my Fellow-Countrymen: I do now declare, that at the Time of signing said Address, I did suppose it might serve us, but am convinced of my Error, and do now renounce said Address in all its Parts, and stand ready with my Life and Fortune to defend my injured Country, and hope for the Forgiveness of all Mankind.

JOHN PEDRICK.

*Marblehead*, April 28, 1775.

---

To the Inhabitants of the Town of *Marblehead*.

WHEREAS I the Subscriber did some Time since sign an Address to Governor *Hutchinson*, which has given just Offence to my Town and Country: I now declare, that I had not the least Design to offend either, but at the Time of signing said Address I thought it might be of Service to my Town and Country, but finding that it has not had the desired Effect, I do now renounce said Address in all its Parts, and beg that my Town and Country would forgive the Error, and I now assure them that at all Times I have been, and still am ready to the utmost of my Power, to support and defend the just Rights and Liberties of my Town and Country with my Life and Fortune.

ROBERT HOOPER, Jun.

*Marblehead, May* 1, 1775.

---

Mr. MODERATOR,

MY not acknowledging my Error and Sorrow in the last Meeting, for having signed an Address to the late Governor *Hutchinson*, which justly incensed this Town and Country, was, because I did not know what Business they were to proceed upon until it was too late: I now publicly and solemnly declare, that the Welfare of this Land was the only Motive that induced me to sign it. And as I find myself mistaken, am as ready as any other (as far as in me lies) to support its Rights and Liberties with my Life and Fortune. I humbly ask Pardon of those whose Sentiments then differed from mine, respecting Governor *Hutchinson*, for the high Reflection, which by signing said Address, I cast upon their Sense and Temper, and hope that my Townsmen and the Public will restore me to their Favor and Friendship.

GEORGE M'CALL.

*Marblehead*, May 3, 1775.

---

To the Gentlemen Select-Men of *Marblehead*.

WHEREAS I the Subscriber signed an Address to Governor *Hutchinson*, which I supposed would answer a good Purpose and be generally adopted, and being now convinced from a further Attention to the Matter, as well as the public Opinion, that it will greatly injure the Cause of *America*; I do now publicly declare, that I had no such Design, and therefore renounce the said Address in every Respect, and am heartily sorry that I ever signed it, and hope to be forgiven by my Town and Countrymen. I now stand ready with my Life and Interest to defend my injured Country whenever called upon.

RICHARD REED.

*Marblehead*, May 3, 1775.

---

GENTLEMEN,

WHEREAS I the Subscriber signed an Address to Governor *Hutchinson*, which I supposed would answer a good Purpose, and be generally adopted, and being now convinced from a a further Attention to the Matter, as well as the public Opinion, that it will greatly injure the Cause of *America*, I do now publicly declare, that I had no such Design, and therefore renounce the said Address in every Respect, and am heartily sorry that I ever signed it, and hope to be forgiven by my Town and Countrymen. I now stand ready with my Life and Interest to defend my injured Country whenever called upon.

HENRY SANDERS.

*Marblehead*, May 3, 1775.

---

*SALEM*: Printed by E. RUSSELL, next Door to JOHN TURNER, Esq; in the Main-street.

## 20. By His Excellency, The Hon. Thomas Gage, Esq. [Boston: Margaret Draper, 1775]

THIS broadside is one strong response to the events of April 18 and 19, 1775. General Gage, Commander in Chief of the British forces in America, was at the center of the events leading up to Lexington and Concord, since he assumed personal responsibility for the execution of the "Intolerable Acts," the name given to the various coercive measures passed by Parliament. These included the Boston Port Bill, the Administration of Justice Act, the Massachusetts Government Act, the Quartering Act, and the Quebec Act. Gage's Proclamation of June 12 effectively summarizes the status of the colony on the eve of Bunker Hill, shortly after Lexington and Concord.

If the Intolerable Acts rallied the other colonies to display sympathy with Massachusetts Bay, they provided Gage with an opportunity to force his will upon the colony, resulting tragically in armed conflict at Lexington green. On the assumption that a colonial militia was forming in Concord, and that ammunition was stored there, and in an effort to arrest Samuel Adams and John Hancock, who were in Lexington, Gage sent an expedition led by Lt. Colonel Smith and Major John Pitcairn to Concord with the following orders:

> Sir, A Quantity of Ammunition and Provision together as Number of Canon and small Arms having been collected at Concord for the avowed Purpose of asserting a Rebellion against His Majesty's Government, You will march with the Corps of Grenadiers and Light Infantry put under your Command with the utmost expedition and secrecy to Concord, where you will seize and destroy all the Artillery and Ammunition . . .

According to Mark Boatner's *Encyclopedia of the American Revolution*, Paul Revere made a preliminary ride to warn Adams and Hancock and to alert citizens of a possible British plan to attack. Returning to Charlestown, he arranged the "one if by land, two if by sea" signal as preparation for the more famous ride made the night of April 18. The stage was set, and the central question of "who fired first" is still asked today. The ultimate responsibility for the battle and its consequences also became a matter of opinion, so the broadsides in this collection represent differing and opposing points of view on the same historical event. As a last resort, Gage here declares martial law in his determined response to the rebellious uprising that took place at Lexington and Concord.

NATIONAL INDEX 14184
FORD 1814
HENRY E. HUNTINGTON LIBRARY
49.5 x 32.4 cm.

By His EXCELLENCY,

# The Hon. *THOMAS GAGE*, Esq.

Governor, and Commander in Chief, in and over his Majeſty's Province of MASSACHUSETTS-BAY, and Vice-Admiral of the ſame.

# A PROCLAMATION.

WHEREAS the infatuated Multitudes, who have long ſuffered themſelves to be conducted by certain well known Incendiaries and Traitors, in a fatal Progeſſion of Crimes, againſt the conſtitutional Authority of the State, have at length proceeded to avowed Rebellion; and the good Effects which were expected to ariſe from the Patience and Lenity of the King's Government, have been often fruſtrated, and are now rendered hopeleſs, by the Influence of the ſame evil Counſels; it only remains for thoſe who are entruſted with ſupreme Rule, as well for the Puniſhment of the guilty, as the Protection of the well-affected, to prove they do not bear the Sword in vain.

The Infringements which have been committed upon the moſt ſacred Rights of the Crown and People of Great-Britain, are too many to enumerate on one Side, and are all too atrocious to be palliated on the other. All unprejudiced People who have been Witneſſes of the late Tranſactions, in this and the neighboring Provinces, will find upon a tranſient Review, Marks of Premeditation and Conſpiracy that would juſtify the fulneſs of Chaſtiſement: And even thoſe who are leaſt acquainted with Facts, cannot fail to receive a juſt Impreſſion of their Enormity, in Proportion as they diſcover the Arts and Aſſiduity by which they have been falſified or concealed. The Authors of the preſent unnatural Revolt never daring to truſt their Cauſe or their Actions, to the Judgment of an impartial Public, or even to the diſpaſſionate Reflection of their Followers, have uniformly placed their chief Confidence in the Suppreſſion of Truth: And while indefatigable and ſhameleſs Pains have been taken to obſtruct every Appeal to the real Intereſt of the People of America; the groſſeſt Forgeries, Calumnies and Abſurdities that ever inſulted human Underſtanding, have been impoſed upon their Credulity. The Preſs, that diſtinguiſhed Appendage of public Liberty, and when fairly and impartially employed it's beſt Support, has been invariably proſtituted to the moſt contrary Purpoſes: The animated Language of ancient and virtuous Times, calculated to vindicate and promote the juſt Rights, and Intereſt of Mankind, have been applied to countenance the moſt abandoned Violation of thoſe ſacred Bleſſings; and not only from the flagitious Prints, but from the popular Harrangues of the Times, Men have been taught to depend upon Activity in Treaſon, for the Security of their Perſons, and Properties; 'till to compleat the horrid Profanation of Terms, and of Ideas, the Name of GOD, has been introduced in the Pulpits to excite and juſtify Devaſtation and Maſſacre.

The Minds of Men having been thus gradually prepared for the worſt Extremities, a Number of armed Perſons, to the amount of many Thouſands aſſembled on the 19th of April laſt, and from behind Walls, and lurking Holes, attacked a Detachment of the King's Troops who not expecting to conſummate an Act of Phrenzy, unprepared for Vengeance, and willing to decline it, made uſe of their Arms only in their own Defence. Since that Period the Rebels, deriving Confidence from Impunity, have added Inſult to Outrage; have repeatedly fired upon the King's Ships and Subjects, with Cannon and ſmall Arms, have poſſeſſed the Roads, and other Communications by which the Town of Boſton was ſupplied with Proviſions; and with a prepoſterous Parade of Military Arrangement, they affect to hold the Army beſieged; while Part of their Body make daily and indiſcriminate Invaſions upon private Property, and with a Wantoneſs of Cruelty ever incident to lawleſs Tumult, carry Depredation and Diſtreſs wherever they turn their Steps. The Actions of the 19th of April are of ſuch Notoriety, as muſt baffle all Attempts to contradict them, and the Flames of Buildings and other Property from the Iſlands, and adjacent Country, for ſome Weeks paſt, ſpread a melancholly Confirmation of the ſubſequent Aſſertions.

In this Exigency of complicated Calamities, I avail myſelf of the laſt Effort within the Bounds of my Duty, to ſpare the Effuſion of Blood; to offer, and I do hereby in his Majeſty's Name, offer and promiſe, his moſt gracious Pardon to all Perſons who ſhall forthwith lay down their Arms and return to the Duties of peaceable Subjects, excepting only from the Benefit of ſuch Pardon, *Samuel Adams* and *John Hancock*, whoſe Offences are of too flagitious a Nature to admit of any other Conſideration than that of condign Puniſhment.

And to the End that no Perſon within the Limits of this proffered Mercy, may plead Ignorance of the Conſequences of refuſing it, I by theſe Preſents proclaim not only the Perſons above-named and excepted, but alſo all their Adherents, Aſſociates, and Abettors, meaning to comprehend in thoſe Terms, all and every Perſon, and Perſons of what Claſs, Denomination or Deſcription ſoever, who have appeared in Arms againſt the King's Government, and ſhall not lay down the ſame as afore-mentioned; and likewiſe all ſuch as ſhall ſo take Arms after the Date hereof, or who ſhall in any-wiſe protect or conceal ſuch Offenders, or aſſiſt them with Money, Proviſion, Cattle, Arms, Ammunition, Carriages, or any other Neceſſary for Subſiſtence or Offence; or ſhall hold ſecret Correſpondence with them by Letter, Meſſage, Signal, or otherwiſe, to be Rebels and Traitors, and as ſuch to be treated.

AND WHEREAS, during the Continuance of the preſent unnatural Rebellion, Juſtice cannot be adminiſtred by the common Law of the Land, the Courſe whereof has, for a long Time paſt, been violently impeded, and wholly interrupted; from whence reſults a Neceſſity for uſing and exerciſing the Law Martial; I have therefore thought fit, by the Authority veſted in me, by the Royal Charter to this Province, to publiſh, and I do hereby publiſh, proclaim and order the Uſe and Exerciſe of the Law Martial, within and throughout this Province, for ſo long Time as the preſent unhappy Occaſion ſhall neceſſarily require; whereof all Perſons are hereby required to take Notice, and govern themſelves, as well to maintain Order and Regularity among the peaceable Inhabitants of the Province, as to reſiſt, encounter and ſubdue the Rebels and Traitors above-deſcribed by ſuch as ſhall be called upon for thoſe Purpoſes.

To theſe inevitable, but I truſt ſalutary Meaſures, it is a far more pleaſing Part of my Duty, to add the Aſſurances of Protection and Support, to all who in ſo trying a Criſis, ſhall manifeſt their Allegiance to the King, and Affection to the Parent State. So that ſuch Perſons as may have been intimidated to quit their Habitations in the Courſe of this Alarm, may return to their reſpective Callings and Profeſſions; and ſtand diſtinct and ſeparate from the Parricides of the Conſtitution, till GOD in his Mercy ſhall reſtore to his Creatures, in this diſtracted Land, that Syſtem of Happineſs from which they have been ſeduced, the Religion of Peace, and Liberty founded upon Law.

*GIVEN at* Boſton, *this Twelfth Day of* June, *in the Fifteenth Year of the Reign of His Majeſty* GEORGE *the Third, by the Grace of GOD, of* Great-Britain, France *and* Ireland, KING, *Defender of the Faith,* &c. Annoque Domini, 177

By His Excellency's Command,
THO'S FLUCKER, Secr'y.

THO'S GAGE.

## *GOD* Save the KING.

Mr. Gage you have forgot the Congreſs

## 21. By the Governor. June 19, 1775
[Boston: Margaret Draper?, 1775]

GENERAL Gage's Proclamation of June 12, 1775 [plate 20] apparently had little effect on the people of Boston. They simply did not "lay down their arms!" A week later, he issued another proclamation in stronger terms requiring "all Persons who have yet Fire-Arms in their Possession, immediately to surrender them at the Court-House." He further declares that "all Persons in whose Possession any Fire-Arms may hereafter be found, will be deemed Enemies to his Majesty's Government." Even after the Battle of Bunker Hill, Gage thought the British could regain control of Massachusetts Bay Colony.

This proclamation, issued just after the Bunker Hill battle, is an early attempt at gun control. The requirement, however, is not for registration of handguns; rather, it is for the total surrender of firearms "to such persons as shall be authorized to receive them," and there is a declaration of hostility against those "enemies" who retained guns in their possession. No wonder that the early legislators regarded the "right to possess and bear arms" an important aspect of civil liberty, including it in the Bill of Rights.

Gage's proclamation is also evidence of how poorly he and the British authorities had perceived the situation during the years of hostilities immediately prior to the Declaration of Independence. The facts that Francis Bernard had been recalled to England in 1769 and that Gage himself was recalled soon after this illustrate the attention given to colonial sentiment, even by Parliament. Nevertheless, Gage's proclamation is delivered in the spirit of the Coercive Acts, which Parliament had supported, and it represents the strong line of forced authority through which the British thought they could reassert their control over the colonial government. As other broadsides in this collection clearly show [e.g., plate 29], Thomas Gage was to become a subject of rebuke, and would be much satirized at the time of his recall to England.

Two features of the broadside deserve special mention. The cartouche at the top adorns a number of official proclamations of this period, but was soon to be replaced by the official shield of the Commonwealth of Massachusetts. The apostrophe GOD SAVE THE KING was in use only briefly after 1775, as more patriotic sentiments were expressed by revolutionary printers [plate 5]. The format of the pronouncements, however, did not change, and, as other broadsides reproduced in this book show, the wording and seals were changed while the visual style of the proclamations remained standard.

NATIONAL INDEX 42865
BRISTOL 4041
FORD 1817
MASSACHUSETTS HISTORICAL SOCIETY
37 x 21 cm.

# By the GOVERNOR.

# A PROCLAMATION.

WHEREAS, notwithstanding the repeated Assurances of the Selectmen and others, That all the Inhabitants of the Town of BOSTON had *bona Fide*, delivered their Fire-Arms unto the Persons appointed to receive them, though I had Advices at the same Time of the contrary, and whereas I have since had full Proof that many have been perfidious in this Respect and have secreted great Numbers:

I HAVE thought fit to issue this Proclamation, to require of all Persons who have yet Fire-Arms in their Possession, immediately to surrender them at the Court-House, to such Persons as shall be authorized to receive them; and hereby to declare that all Persons in whose Possession any Fire-Arms may hereafter be found, will be deemed Enemies to his Majesty's Government.

*GIVEN at* Boston, *the Nineteenth Day of June,* 1775, *in the Fifteenth Year of the Reign of our Sovereign Lord,* GEORGE *the Third, by the Grace of* GOD, *of* Great-Britain, France, *and* Ireland, KING, *Defender of the Faith,* &c.

THO'S GAGE.

By His Excellency's Command,
THO'S FLUCKER, Secr'y.

***GOD*** **Save the KING.**

## 22. The American Hero
[n.p., 1775?]

THE Battle of Bunker Hill, June 17, 1775, is second only to Lexington and Concord in the popular folklore of the American Revolution. Unlike the earlier skirmishes, however, Bunker Hill was a large battle with many casualties. Mark Boatner records that some 441 Americans were killed or wounded, against 1,150 for the British. His *Encyclopedia of the American Revolution* suggests that the significance of the battle has always been vague. The British learned that they were contending with a stronger military force than they had imagined, but some Americans viewed the conflict as unnecessary, though they did discover that the British regulars were far from invincible. Patriotism and nationalism became the hallmark of America's new beginning in independence, and the folk-heroes who emerged, like Patrick Henry and George Washington (who had been named Commander-in-Chief on June 17, 1775, but whose command actually commenced on July 3, after the Battle of Bunker Hill) were first, last and always patriots of unswerving loyalty to the united colonies and their independence from Britain.

This poem by Nathaniel Niles was published many times, frequently with the subtitle, "A Sapphic Ode." Although it refers directly to the events of the Battle of Bunker Hill, there is evidence that it was first printed as late as 1776 or 1777. The most convincing argument for a later date is that the tune for the poem-song was composed after the Bunker Hill episode. According to Richard Crawford's *Andrew Law: an American Psalmodist*, "The American Hero" appeared in Andrew Law's *Select Number of Plain Tunes* (Norwich, Connecticut, 1776?), and the poem and the tune were probably composed together to celebrate the earlier battle.

NATIONAL INDEX 42911
BRISTOL 4083
FORD 1787
WEGELIN 487
HENRY E. HUNTINGTON LIBRARY
25 x 21 cm.

# THE AMERICAN HERO.

## Made on the battle of Bunker-Hill, and the burning of Charleſtown.

WHY ſhould vain mortals tremble at the
ſight of
Death and deſtruction in the field of battle,
Where blood and carnage clothe the ground
in crimſon,
Sounding with death groans?

Death will invade us by the means appointed,
And we muſt all bow to the king of terrors;
Nor am I anxious, if I am prepared,
What ſhape he comes in.

Infinite goodneſs teaches us ſubmiſſion;
Bids us be quiet under all his dealings:
Never repining, but forever praiſing
God our Creator.

Well may we praiſe him—all his ways are
perfect;
Though a reſplendence, infinitely glowing,
Dazzles in glory on the ſight of mortals
Struck blind by luſtre.

Good is Jehovah in beſtowing ſun-ſhine,
Nor leſs his goodneſs in the ſtorm & thunder,
Mercies and judgments both proceed from
kindneſs;
Infinite kindneſs.

O then exult, that God forever reigneth;
Clouds, which around him hinder our pre-
ception,
Bind us the ſtronger to exalt his name, and
Shout louder praiſes.

Then to the wiſdom of my Lord and Maſter,
I will commit all that I have or wiſh for;
Sweetly as babes ſleep will I give my life up
When call'd to yield it.

Now, Mars, I dare thee, clad in ſmoky pillars,
Burſting from bomb-ſhells, roaring from
the cannon,
Rattling in grape ſhot, like a ſtorm of hail-
ſtones,
Torturing æther!

Up the bleak heavens let the ſpreading flames
riſe,
Breaking like Ætna thro' the ſmoky columns,
Low'ring like Egypt o'er the falling city,
Wantonly burnt down.

While all their hearts quick palpitate for
havoc,
Let ſlip your blood hounds, nam'd the Britiſh lions,
Dauntleſs as death ſtares; nimble as the
whirlwind;
Dreadful as demons.

Let oceans waft on all your floating caſtles,
Fraught with deſtruction, horrible to nature;
Then with your ſails fill'd by a ſtorm of ven-
geance,
Bear down to battle!

From the dire caverns made by ghoſtly miners,
Let the exploſion, dreadful as volcanoes,
Heave the broad town, with all its wealth
and people,
Quick to deſtruction.

Still ſhall the banners of the King of heaven
Never advance where I'm afraid to follow:
While that preceds me, with an open boſom,
War, I defy thee.

Fame and dear freedom lure me on to battle,
While a fell deſpot, grimer than a death's
head,
Stings me with ſerpents, fiercer than Meduſa's
To the encounter.

Life for my country, and the cauſe of free-
dom,
Is but a trifle for a worm to part with;
And if preſerved in ſo great a conteſt,
Life is redoubled.

## 23. A Song Composed by the British Soldiers, June, 1775
[n.p., 1775]

THE Battle of Bunker Hill produced its own folklore and balladry, like "The American Hero" [plate 22]. It was a difficult and costly battle for both sides; the British were under the command of General Thomas Gage, and the Americans were commanded by Colonel Prescott. Although the Americans were forced to withdraw from positions they had occupied around Bunker Hill and Breed's Hill because their ammunition had been depleted, they were able to inflict heavy casualties on the British, who emerged from the battle with a mixed victory and with a new awareness of colonial determination.

The song here was used by both sides. On other versions of this song, the title is "A Song Composed by the British Butchers," although the text, curiously, remains the same. Ola Winslow suggests these verses were printed many times, and in such varying versions that they show both Tory and colonial sympathies. With slight alterations of the broadside text, the story of any significant event could be told from the point of view of either side. "A Song Composed by the British Soldiers" was sung by both choral societies and smaller tavern groups. It has been revived in several bicentennial celebrations, and has a melodic tune that is easily remembered.

NATIONAL INDEX 42939
BRISTOL 4119
FORD 1934
WEGELIN 779 variant issue
AMERICAN ANTIQUARIAN SOCIETY
40.3 x 17 cm.

A

# SONG

## Compoſed by the *Britiſh Soldiers*, after the Battle at *Bunker-Hill*, on the 17th of June, 1775.

IT was on the ſeventeenth by break of Day, the Yankees did ſurpriſe us,
With their ſtrong works they had thrown up, to burn the town and drive us ;
But ſoon we had an order came, an order to defeat them,
Like rebels ſtout they ſtood it out, and thought we ne'er could beat them.

About the hour of twelve that day, an order came for marching,
With three good flints and ſixty rounds, each man hop'd to diſcharge them ;
We marched down to the long wharf, where boats were ready waiting,
With expedition we embark'd, our ſhips kept cannonading.

And when our boats all filled were, with officers and ſoldiers,
With as good troops as England had, to oppoſe who dare controul us ;
And when our boats all filled were, we row'd in line of battle,
Where ſhowers of balls like hail did fly, our cannon loud did rattle.

There was Cops-Hill battery near Charleſtown, our twenty-fours they play'd,
And the three frigates in the ſtream, that very well behav'd ;
The Glaſgow frigate clear'd the ſhore, all at the time of landing,
With her grape ſhot and cannon balls, no Yankees e'er could ſtand them.

And when we landed on the ſhore, we draw'd up all together,
The Yankees they all mann'd their works & thought we'd ne'er come thither :
But ſoon they did perceive brave Howe, brave Howe our bold commander,
With grenadiers and infantry, we made them to ſurrender.

Brave William Howe on our right wing, cry'd boys fight on like thunder,
You ſoon will ſee the rebels flee, with great amaze and wonder ;
Now ſome lay bleeding on the ground, and ſome full faſt a running,
O'er hills & dales & mountains high, crying zounds brave Howe's a coming.

They began to play on our left wing, where Pigot he commanded,
But we return'd it back again, with courage moſt undaunted ;
To our grape ſhot and muſquet ball, to which they were but ſtrangers,
They thought to come with ſword in hand, but ſoon they found their danger.

And when their works we got into, and put them to the flight, ſir,
Some of them did hide themſelves, and others died with fright, ſir ;
And when their works we got into, without great fear or danger,
Their works were made ſo firm and ſtrong, the Yankees are great ſtrangers.

But as for our artillery, they all behaved dinty,
For while their ammunition held, we gave it to them plenty ;
But our conductor he got broke, for his miſconduct ſure, ſir,
The ſhot he ſent for twelve pound guns, were made for twenty-four, ſir.

There is ſome in Boſton pleaſe to ſay, as we the field were taking,
We went to kill their countrymen, while they their hay were making ;
But ſuch ſtout whigs I never ſaw, to hang them all I'd rather,
For making hay with muſquet balls, and buck-ſhot mix'd together.

Brave Howe is ſo conſiderate, as to prevent all danger,
He allows us half a pint a day, to rum we are not ſtrangers ;
Long may he live by land and ſea, for he's belov'd by many,
The name of Howe the Yankees dread, we ſee it very plainly.

And now my ſong is at an end, and to conclude my ditty,
It is the poor and ignorant, and only them I pity ;
And as for their king that John Hancock, and Adams if they're taken,
Their heads for ſigns ſhall hang up high upon that hill call'd Beacon.

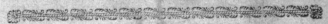

## 24. A Poem, on the Bloody Engagement That Was Fought on Bunker Hill
[Chelmsford: Nathaniel Coverly, 1775]

ELISHA Rich, a minister, wrote several occasional poems celebrating the events of the Revolutionary War. His *Poetical Dialogues* appeared in 1775, published by Nathaniel Coverly of Chelmsford. More interesting in relation to the present broadside poem, however, is the poem, *Poetical Remarks Upon the Fight at the Boston Light-House, Which happen'd between a Party of Troops belonging to the United Colonies, Commanded by Major Tupper. . . .* [Chelmsford: Presented by Nathaniel Coverly]

Rich's "Poem . . . Bunker's Hill," is composed in rhythmic quatrains, with a simple aa/bb rhyme scheme throughout. The twenty-six stanzas give mythic dimension to the military event by invoking God's sanction of the colonial cause and by suggesting that an international union of nations will someday usher in a millennium of peace (stanza xxv). The illustration appears to be a crude representation of the battle, and the coffin shown at the top commemorates the death of General Joseph Warren.

NATIONAL INDEX 14426
FORD 1922
WEGELIN 322
HENRY E. HUNTINGTON LIBRARY
39 x 24.5 cm.

# POEM

On the Bloody engagement that was Fought on

# BUNKER's HILL

In Charleſtown

# NEW-ENGLAND,

On the 17th of JUNE, 1775: Together with ſome Remarks of the Cruelty and Barbarity of the BRITISH Troops, by Deſtroying the above mention'd TOWN by FIRE, by which a Number of Diſtreſs'd Inhabitants were forced to Flee from the Flames, to ſeek Relief and Shelter among their Sympathizing Brethren in the neighbouring TOWNS.

BY ELISHA RICH, Miniſter of the Goſpel.

I.

AMERICANS pray lend an Ear,
And you a ſolemn Tale ſhall hear
'Twas on the ſeventeenth of JUNE,
Men were cut down all in their bloom.

II.

GOD grant it's memory may lye
A witneſs againſt TYRANNY,
Alſo againſt NEW-ENGLAND's ſin,
Which hath let cruel TYRANTS in.

III.

Whoſe bloody minds are to devour,
For which they do Exert their power;
They would eſtabliſh SLAVARY
Or elſe our LAND in ruin lay,

IV.

Laſt JUNE, upon the ſeventeenth day.
Theſe Troops for CHARLESTOWN made their way,
For to reſiſt our SOLDIERS there,
Who a ſtrong FORT prepairing were.

V.

The SHIPS of WAR had gather'd round,
To make our Soldiers quit the ground.
And tho' ſome Men by them were ſlain,
Yet ſtill their courage they retain.

VI.

But when theſe Troops had landed there,
Our Men to fight them did prepare,
And when our Men ſhot their firſt round,
Many BRITAINS gaſped on the ground.

VII.

They Fought like brave MEN on both ſides,
And many a valiant HERO dy'd,
The Earth was ſoaked with their blood,
And wounded wallow'd in the Flood.

VIII.

So warm a Fight is ſeldom known,
Men were cut down like Graſs that's mown,
And ſome ſay Gage who did them 'ſpie,
Said we that ground too dear ſhall buy,

IX.

Our Men that fought, they were but few,
Their POWDER being ſpent, withdrew,
And left the ground unto their foe,
And back again were forſt to go.

X.

Tho' BRITISH TROOPS the ground did gain,
Yet many more of them were ſlain,
The beſt intelligence doth tell,
One THOUSAND and near FIFTY fell.

XI.

'Tis thought they loſt five to our one,
Altho' our Men were forc'd to run,
They bought the victory ſo dear
It did not much increaſe our fear,

XII.

Theſe Savage Troops CHARLESTOWN, did Fire
And it to Aſhes did expire,
The TOWN now in deſtruction lies,
The ſight affects our hearts and eyes.

XIII.

Why is this deſolation made?
Why is the Tyrants banner ſpread?
Why is he ſuffer'd thus to reign
And ſo far Victory obtain.

XIV.

NEW-ENGLAND ſearch and know the cauſe,
Haſt thou not broken GOD's bleſt LAWS,
For which thy GOD doth thee chaſtize,
And turns thy Friends to Enemies.

XV.

Would thou obtain thy LIBERTY,
Then break all bands of ſlavery,
And do thou LIBERTY proclaim
To all that have a human frame.

XVI.

But if oppreſſion here is found?
Can you with victory be crown'd,
No no, be ſure this cannot be,
While thou thy neighbours do not free.

XVII.

O may we ne'er forget the Day,
When Charleſtown in it's ruins lay,
And many of our Sons did die
And fled before their enemy.

XVIII.

MOTHERS Lament their Sons that fell.
And Wife's the loſs of Huſbands tell,
Their Cries may cauſe the hardeſt heart,
With their diſtreſs to bear a part.

XIX.

Come mourn with them and for them pray
That GOD would turn their night to day,
Make up their loſs by ſpecial Grace,
That they with joy may ſee his face.

XX

Let's view the rod that GOD hath ſent
And for our many ſins relent,
So that God's wrath again may ceaſe
And may reſtore our land to peace.

XXI.

That TYRANTS may no more ariſe
And brand their Swords with haughty eyes,
May Heaven cauſe their pride to ceaſe,
That ſo Chriſt's kingdom may encreaſe.

XXII.

May GOD bring on the happy day
When carnal Swords no more ſhall ſlay,
And CHRIST as Prince of peace ſhall reign,
And War be learnt no more again.

XXIII.

Then men ſhall lay oppreſſion by,
Their neighbours good ſhall not envy,
Nor covet what is not their own
Nor tread the poorer people down.

XXIV.

That day will bring great joy to all,
That on the name of GOD do call,
When Wars and fightings ſhall no more,
Spread deſolation as before.

XXV.

Then Nations ſhall together join,
And Kings their ſeptres ſhall reſign,
To JESUS as their Prieſt and KING,
And ſhall to him their honours bring.

XXVI.

Thus CHRIST ſhall have a large encreaſe,
And ſhall his kingdom rule in peace,
The CHURCH in him ſhall reſt ſecure
While SUN and MOON and STARS endur.

CHELMSFORD: Printed and ſold by Nathaniel Coverly, 1775.

25. Boston, 26th of June, 1775
[Boston: John Howe, 1775]

THIS is an account of the Battle of Bunker Hill from the British point of view. Characteristically, the battle is described with restraint, and the casualties (which were great for the British) are minimized. The spirit of the British soldiers—present in verse broadsides celebrating the battle—is missing from this account, and the final paragraph is anticlimactic: "This Action has shown the Bravery of the King's Troops, who under every Disadvantage, gained a compleat Victory over Three Times their Number, strongly posted, and covered by Breastworks. But they fought for their *King*, their *Laws*, and *Constitution*."

NATIONAL INDEX 13842
FORD 1801
AMERICAN ANTIQUARIAN SOCIETY
35.8 x 21.3 cm.

BOSTON, 26th of JUNE, 1775.

THIS Town was alarmed on the 17th Inſtant at break of Day, by a Firing from the Lively Ship of War; and a Report was immediately ſpread that the Rebels had broke Ground, and were raiſing a Battery on the Heights of the Peninſula of Charleſtown, againſt the Town of Boſton. They were plainly ſeen, and in a few Hours a Battery of Six Guns, played upon their Works. Preparations were inſtantly made for the landing a Body of Men; and ſome Companies of Grenadiers and Light Infantry, with ſome Battallions, and Field Artillery; amounting in the whole to about 2000 Men, under the Command of Major General HOWE, and Brigadier General PIGOT, were embarked with great Expedition, and landed on the Peninſula without Oppoſition; under Cover of ſome Ships of War, and armed Veſſels.

The Troops formed as ſoon as landed: The Rebels upon the Heights, were perceived to be in great Force, and ſtrongly poſted. A Redoubt thrown up on the 16th at Night, with other Works full of Men, defended with Cannon, and a large Body poſted in the Houſes of Charleſtown, covered their Right; and their Left was covered by a Breaſtwork, Part of it Cannon Proof, which reached from the Left of the Redoubt to the Myſtick River.

Beſides the Appearance of the Rebels Strength, large Columns were ſeen pouring in to their Aſſiſtance; but the King's Troops advanced; the Attack began by a Cannonade, and notwithſtanding various Impediments of Fences, Walls, &c. and the heavy Fire they were expoſed to, from the vaſt Numbers of Rebels, and their Left galled from the Houſes of Charleſtown, the Troops made their Way to the Redoubt, mounted the Works, and carried it. The Rebels were then forced from other ſtrong Holds, and purſued 'till they were drove clear of the Peninſula, leaving Five Pieces of Cannon behind them. Charleſtown was ſet on Fire during the Engagement, and moſt Part of it conſumed. The Loſs they ſuſtained, muſt have been conſiderable, from the vaſt Numbers they were ſeen to carry off during the Action, excluſive of what they ſuffered from the ſhipping. About a Hundred were buried the Day after, and Thirty found wounded on the Field, ſome of which are ſince Dead. About 170 of the King's Troops were killed, and ſince dead of their Wounds; and a great many were wounded.

This Action has ſhown the Bravery of the King's Troops, who under every Diſadvantage, gained a compleat Victory over Three Times their Number, ſtrongly poſted, and covered by Breaſtworks. But they fought for their KING, their LAWS and CONSTITUTION.

## 26. A Proclamation for a Public Thanksgiving
## [Watertown: Benjamin Edes, 1775]

THE purpose of fast days, and "days of Thanksgiving," was to provide times for reflection on the generosity of Providence in guiding the colony through the perils of the original "errand into the wilderness," as the early settlers conceived their mission for God. In the years preceding the Revolution, a civil dimension to this divine purpose was developed in the gratitude expressed for God's assistance in throwing off the yoke of Great Britain [plate 37]. Of course, the theme of freedom from tyranny was easily associated with divine intention, and the broadsides of this period are rich with allusions to God's sanction of the colonial cause. The first paragraph of this broadside states the general theme, showing the tradition of God's support for the American settlement; the second paragraph specifically develops this theme in the context of revolutionary events. The broadside concludes with an apostrophe to God to "Save the People," rather than the King.

NATIONAL INDEX 14199
FORD 1874
AMERICAN ANTIQUARIAN SOCIETY
42.2 x 33 cm.

# A PROCLAMATION

### FOR A

# PUBLIC THANKSGIVING.

*A*LTHO' *in Consequence of the unnatural, cruel, and barbarous Measures, adopted and pursued by the British Administration, great and distressing Calamities are brought upon our oppressed Country, and on this Colony in particular ; we feel the dreadful Effects of Civil War, by which America is stained with the Blood of her valiant Sons, who have bravely fallen in the laudable Defence of our Rights and Priviledges ;—Our Capital, once the Seat of Justice, Opulence and Virtue, is unjustly wrested from its proper Owners, who are obliged to flee from the Iron Hand of Tyranny, or are held in the unrelenting Arms of Oppression :—Our Sea-Ports greatly distressed, and Towns burnt by the Foes, who have acted the Part of barbarous Incendiaries. —And altho' the wise and holy Governor of the World, has, in his righteous Providence, sent Droughts into this Colony, and wasting Sickness into many of our Towns ; yet we have the greatest Reason to adore and praise the Supreme Disposer of Events, who deals infinitely better with us than we deserve ; and amidst all his Judgments hath remembered Mercy, by causing the Voice of Health again to be heard amongst us ;—Instead of Famine, affording to an ungrateful People a Competency of the Necessaries and Comforts of Life ; in remarkably preserving and protecting our Troops, when in apparent Danger, while our Enemies, with all their boasted Skill and Strength, have met with Loss, Disappointment, and Defeat ;—and in the Course of his good Providence, the Father of Mercies hath bestowed upon us, many other Favours, which call for our grateful Acknowledgements.*

Therefore,

WE have thought fit, with the Advice of the Council and House of Representatives, to appoint THURSDAY the *Twenty-third* Day of *November* Instant, to be observed as a Day of public *THANKSGIVING*, throughout this Colony ; hereby calling upon Ministers and People, to meet for religious Worship on said Day, and *devoutly* to offer up their unfeigned Praises to Almighty GOD, the Source and benevolent Bestower of all Good, for his affording the necessary Means of Subsistance, tho' our Commerce has been prevented, and the Supplies from the Fishery denied us.—That such a Measure of Health is enjoyed among us ; that the Lives of our Officers and Soldiers have been so remarkably preserved, while our Enemies have fell before them :—That the vigorous Efforts which have been used to excite the Savage Vengeance of the Wilderness, and rouse the *Indians* to Arms, that an unavoidable Destruction might come upon our Frontiers, have been almost miraculously defeated :—That our unnatural Enemies, instead of Ravaging the Country with uncontrouled Sway, are confined within such narrow Limits, to their own Mortification and Distress, environed by an *American* Army, brave and determined ;—That such a Band of Union, founded upon the best Principles, unites the *American* Colonies :—That our Rights and Priviledges, both Civil and Religious, are so far preserved to us, notwithstanding all the Attempts of our barbarous Enemies to deprive us of them.——

And to offer up humble and fervent Prayers to Almighty GOD, for the whole *British* Empire ; especially for the UNITED *AMERICAN* COLONIES :—That he would bless our Civil Rulers, and lead them into wise and prudent Measures in this dark, and difficult Day :—That he would endow our General Court with all that Wisdom which is profitable to direct :—That he would graciously Smile upon our Endeavours to restore Peace, preserve our Rights and Priviledges, and hand them down to Posterity :—That he would give Wisdom to the *American* Congress, equal to their important Station :—That he would direct the Generals, and the *American* Armies, wherever employed, and give them Success and Victory :—That he would preserve and strengthen the Harmony of the UNITED COLONIES :—That he would pour out his Spirit upon all Orders of Men, thro' the Land, bring us to a hearty Repentance and Reformation ; purify and sanctify all his Churches :—That he would make Our's Emanuel's Land :—That he would spread the Knowledge of the Redeemer thro' the whole Earth, and fill the World with his Glory.

And all servile Labour is forbidden on said Day.

*GIVEN under our Hands at the Council-Chamber, in Watertown, this Fourth Day of November, in the Year of the LORD, One Thousand seven Hundred and Seventy-five.*

By their Honor's Command,
PEREZ MORTON, Dep'y. Secr'y.

JAMES OTIS,
W. SPOONER,
CALEB CUSHING,
JOSEPH GERRISH,
JOHN WHETCOMB,
JEDEDIAH FOSTER,
JAMES PRESCOTT,
ELDAD TAYLOR,
BENJA. LINCOLN,
MICHAEL FARLEY,
JOSEPH PALMER,
SAMUEL HOLTEN,
JABEZ FISHER,
MOSES GILL,
BENJA. WHITE.

# GOD SAVE THE PEOPLE.

*WATERTOWN*: Printed by *Benjamin Edes*, Printer to the Honorable COUNCIL, and House of REPRESENTATIVES. M,DCC,LXXV.

## 27. By the Great and General Court of the Colony of Massachusetts Bay
[Watertown: Benjamin Edes, 1776]

THIS broadside is important because it so eloquently foreshadows the Declaration of Independence. It is more than an official proclamation; the rhetoric, and the general subject of human freedom, are focussed sharply in an assessment of England's tyranny over the colonies: "The Administration of *Great Britain*, despising equally the Justice, Humanity, and Magnanimity of their Ancestors, and the Rights, Liberties, and Courage of AMERICANS, have, for a Course of Years, laboured to establish a Sovereignty in *America*, not founded in the Consent of the People, but in the mere Will of Persons a Thousand Leagues from Us, whom we know not, and have endeavoured to establish this Sovereignty over Us, against our Consent, in all Cases, whatsoever." Moreover, the line "When Kings, Ministers, Governors. . . ." is very similar to "When, in the Course of Human Events. . . ." the opening phrase of the Declaration of Independence. Throughout the document, the relationship between the specific circumstances of the American colonies and some broader, more general principles of human nature has been drawn. Like the Declaration of Independence, this proclamation is a philosophical statement as well as a list of specific grievances, and its publication, six months before the final adoption of many similar principles by all of the colonies, shows clearly how strong the impulse for severance from England was in the Massachusetts Bay Colony.

The broadside is also interesting because it follows the formulaic structure for official broadside proclamations, concluding, as did so many revolutionary statements, with *"God Save the People."*

NATIONAL INDEX 14839
FORD 1973
AMERICAN ANTIQUARIAN SOCIETY
43.8 x 35.6 cm.

By the Great and General Court of the Colony of *MASSACHUSETT'S-BAY.*

# A PROCLAMATION.

THE Frailty of human Nature, the Wants of Individuals, and the numerous Dangers which ſurround them, through the Courſe of Life, have in all Ages, and in every Country, impell'd them to form Societies, and eſtabliſh Governments.

As the Happineſs of the People is the ſole End of Government, ſo the Conſent of the People is the only Foundation of it, in Reaſon, Morality, and the natural Fitneſs of Things: And therefore every Act of Government, every Exerciſe of Sovereignty, againſt, or without, the Conſent of the People, is Injuſtice, Uſurpation, and Tyranny.

It is a Maxim, that in every Government, there muſt exiſt ſomewhere, a ſupreme, ſovereign, abſolute, and uncontroulable Power: But this Power reſides always in the Body of the People; and it never was, or can be delegated to one Man, or a few; the Great Creator having never given to Men a Right to veſt others with Authority over them, unlimitted either in Duration or Degree.

When Kings, Miniſters, Governors, or Legiſlators therefore, inſtead of exerciſing the Powers intruſted with them, according to the Principles, Forms, and Proportions ſtated by the Conſtitution, and eſtabliſhed by the original Compact, proſtitute thoſe Powers to the Purpoſes of Oppreſſion;—to ſubvert, inſtead of ſupporting a free Conſtitution;—to deſtroy, inſtead of preſerving the Lives, Liberties and Properties of the People;—they are no longer to be deemed Magiſtrates veſted with a ſacred Character, but become public Enemies, and ought to be reſiſted.

The Adminiſtration of *Great Britain*, deſpiſing equally the Juſtice, Humanity and Magnanimity of their Anceſtors; and the Rights, Liberties and Courage of *AMERICANS*, have, for a Courſe of Years, laboured to eſtabliſh a Sovereignty in *America*, not founded in the Conſent of the People, but in the mere Will of Perſons a Thouſand Leagues from Us, whom we know not, and have endeavoured to eſtabliſh this Sovereignty over Us, againſt our Conſent, in all Caſes whatſoever.

The Colonies, during this Period, have recurred to every peaceable Reſource in a free Conſtitution, by Petitions and Remonſtrances, to obtain Juſtice; which has been not only denied to them, but they have been treated with unexampled Indignity and Contempt; and at length, open War of the moſt atrocious, cruel and ſanguinary Kind, has been commenced againſt them. To this, an open, manly and ſucceſsful Reſiſtance has hitherto been made. Thirteen Colonies are now firmly united in the Conduct of this moſt juſt and neceſſary War, under the wiſe Councils of their Congreſs.

It is the Will of Providence, for wiſe, righteous, and gracious Ends that this Colony ſhould have been ſingled out, by the Enemies of *America*, as the firſt Object both of their Envy and their Revenge; and after having been made the Subject of ſeveral mercileſs and vindictive Statutes, one of which was intended to ſubvert our Conſtitution by Charter, is made the Seat of War.

No effectual Reſiſtance to the Syſtem of Tyranny prepared for us, could be made without either inſtant Recourſe to Arms, or a temporary Suſpenſion of the ordinary Powers of Government, and Tribunals of Juſtice: To the laſt of which Evils, in Hopes of a ſpeedy Reconciliation with *Great-Britain*, upon equitable Terms, the Congreſs adviſed Us to ſubmit:——And Mankind has ſeen a Phænomenon, without Example in the political World, a large and populous Colony, ſubſiſting in great Decency and Order, for more than a Year, under ſuch a Suſpenſion of Government.

But as our Enemies have proceeded to ſuch barbarous Extremities, commencing Hoſtilities upon the good People of this Colony, and with unprecedented Malice exerting their Power to ſpread the Calamities of Fire, Sword and Famine through the Land, and no reaſonable Proſpect remains of a ſpeedy Reconciliation with *Great-Britain*, the Congreſs have reſolved:

"That no Obedience being due to the Act of Parliament for altering the Charter of the Colony of *Maſſachuſetts-Bay*, nor to a Governor or Lieutenant Governor, who will not obſerve the Directions of, but endeavour to ſubvert that Charter; the Governor and Lieutenant Governor of that Colony, are to be conſidered as abſent, and their Offices vacant; and as there is no Council there, and Inconveniences ariſing from the Suſpenſion of the Powers of Government, are intolerable, eſpecially at a Time when General *Gage* hath actually levied War, and is carrying on Hoſtilities againſt his Majeſty's peaceable and loyal Subjects of that Colony; that, in order to conform as near as may be to the Spirit and Subſtance of the Charter, it be recommended to the Provincial Convention, to write Letters to the Inhabitants of the ſeveral Places which are intitled to Repreſentation in Aſſembly, requeſting them to chuſe ſuch Repreſentatives; and that the Aſſembly when choſen, do elect Counſellors; and that ſuch Aſſembly and Council, exerciſe the Powers of Government, until a Governor of his Majeſty's Appointment will conſent to govern the Colony, according to it's Charter."

In Purſuance of which Advice, the good People of this Colony have choſen a full and free Repreſentation of themſelves, who, being convened in Aſſembly, have elected a Council; who, as the executive Branch of Government, have conſtituted neceſſary Officers through the Colony. The preſent Generation, therefore, may be congratulated on the Acquiſition of a Form of Government, more immediately in all it's Branches, under the Influence and Controul of the People; and therefore more free and happy than was enjoyed by their Anceſtors: But as a Government ſo popular can be ſupported only by univerſal Knowledge and Virtue, in the Body of the People, it is the Duty of all Ranks, to promote the Means of Education, for the riſing Generation, as well as true Religion, Purity of Manners, and Integrity of Life, among all Orders and Degrees.

As an Army has become neceſſary for our Defence, and in all free States the Civil muſt provide for and controul the Military Power, the major Part of the Council have appointed Magiſtrates and Courts of Juſtice in every County, whoſe Happineſs is ſo connected with that of the People, that it is difficult to ſuppoſe they can abuſe their Truſt. The Buſineſs of it is to ſee thoſe Laws inforced, which are neceſſary for the Preſervation of Peace, Virtue and good Order. And the Great and General Court expects and requires, that all neceſſary Support and Aſſiſtance be given, and all proper Obedience yielded to them; and will deem every Perſon, who ſhall fail of his Duty in this Reſpect towards them, a Diſturber of the Peace of this Colony, and deſerving of exemplary Puniſhment.

That Piety and Virtue, which alone can ſecure the Freedom of any People, may be encouraged, and Vice and Immorality ſuppreſſed, the Great and General Court have thought fit to iſſue this Proclamation, commanding and enjoining it upon the good People of this Colony, that they lead ſober, religious and peaceable Lives; avoiding all Blaſphemies, Contempt of the Holy Scriptures, and of the Lord's Day, and all other Crimes and Miſdemeanors, all Debauchery, Prophaneneſs, Corruption, Venality, all riotous and tumultuous Proceedings, and all Immoralities whatſoever: And that they decently and reverently attend the public Worſhip of GOD, at all Times acknowledging with Gratitude his merciful Interpoſition in their Behalf, devoutly confiding in Him, as the GOD of Armies, by whoſe Favour and Protection alone they may hope for Succeſs, in their preſent Conflict.

And all Judges, Juſtices, Sheriffs, Grand Jurors, Tythingmen, and all other Civil Officers within this Colony, are hereby ſtrictly enjoined and commanded that they contribute all in their Power, by their Advice, Exertions and Examples, towards a general Reformation of Manners; and that they bring to condign Puniſhment, every Perſon, who ſhall commit any of the Crimes or Miſdemeanors aforeſaid, or that ſhall be guilty of any Immoralities whatſoever; and that they uſe their utmoſt Endeavours, to have the Reſolves of the Congreſs, and the good and wholſome Laws of this Colony duly carried into Execution.

And as the Miniſters of the Goſpel, within this Colony, have, during the late Relaxation of the Powers of Civil Government, exerted themſelves for our Safety, it is hereby recommended to them, ſtill to continue their virtuous Labours for the Good of the People, inculcating by their public Miniſtry, and private Example, the Neceſſity of Religion, Morality, and good Order.

In Council *January* 19. 1776.

*ORDERED*, That the foregoing Proclamation be read at the Opening of every Superiour Court of Judicature, &c. and Inferiour Court of Common Pleas, and Court of General Seſſions for the Peace within this Colony, by their reſpective Clerks; and at the annual Town Meetings in *March*, in each Town. And it is hereby recommended to the ſeveral Miniſters of the Goſpel, throughout this Colony, to read the ſame in their reſpective Aſſemblies on the Lord's Day next after their receiving it, immediately after Divine Service.

Sent down for Concurrence.

*PEREZ MORTON*, Dep'y Sec'ry.

In the Houſe of Repreſentatives, *January* 23, 1776. Read and concurr'd.

*WILLIAM COOPER*, Speaker pro Tem.

Conſented to,

| | |
|---|---|
| *WILLIAM SEVER,* | *MOSES GILL,* |
| *WALTER SPOONER,* | *MICHAEL FARLEY,* |
| *CALEB CUSHING,* | *SAMUEL HOLTEN,* |
| *JOHN WINTHROP,* | *CHARLES CHAUNCY,* |
| *THOMAS CUSHING,* | *JOSEPH PALMER,* |
| *JOHN WHETCOMB,* | *JOHN TAYLOR,* |
| *JEDIDIAH FOSTER,* | *BENJAMIN WHITE,* |
| *ELDAD TAYLOR,* | *JAMES PRESCOTT.* |

By Order of the General Court,

PEREZ MORTON, Dep. Sec'ry.

GOD Save the PEOPLE.

## 28. On the Evacuation of Boston by the British Troops
[Boston, 1776]

THE illustration on this broadside was used previously on a broadside printed by Thomas Fleet, entitled "New England Bravery," a poem that described the successful siege executed by General William Pepperell and his New England forces at Louisburg in 1745. The illustration is a good example of the longevity of some eighteenth-century cuts, which were passed from one printing house to another, and reused whenever the occasion demanded an illustration. According to Ola Winslow, the text of this "Evacuation of Boston" broadside is almost the same as one entitled, "Two favorite Songs made on the Evacuation of the Town of Boston." The spelling of certain words and the kind of typeface used are different, which suggests that if two separate presses were not involved, then the original poem must have been edited and issued for a second time.

The background of the evacuation of Boston was complex, but it was an episode unusually free from casualty and conflict. The British move from Boston was the result of cunning strategy on George Washington's part, and the consequence of a long-standing plan to remove most of the troops to New York. According to Mark Boatner's *Encyclopedia of the American Revolution*, "Washington had fortified Dorchester Heights to threaten the British ship movement, and thus gained bargaining power for British-occupied Boston during their withdrawal. The British were allowed to depart without interference, and the town was not burned by the withdrawing troops in exchange. In fact, the colonials gained large stores of medical supplies and munitions in resuming their occupation of Boston, in addition to some sixty functioning cannon. The evacuation was a maneuver of strategy rather than bloodshed; including the siege of Boston and the withdrawal of British troops, the colonial army lost fewer than twenty men."

The two songs represented here were probably sung. Their lines are sufficiently brief to permit spontaneous group response; the reprinting, in several separate versions with substantive alterations in each text, indicates widespread popularity and a general acceptance by people whose public singing may have suggested some of the changes and variants.

NATIONAL INDEX 43113
BRISTOL 4305
THE BOSTONIAN SOCIETY
35.7 x 19.7 cm.

# ON THE EVACUATION OF BOSTON

## by the *British Troops*, March 17th, 1776.

IN seventeen hundred and seventy six,
On March the eleventh, the time was prefix'd,
Our forces march'd on upon Dorchester neck,
Made fortifications against an attack.
The morning next following, as HOWE did espy,
The banks we cast up were so copious and high,
Said he in three months, all my men with their might,
Cou'd not make two such forts as they've made in a night.
Now we hear that their Admiral was very wroth,
And drawing his sword, he bids Howe to go forth,
And drive off the Yankees from Dorchester hill,
Or he'd leave the harbor and him to their will.
Howe rallies his forces upon the next day,
One party embark'd for the castle they say,
But the wind and the weather against them did fight,
On Governor's Island it drove them that night.
Then being discourag'd they soon did agree,
From Bunker and Boston, on board ship to flee:
Great Howe lost his senses, they say for a week,
For fear our next fort should be rais'd in King-street.
But yet notwithstanding the finger of God,
In the wind and the weather that often occurr'd;
Still Howe, Pharaoh like, did harden his heart,
Being thirsty for victory to maintain his part.
He gives out fresh orders on Thurday it's said,
Forms his men in three branches upon the parade;
Acknowledging it was a desperate case,
In their situation the Yankees to face:
Yet nevertheless being haughty of heart,
On Friday one branch of his men did embark:
A second stood ready down by the sea side:
His Dragoons were mounted all ready to ride.
Great Howe he now utters a desperate oration,
Saying fight my brave boys for the crown of our nation;
Take me for your pattern, and fight ye as I,
Let it be till we conquer, or else till we die.
But all of a sudden with an eagle ey'd glance,
They espied a fire being kindled by chance,
In a barrack at Cambridge, as many do know,
And then in confusion they ran to and fro.
Moreover as Providence order'd the thing,
Our drums beat alarm, our bell it did ring,
Which made them cry out, O the Yankees will come!
O horror they'll have us! so let us be gone.
Then hilter skilter they ran in the street,
Sometimes on their heads, and sometimes on their feet,
Leaving cannon and mortars, packsaddles and wheat,
Being glad to escape with the skin of their teeth.
Now off goes Pilgarlic with his men in a fright,
And altho' they show cowards, yet still they show spite,
In burning the Castle as they pass'd along,
And now by Nantasket they lie in a throng.
Let e'm go, let e'm go, for what they will fetch,
I think their great Howe is a miserable wretch;
And as for his men they are fools for their pains,
So let them return to Old England again.

IT was'nt our will that Bunker Hill,
From us should ne'er be taken,
We thought 'twould never be retook,
But we find we are mistaken.

The soldiers bid the hill farewel,
Two images left sentries,
This they had done all out of fun
To the American Yankies.

A flag of truce was sent thereon,
To see the hill was clear,
No living soul was found thereon,
But these images stood there.

Their hats they wave, come if you please,
There's none here to molest us,
These wooden men that here do stand,
Are only to defy us.

These images they soon threw down,
Not one man's life was lost then,
No sooner they were on the hill,
But some landed into Boston.

The women come and children run,
To brave PUTNAM rejoicing,
Saying now is the time to man your lines,
For the soldiers have left Boston.

The troops you've fairly scar'd away,
On board the ships they're quarter'd,
The children laugh'd, saying over the wharf,
They threw their best bomb mortar.

With the blazing of your guns that night,
And roaring of your mortars,
The soldiers cry'd the Yankees come
To tear us all in quarters.

The barracks being set on fire,
Which made the soldiers quiver,
They soon embark on board their ships,
May they stay there forever.

Soon after this the fleet fell down,
It's what we long desir'd,
We think their Gen'rals were afraid,
That they'd be set on fire.

The shipping now have all set sail,
No cause have we to mourn,
But seem afraid because 'tis said
That they will soon return.

Some say they're sail'd for Halifax,
And others for New York;
Howe let none know where he was bound,
When the soldiers did embark.

Where they are bound there's none can tell,
But the great GOD on high,
May all our heads be cover'd well,
When cannon balls do fly.

## 29. Gage's Folly: or, the Tall Fox Out-Witted
[Salem: Ezekiel Russell, 1776]

THIS broadside is doubly interesting, since in addition to the text it also carries an advertisement for the twelfth edition of Thomas Paine's *Common Sense*. Probably the most important pamphlet to emerge from the controversy preceding the Declaration of Independence, *Common Sense* sets out the philosophical arguments against reconciliation with England, and advocates complete severence of economic and political ties.

Thomas Gage, British Commander in Chief in America, was "a villain in America for doing his job too well and a villain in England for not doing it well enough," according to Mark Boatner. He was in charge of British operations during the Battles of Lexington and Concord and Bunker Hill, but he was replaced by Generals Howe and Clinton, for not having demonstrated sufficient initiative and aggressiveness in the spring and summer of 1775. Gage's coercive posture toward the colonies, and his inflexible attitude toward enforcement of the "Intolerable Acts," led to his unpopularity in America. His insensitivity to colonial problems compounded the image of an unauthorized tyrant-in-residence, which was how the colonists viewed him. His recall occasioned numerous expressions of joy, one of which was this original song, written to commemorate the happy event.

NATIONAL INDEX 43026
BRISTOL 4216
HENRY E. HUNTINGTON LIBRARY
32.5 x 22 cm.

# GAGE's FOLLY: OR, THE TALL FOX OUT-WITTED.

An excellent NEW SONG, never before Printed. By a FARMER, in the County of WORCESTER.

FROM Briton's ſhore Gage ſailed o'er
To Maſſachuſetts-Bay,
Quite void of fear he landed here
About the firſt of May.

With courage ſtout he made no doubt
But he ſhould win the field,
Tho' Rebels call'd, he thought for all,
To make thoſe Rebels yield.

And on our backs to lay thoſe acts
Which parliament had made,
And troops were ſent with an intent
To be poor Tommy's aid.

But now poor Gage ſeems in a rage,
To think he croſs'd the ſea,
Becauſe he finds the People's minds
Are bent on LIBERTY.

Their helliſh plot we value not,
Nor will we be enſlav'd,
Our CHARTER they have took away,
Tho' we ha'nt meſbehav'd.

They've ſtop'd our Port, remov'd the Court
From Boſton unto Salem,
But yet it ſeems that all their ſchemes,
And ſtratagems will fail 'em.

Tories ſhall fall, each one and all,
We value none of thoſe,
Tho' they 'trench deep, themſelves to keep,
Secure from Country Foes.

Thoſe ſtrifes and ſtruggles caus'd by old
Gage, Edſon, Murrey too, (Ruggles,
We truſt will ceaſe, then happy peace
Will inſtantly enſue.

Twas Hutchinſon the rout begun,
Who ſhould have been our friend,
But Gage we ſee is worſe than he,
And who knows where 'twill end.

Say, an't it ſtrange that ſuch a ſot
Whoſe conduct is a ſlander,
Should thus be ſent by parliament
To be our Chief Commander?

He lives in hopes than Prieſts and Popes
Will be eſtabliſh'd here,
Then thinks that he ſhall pardon'd be,
For crimes he's done this year.

May Edſon 'bide at his backſide,
The fitteſt place for him,
Bind Murrey faſt unto his arſe,
And then drive on old Tim.

It ſeems to me they ought to be
Bound hand and foot together,
Then daub their britch with tar and pitch,
And roul them well in feathers.

At ſuch a ſight the devil might
Addreſs them thus and ſay,
"You are my brothers, or elſe ſome others
"That look as bad as they."

But to conclude and not be rude,
May enemies to Freedom
Tranſported be beyond the ſea,
For ſurely we don't need e'm.

*SALEM*: Printed by E. RUSSELL, next to JOHN TURNER, Eſq; Upper End of Main-ſtreet.—Sold alſo by G. ALLEN, Travelling-Trader, in Concord.—☞ Shopkeepers, Travelling-Traders, &c. are deſired to call at the above Place, where is juſt Publiſhed, The Twelfth and laſt Edition of an excellent and much-admired Pamphlet, entitled, COMMON SENSE; addreſſed to the Continent, on the Subject of Independency.—In this new and compleat Edition is annexed, an Appendix; alſo, An Addition to COMMON SENSE, lately publiſhed at Philadelphia; or an Addreſs to the Repreſentatives of the religious Society of the People called Quakers, or to ſo many of them as were concerned in publiſhing a late Piece, entitled, The ancient Teſtimony and Principles of the People called Quakers renewed, with reſpect to the King and Government, and touching the Commotions now prevailing in theſe and other Parts of America, addreſſed to the People in general.—☞ This uſeful Book, (which is at this Time very juſtly eſteemed, by every hearty Friend to the civil and religious RIGHTS of Mankind, the American's

## 30. Gen. Washington, a New Favourite Song
[Boston?, 1776] Composed and written by Jonathan Mitchell Sewall

AMONG the songs represented in this collection, "General Washington" and "Yankee Doodle" would be the most readily recognizable tunes today. Both broadside poems follow early tune patterns, which have survived into our own time. The history of the grenadiers' song, however, is complex. The tune intended for "General Washington" was popular during the Revolution, and had a rhythm suitable for accompaniment by fife and drum. This version closely follows the tune for "All You that Love Good Fellows," originally a seventeenth-century Dutch tune, which was popular in England in the late seventeenth and early eighteenth centuries. Claude Simpson follows this musical history further in *The British Broadside Ballad and Its Music:* "As 'London Apprentice,' it is one of the airs in Charles Coffey's opera, *The Devil to Pay*, 1731. The eighteenth-century 16-measure versions of the air—in *Pills* and *The Devil to Pay*, fit the double ballad stanza of pieces associated with the tune, while earlier music . . . contains an additional eight-measure phrase at the end. 'The British Grenadiers' clearly descends from this old tune." This should not be confused with the tune of "The Grenadier's March," which appeared first in *A Collection of the Newest and Choicest Songs*, London, 1683.

The publication of this new song indicates how Washington, who had assumed command of the continental forces only a few hours before Bunker Hill, and who had not been in actual command there, was to be celebrated as a folk-hero within a few months of his rise to power. The colonists needed inspirational leaders like Washington, not only for the practical purpose of achieving victory, but also to provide a mythic dimension for the revolutionary cause. The association of Washington with classical and biblical heroes gave instant historical authority to the revolutionary venture.

NATIONAL INDEX 43158
BRISTOL 4361
FORD 2038
WEGELIN 352
NEW-YORK HISTORICAL SOCIETY
32.5 x 19.5 cm.

# Gen. WASHINGTON,

## A New Favourite SONG, at the AMERICAN CAMP.

### To the Tune of the *British Grenadiers.*

VAIN Britons boast no longer, with proud Indignity,
By Land your conquering Legions, your matchless Strength by Sea,
Since we your SONS incensed, our Swords have girded on;
Huzza, huzza,—huzza, huzza, for War and WASHINGTON.

Urg'd on by North and Vengeance, these valiant Champions came,
Bellowing TEA and Treason, and George was all on Flame;
Yet sacreligious as it seems, we REBELS still live on,
And laugh at all your empty Puffs, and so does WASHINGTON.

Still deaf to mild intreaties, still blind to England's Good,
You have for thirty Pieces, betrayed your Country's Blood;
Like Æsop's Cur you'll gain, a shadow for your Bone,
Yet find us fearful shades indeed inspired by WASHINGTON.

Mysterious, unexampled, incomprehensible,
The blund'ring Schemes of Britain, their downfall well foretell,
Like Lions roar and grumble, meer Asses have ye shown;
And ye shall share an Ass's Fate, and drudge for WASHINGTON.

Your dark unfathom'd Councils, our weakest Heads defeat,
Our Children rout your Armies, our Boats destroy your Fleet;
And to complete the dire Disgrace, cooped up within a Town,
You live the Scorn of all our Host, the Slaves of WASHINGTON.

Great Heaven! is this the Nation, whose thundering Arms were hurl'd,
Thro' Europe, Afric, India; whose Navy rul'd the World;
The Lustre of your former Deeds, whole Ages of Renown,
Lost in a moment or transferr'd to US and WASHINGTON.

Yet think not thirst of Glory, unsheaths our vengeful Swords,
To rend your Bands asunder, and cast away your Cords;
'Tis Heav'n-born FREEDOM fires us all, and strengthens each brave SON.
From him who humbly guides the Plough, to God-like WASHINGTON.

For this, O! could our Wishes, your ancient Rage inspire,
Your Armies should be doubled, in Numbers, Force, and Fire;
Then might the glorious Conflict prove, which best deserv'd the Boon,
AMERICA or Albion, great GEORGE or WASHINGTON.

Fired with the great Idea, our Father's Shades would rise,
To view the stern Contention, the gods desert their Skies;
And WOLFE mid' Hosts of Heroes, superior bending down
Cry out with eager Transport, *Well done brave WASHINGTON.*

Should George too choice of Britons, to foreign Realms apply,
And madly arm half Europe, yet still we would defy,
Turk, Russian, Jew, or Infidel, or all these Powers in one,
While HANCOCK crowns our Senate, our Camp great WASHINGTON.

Tho' warlike Weapons fail'd us, disdaining slavish Fears,
To Swords we'd beat our Ploughshares, our Pruning-hooks to Spears,
And rush all desp'rate on our Foes, nor breathe 'till Battle won,
Then Shout and Shout,—AMERICA and conquering WASHINGTON.

Proud France should view with Terror, and haughty Spain should fear,
While every warlike Nation would court Alliance here,
And ———, his Minions trembling, dismounted from his T——,
Pay Homage to AMERICA, and glorious WASHINGTON.

## 31. Two Favorite New Songs at the American Camp
[n.p., 1776?]

THE portrait at the top of this document was executed by Paul Revere in 1771, for use in Nathaniel Ames' *Almanack* for 1772, which was published by Ezekiel Russell. It is quite probable, therefore, that this broadside from the year 1776 was also published by Russell. The subject of the original portrait was John Dickinson, but here it is used merely as a decoration.

Both of the songs on this broadside celebrate the subject of liberty, but the second, "The American Liberty Song," is a broadside ballad, while the first is an exhortation. The term "ballad" has been used in so many different contexts that more specific classification is difficult. Malcolm Laws, in *The British Literary Ballad,* describes three classes of ballads: "The most familiar is that of the folk ballads or popular ballads, traditional narrative songs carried in the memories of the folk from one generation to another and sung in public or private, usually among country people. The second class, the broadside ballads, consists of journalistic verse narratives composed and printed for sale at a penny or so and hawked about the streets . . . by balladmongers and peddlers. . . . The third class comprises the literary ballads or ballads of art." "The American Liberty Song" is hardly a narrative with a beginning, middle, and end, but it does tell the story of the dramatic origins of colonial liberty from Britain.

Both songs are written in the conventional six-line stanzaic form that was popular among balladeers in the seventeenth and eighteenth centuries. Since the writers and readers of the early American broadside ballads were transplanted Englishmen, the literary conventions which were followed in England persisted in this country even during the Revolution. The subjects and their treatment, however, clearly reflect the colonial point of view.

NATIONAL INDEX 43178
BRISTOL 4384
FORD 2042
HISTORICAL SOCIETY OF PENNSYLVANIA
32.5 x 21.9 cm.

Two Favorite new SONGS at the American Camp.

## EXHORTATION

### To the FREEMEN OF AMERICA.

*Aut Mors aut Vita decora.*

HARK ! the goddeſs of fame,
Fair LIBERTY's dame,
Has ſounded her trumpet victorious ;
To AMERICANS all,
She ſounds her loud call,
To rouſe in a cauſe that is glorious.

For your Freedom and lives,
Your children and wives,
To defend is the time, now or never ;
Then tyrants oppoſe,
AMERICA's foes,
And live Freemen both now and forever.

Your Grandſires of old
Were courageous and bold,
By the ſmiles and the bleſſings of Heav'n,
Obtained this land,
And by their command,
To you as their heirs it was giv'n.

May Heaven inſpire
Their ſons with their fire,
For greater your dangers were never,
And ſhould trumpets alarms
Now ſound you to arms,
Be valiant your Rights to recover.

Future æra's of time
Shall gratefully ſing,
To the praiſe of true patriot Sages,
"AMERICA *free*
"*Forever ſhall be*
"*Thro' all the vaſt volumes of ages.*"

---

## THE AMERICAN LIBERTY SONG.

IN ſtory we're told
How our Fathers of old
Brav'd the rage of the wind and the waves,
And croſs'd the deep o'er
To this deſolate ſhore,
All, becauſe they were loth to be ſlaves, *brave Boys.*
All, becauſe they were loth to be ſlaves, &c.

Yet a ſtrange ſcheme of late
Has been form'd in the ſtate,
By a knot of political knaves,
Who in ſecret rejoice,
That the parliament's voice
Has condemn'd us by law to be ſlaves, &c.

But ſhould we obey
Theſe vile ſtatutes, the way
To more baſe future ſlav'ry paves,
Nor in ſpite of our pain
Muſt we ever complain,
If we now tamely yield ourſelves ſlaves, &c.

Counteract then we muſt
A decree ſo unjuſt,
Which our wiſe conſtitution depraves,
Lo ! all nature conſpire
To approve our deſires,
For ſhe cautions us not to be ſlaves, &c.

As the ſun's lucid ray
To all nature gives day,
And a world from obſcurity ſaves,
So all happy and free
*George's* ſubjects ſhall be,
Then *Americans* muſt not be ſlaves, &c.

Hark ! the wind as it flies
Tho' controul'd by the ſkies,
While it each meaner obſtacle braves,
Seems to ſay be like me,
Ever loyally free,
But ah ! ne'er conſent to be ſlaves, &c.

To our Monarch we know,
Due allegiance we owe,
Who the ſceptre ſo rightfully waves,
But no ſov'reign we own
But the King on the throne,
And we cannot to ſubjects be ſlaves, &c.

Stupid ſimpletons tell
How we mean to rebel,
And yet all each *American* craves,
Is but to be free,
As we ſurely muſt be,
For we never were born to be ſlaves, &c.

But whoever in ſpite
At *American*'s Right,
Like inſolent *Haman* behaves,
Or would wiſh to grow great
On the ſpoils of the ſtate,
May he and his children be ſlaves, &c.

The State-Bunglers ſhall ſee,
We deſpiſe their curs'd TEA,
Since a way for oppreſſion it paves,
They plan odious taxes
To teaze and perplex us,
And make us, like themſelves, venal ſlaves, &c.

Vain fooliſh Curmudgeons !
To think we, like gudgeons,
Swallow baits that of Freedom bereaves,
Tea, Nabobs, and Minions,
With their dire opinions,
May be damn'd but we'll not be ſlaves, &c.

With the beaſts of the wood
We will ramble for food
And live in wild deſerts and caves,
And live poor as *Job*
On the ſkirts of the globe,
Before we'll ſubmit to be ſlaves, &c.

The birthright we hold
Shall never be ſold,
But ſacred maintain'd to our graves,
Nay, and e'er we'll comply
We'll gallantly die,
For we muſt not, and will not, be ſlaves,
We muſt not, and will not, be ſlaves, *brave Boys.*

## 32. July 4, 1776. A Declaration [Newburyport?, 1776]

THE introductory essay for this collection explains that the Declaration of Independence was originally a broadside, printed by the Philadelphia printer, John Dunlap, early in the morning of July 5, 1775. Although a much-revised draft of Jefferson's manuscript exists, the engrossed parchment that is housed in the National Archives in Washington was prepared by a scribe specifically for signature by members of the Continental Congress, who had not signed the earlier printed broadside copy that had been inserted into the journal of the Congress. August 2, 1775, is the earliest date when the parchment manuscript could possibly have been signed, and many signatures were probably added later in the year. There is speculation that one or two final signatures were added as late as 1781.

No manuscript or printed copy of the Declaration of Independence ever carried that title, although this is its popular name. In the manuscript it is called "A Declaration by the Representatives of America in General Congress Assembled," the same title it was given by the printer of this broadside. In the final parchment copy, it is entitled, "The Unanimous Declaration of the Thirteen United States of America." The unique printing shown here is housed in the library of the American Antiquarian Society. It is the only copy on record having an incorrect spelling for Hancock's name, here John "Hacock." Clearly a printer's error, it is perhaps an indication of the haste with which broadsides of this kind were frequently assembled. This unusual copy was presented to the Antiquarian Society in 1822, by Simon Greenleaf. In the letter which accompanied the broadside, he notes that, "it was posted up in Newburyport and afterwards preserved by my grandfather the late Honorable Jonathan Greenleaf." It may well have been printed in Newburyport by John Mycall, who had just begun his own printing business in 1776.

NATIONAL INDEX 43199
BRISTOL 4407
FORD 1952
AMERICAN ANTIQUARIAN SOCIETY
50.2 x 38.4 cm.

*In* *July* 4, 1776.

# DE TION,

## By the REPRESENTATIVES of the UNITED STATES OF AMERICA, *In GENERAL CONGRESS Assembled.*

WHEN in the course of human events, it becomes necessary for one people to dissolve the Political Bands which have connected them with another, and to assume among the powers of the earth, the seperate and equal station to which the laws of nature and of nature's God entitle them, a decent respect to the opinions of mankind require that they should declare the causes which impel them to the separation.

We hold these truths to be self-evident, that all men are created equal, that they are endowed by their Creator with certain unalienable rights, that among these are Life, Liberty, and the Pursuit of Happiness.—That to secure these rights, governments are instituted among men, deriving their just powers from the consent of the governed, that whenever any form of government becomes destructive of these ends, it is the right of the people to alter or to abolish it, and to institute new government, laying its foundation on such principles, and organizing its powers in such form, as to them shall seem most likely to effect their safety and happiness. Prudence, indeed, will dictate that governments long established should not be changed for light and trancient causes, and accordingly all experience hath shewn, that mankind are more disposed to suffer, while evils are sufferable, than to right themselves by abolishing the forms to which they are accustomed. But when a long train of abuses and usurpations, pursuing invariably the same object, evinces a design to reduce them under absolute despotism, it is their right, it is their duty, to throw off such government, and to provide new guards for their future security. Such has been the patient sufferance of these Colonies; and such is now the necessity which constrains them to alter their former systems of government. The history of the present King of Great-Britain is a history of repeated injuries and usurpations, all having in direct object the establishment of an absolute Tyranny over these States. To prove this, let facts be submitted to a candid World.

He has refused his assent to laws, the most wholesome and necessary for the public good.

He has forbidden his governors to pass laws of immediate and pressing importance, unless suspended in their operation till his assent should be obtained; and when so suspended, he has utterly neglected to attend to them.

He has refused to pass other laws for the accommodation of large Districts of people, unless those people would relinquish the right of representation in the legislature, a right inestimable to them, and formidable to Tyrants only.

He has called together legislative bodies at places unusual, uncomfortable, and distant from the depository of their public records, for the sole purpose of fatiguing them into compliance with his measures.

He has dissolved Representative Houses repeatedly, for opposing with manly firmness his invasions on the rights of the people.

He has refused for a long time, after such dissolutions, to cause others to be elected; whereby the legislative powers, incapable of annihilation, have returned to the people at large for their exercise; the state remaining in the mean time exposed to all the dangers of invasion from without, and convulsions within.

He has endeavoured to prevent the population of these States; for that purpose obstructing the laws for naturalization of foreigners; refusing to pass others to encourage their migrations hither, and raising the conditions of new appropriations of lands.

He has obstructed the administration of justice, by refusing his assent to laws for establishing judiciary powers.

He has made Judges dependent on his will alone, for the tenure of their offices, and the amount and payment all their salaries.

He has erected a multitude of, new offices, and sent hither swarms of officers to harrass our people, and eat out their substance.

He has kept among us, in times of peace, standing armies, without the consent of our legislatures.

He has affected to render the military independent of and superior to the civil power.

He has combined with others to subject us to a jurisdiction foreign to our constitution, unacknowledged by our laws; given his assent to their acts of pretended legislation.

For quartering large Bodies of armed Troops among us:

For protecting them by a mock Trial, from punishment for any Murders which they should commit on the Inhabitants of these States:

For cutting off our Trade with all parts of the World:

For imposing Taxes on us without our consent:

For depriving us, in many Cases of the benefits of Trial by Jury:

For transporting us beyond Seas to be tried for pretended Offences:

For abolishing the free System of English Laws, in a neighbouring Province, establishing therein an arbitrary Government, and enlarging its Boundaries, so as to render it at once an example and fit instrument for introducing the same absolute rule into these Colonies:

For taking away our Charters, abolishing our most valuable Laws, and altering fundamentally the Forms of our Governments:

For suspending our own Legislatures, and declaring themselves invested with power to legislate for us in all Cases whatsoever.

He has abdicated Government here, by declaring us out of his protection, and waging War against us.

He has plundered our Seas, ravaged our Coasts, burnt our Towns, and destroyed the lives of our people.

He is at this time, transporting large Armies of foreign Mercenaries to compleat the works of Death, Desolation and Tyranny, already begun with circumstances of Cruelty and Perfidy scarcely parallelled in the most barbarous Ages, and totally unworthy the Head of a civilized Nation.

He has constrained our fellow Citizens taken Captive on the high Seas to bear Arms against their Country, to become the Executioners of their Friends and Brethren, or to fall themselves by their hands.

He has excited Domestic Insurrections amongst us, and has endeavored to bring on the Inhabitants of our Frontiers, the merciless Indian Savages, whose known rule of Warfare, is an undistinguished destruction, of all Ages, Sexes and Conditions.

In every Stage of these oppressions we have petitioned for Redress, in the most humble Terms: Our repeated Petitions have been answered only by repeated injury. A Prince whose Character is thus marked by every Act which may define a Tyrant, is unfit to be the ruler of free People.

Nor have we been wanting in attention to our British Brethren. We have warned them from time to time of attempts by their Legislature to extend an unwarrantable Jurisdiction over us. We have reminded them of the circumstances of our Emigration and Settlement here. We have appealed to their native Justice and Magnanimity, and we have conjured them by the ties of common Kindred to disavow these Usurpations, which inevitably interrupt our Connections and Correspondence. They too have been deaf to the voice of Justice and of Consanguinity. We must therefore acquiesce in the Necessity which denounces our Separation, and hold them, as we hold the rest of Mankind, Enemies in War; in peace, Friends.

We, therefore, the Representatives of the UNITED STATES OF AMERICA, in GENERAL CONGRESS assembled, appealing to the Supreme Judge of the World for the rectitude of our intentions, do in the name, and by the Authority of the good people of these Colonies, solemnly Publish and Declare, that these United Colonies are, and of right ought to be, FREE AND INDEPENDENT STATES, that they are absolved from all Allegiance to the British Crown, and that all political Connection between them and the State of Britain, is, and ought to be totally dissolved; and that *as Free and Independant States*, they have full Power to levy War, conclude Peace, contract Alliances, establish Commerce, and to do all other Acts and Things which INDEPENDENT STATES, may of right do. And for the support of this Declaration, with a firm reliance on the protection of Divine Providence, we mutually pledge to each other our Lives, our Fortunes, and our sacred Honor.

*Signed by* Order *and in* Behalf *of the* CONGRESS,

JOHN HACOCK President.

*Attest.*

CHARLES THOMPSON, Secretary.

33. In Congress, July 4, 1776. A Declaration
[Salem: Ezekiel Russell, 1776]

THIS particular copy was sent to the Rev. Caleb Curtis of Charlton, Massachusetts, whose congregation had signed the protest against the Port Bill in June of 1774 [plate 13]. The broadside was printed by Ezekiel Russell of Salem, Massachusetts, and was issued at about the same time when other colonial printers were being urged to circulate the news of a formal declaration. It is especially interesting because it carries the specific terms of the legislative order controlling distribution of the declaration: "*Ordered,* That the Declaration of Independence be printed; and a Copy sent to the Ministers of each Parish, of every Denomination within this State; and that they severally be *required* to read the same to their respective Congregations, as soon as Divine Service is ended. . . ." Although the Constitution guarantees a separation of Church and State, the theocracy of the Massachusetts Bay Colony from 1620 to 1783 made no such provisions. Important announcements were frequently made from the pulpit, and the sermons of the revolutionary era show how ministers adopted political positions, which they defended vigorously by lending the authority of their social and spiritual positions to the revolutionary cause. The fact that ministers were chosen to be such important vehicles for the dissemination of the new announcement also shows how influential they were in the control of public opinion. On the other side of the common, in the tavern, the declaration would have been posted, should the innkeeper have been of the revolutionary "persuasion." It would also have been posted on the door of the meetinghouse.

NATIONAL INDEX 15163
FORD 1955
AMERICAN ANTIQUARIAN SOCIETY
51.4 x 40.5 cm.

IN

# CONGRESS,

JULY 4, 1776.

# A DECLARATION

BY THE

## REPRESENTATIVES

OF THE

# UNITED STATES OF AMERICA,

IN GENERAL CONGRESS ASSEMBLED.

WHEN in the Course of human Events, it becomes necessary for one People to dissolve the political Bands which have connected them with another, and to assume among the Powers of the Earth, the separate and equal Station to which the Laws of Nature and of Nature's God entitle them, a decent Respect to the Opinions of Mankind requires that they should declare the Causes which impel them to the Separation.

WE hold these Truths to be self-evident, that all Men are created equal, that they are endowed by their Creator with certain unalienable Rights, that among these are Life, Liberty, and the Pursuit of Happiness:—That to secure these Rights, Governments are instituted among Men, deriving their just Powers from the Consent of the Governed, that whenever any Form of Government becomes destructive of these Ends, it is the Right of the People to alter or to abolish it, and to institute new Government, laying its Foundation on such Principles, and organizing its Powers in such Form, as to them shall seem most likely to effect their Safety and Happiness. Prudence, indeed, will dictate that Governments long established should not be changed for light and transient Causes; and accordingly all Experience hath shewn, that Mankind are more disposed to suffer, while Evils are sufferable, than to right themselves by abolishing the Forms to which they are accustomed. But when a long Train of Abuses and Usurpations, pursuing invariably the same Object, evinces a Design to reduce them under absolute Despotism, it is their Right, it is their Duty, to throw off such Government, and to provide new Guards for their future Security. Such has been the patient Sufferance of these Colonies; and such is now the Necessity which constrains them to alter their former Systems of Government. The History of the present King of Great-Britain is a History of repeated Injuries and Usurpations, all having in direct Object the Establishment of an absolute Tyranny over these States. To prove this, let Facts be submitted to a candid World.

HE has refused his Assent to Laws, the most wholesome and necessary for the public Good.

HE has forbidden his Governors to pass Laws of immediate and pressing Importance, unless suspended in their Operation until his Assent should be obtained; and when so suspended, he has utterly neglected to attend to them.

HE has refused to pass other Laws for the Accommodation of large Districts of People, unless those People would relinquish the Right of Representation in the Legislature, a Right inestimable to them, and formidable to TYRANTS only.

HE has called together Legislative Bodies at Places unusual, uncomfortable, and distant from the Depository of their public Records, for the sole Purpose of fatiguing them into Compliance with his Measures.

HE has dissolved Representative Houses repeatedly, for opposing with *manly* FIRMNESS his Invasions on the Rights of the People.

HE has refused for a long Time, after such Dissolutions, to cause others to be elected; whereby the Legislative Powers, incapable of Annihilation, have returned to the People at large for their Exercise; the State remaining in the mean Time exposed to all the Dangers of Invasion from without, and Convulsions within.

HE has endeavoured to prevent the Population of these States; for that Purpose obstructing the Laws for Naturalization of Foreigners; refusing to pass others to encourage their Migrations hither, and raising the Conditions of new Appropriations of Lands.

HE has obstructed the Administration of Justice, by refusing his Assent to Laws for establishing Judiciary Powers.

He has made Judges dependent on his Will alone, for the Tenure of their Offices, and the Amount and Payment of their Salaries.

HE has erected a multitude of new Offices, and sent hither Swarms of Officers to harrass our People, and eat out their Substance.

HE has kept among us, in Times of Peace, Standing Armies, without the Consent of our Legislatures.

HE has affected to render the Military independent of, and *superior* to the Civil Power.

HE has combined with others to subject us to a Jurisdiction foreign to our Constitution, and unacknowledged by our Laws; giving his Assent to their Acts of pretended Legislation:

For quartering large Bodies of armed Troops among us:

For protecting them, by a *mock* Trial, from Punishment for any Murders which they should commit on the Inhabitants of these States:

For cutting off our Trade with all Parts of the World:

For imposing Taxes on us *without* our CONSENT:

For depriving us, in many Cases, of the Benefits of Trial by Jury:

For transporting us beyond Seas to be tried for pretended Offences:

For abolishing the free System of English Laws in a neighbouring Province, establishing therein an arbitrary Government, and enlarging its Boundaries, so as to render it at once an Example and fit Instrument for introducing the same absolute Rule into these Colonies.

For taking away our Charters, abolishing our most valuable Laws, and altering fundamentally the Forms of our Governments:

For suspending our own Legislatures, and declaring themselves invested with Power to legislate for us in *all* Cases whatsoever.

He has abdicated Government here, by declaring us out of his Protection and waging War against us.

He has plundered our Seas, ravaged our Coasts, burnt our Towns, and destroyed the Lives of our People.

He is, at this Time, transporting large Armies of *foreign* Mercenaries to compleat the Works of Death, Desolation, and TYRANNY, already begun with Circumstances of Cruelty and Perfidy scarcely paralleled in the most *barbarous* Ages, and *totally* unworthy the Head of a civilized Nation.

He has constrained our Fellow Citizens, taken Captive on the high Seas, to bear Arms *against* their Country; to become the Executioners of their Friends and Brethren, or to fall themselves by *their* Hands.

He has excited Domestic Insurrections amongst us, and has endeavoured to bring on the Inhabitants of our Frontiers, the *merciless* Indian Savages, whose known Rule of Warfare, is an undistinguished Destruction of all Ages, Sexes, and Conditions.

In every Stage of these Oppressions we have petitioned for Redress, in the most humble Terms: Our repeated Petitions have been answered only by *repeated* Injury!—A Prince, whose Character is thus marked by *every* Act which may define a TYRANT, is unfit to be the Ruler of a FREE PEOPLE!

Nor have we been wanting in Attention to our British Brethren. We have *warned* them from Time to Time of Attempts by their Legislature to extend an unwarrantable Jurisdiction over us. We have reminded them of the Circumstances of our Emigration and Settlement here. We have appealed to their native Justice and Magnanimity, and we have conjured them by the Ties of our common Kindred to disavow these *Usurpations*, which would inevitably interrupt our Connexions and Correspondence. They too have been *deaf* to the Voice of Justice and of Consanguinity. We must, therefore, acquiesce in the Necessity which denounces our Separation, and hold *them*, as we hold the rest of Mankind, *Enemies* in War; in Peace, Friends.

We, therefore, the REPRESENTATIVES of the UNITED STATES OF AMERICA, in GENERAL CONGRESS assembled, appealing to the SUPREME JUDGE of the World for the *Rectitude* of our Intentions, do, in the Name and by the Authority of the good People of these Colonies, *solemnly* Publish and Declare, That these United Colonies are, and of Right ought to be, FREE AND INDEPENDENT STATES; that they are absolved from all Allegiance to the British Crown; and that *all* political Connexion between them and the State of Great-Britain, is, and ought to be *totally* dissolved; and that as FREE AND INDEPENDENT STATES, they have full Power to levy War, conclude Peace, contract Alliances, establish Commerce, and to do *all* other Acts and Things which INDEPENDENT STATES may of Right do. And for the Support of this Declaration, with a *firm* Reliance on the Protection of DIVINE PROVIDENCE, we mutually pledge to each other our LIVES, our FORTUNES, and our SACRED HONOR.

*Signed by* ORDER *and in* BEHALF *of the* CONGRESS,

JOHN HANCOCK, PRESIDENT.

ATTEST, CHARLES THOMPSON, SECRETARY.

IN COUNCIL, JULY 17th, 1776.

ORDERED, That the Declaration of Independence be printed; and a Copy sent to the Ministers of each Parish, of every Denomination, within this STATE; and that they severally be *required* to read the same to their respective Congregations, as soon as divine Service is ended, in the Afternoon, on the first Lord's-Day after they shall have received it:---And after such Publication thereof, to deliver the said Declaration to the Clerks of their several Towns, or Districts; who are hereby required to record the same in their respective Town, or District Books, there to remain as a *perpetual* MEMORIAL thereof.

In the Name, and by Order of the COUNCIL, R. DERBY, Jun. President.

A true Copy Attest, JOHN AVERY, Dep. Sec'y.

*SALEM*, MASSACHUSETTS-BAY: Printed by E. RUSSELL, by Order of AUTHORITY.

## 34. For the Encouragement of Those That Shall Inlist
[Boston: Benjamin Edes, 1776]

THE "Continental Army" refers to the regulars of the American Army, as distinguished from the state militia forces. Mark Boatner notes that, "the Continental Army was created in June, 1775, when Congress raised companies of Riflemen, made Washington Commander in Chief, took over the 'Boston Army,' and started naming generals for Continental Commissions. When Washington assumed command at Boston on July 3, 1775, he found 17,000 militiamen whose enlistments would expire before the end of the year. . . . During this first year, Congress authorized the raising of Continental troops in other colonies, and about 27,500 men were reported as being in her pay in 1775."

The conscription of troops was carried out through congressional mandate, and broadsides were used to publish announcements and proclamations of legislative actions governing the raising of troop levels. More important, these announcements also told of the specific pay, provisions, and perquisites of enlistment. Interestingly, this broadside carries added inducements "to each Soldier who shall procure those Articles for himself," indicating the desperate state of colonial provisions at the start of the war.

NATIONAL INDEX 14870
FORD 2003
AMERICAN ANTIQUARIAN SOCIETY
25.5 x 19 cm.

**FOR** the Encouragement of thoſe that ſhall Inliſt in the Continental Army—The CONGRESS in their Reſolves of *September 16th, 18th, 19th, October 8th*, and *November 12th*, 1776, Engage,

THAT *Twenty Dollars* be given as a Bounty to each Non-Commiſſioned Officer and Private Soldier who ſhall Inliſt to ſerve for the Term of Three Years.

That each Non-Commiſſioned Officer and private Soldier ſhall annually receive a Suit of Cloaths, to conſiſt for the preſent Year, of two Linnen Hunting Shirts, two Pair of Overalls, a Leather or Woolen Waiſtcoat with Sleeves, one pair of Breeches, a Hat or Leather Cap, two Shirts, two Pair of Hoſe, and two Pair of Shoes, amounting in the whole to the Value of Twenty Dollars, or that Sum to be paid to each Soldier who ſhall procure thoſe Articles for himſelf, and produces a Certificate thereof from the Captain of the Company to which he belongs, to the Paymaſter of the Regiment.

That each Non-Commiſſioned Officer and private Soldier who ſhall Inliſt and engage to continue in the Service to the Cloſe of the War or until diſcharged by CONGRESS, ſhall receive in Addition to the above Encouragement, One Hundred Acres of Land, and if any are Slain by the Enemy, the Repreſentatives of ſuch Soldiers ſhall be intitled to the aforeſaid Hundred Acres of Land.

And for their further Encouragement, the State of *Maſſachuſetts-Bay*, has, by a Reſolve of *November* 25 laſt engaged,

That each Non-Commiſſioned Officer and private Soldier who ſhall Inliſt into the Continental Army, either during the War or for the Term of Three Years, as Part of the Quota of Men aſſigned this State, the Sum of *Twenty Pounds* on his paſſing Muſter, the ſaid *Twenty Pounds* to be paid in Treaſurers Notes of *Ten Pounds* each, payable to the Poſſeſſor in Four Years, with Intereſt to be paid annually, at the Rate of *ſix per Cent*.

**In the Houſe of REPRESENTATIVES, Dec. 4, 1776.**

THE foregoing Extracts were Read and *Ordered* to be Printed.

JAMES WARREN, Speaker.

## 35. Great Encouragement for Seamen
## [Danvers: Ezekiel Russell, 1777]

THIS broadside was issued to find men to sail on the *Ranger* under the command of John Paul Jones. The ship was a naval vessel, not a privateer, and was bound for Europe. From the coast of France, Jones ventured into the Irish Sea. These exploits are well told by Samuel Eliot Morison in his biography, *John Paul Jones: A Sailor's Biography.*

The Continental Navy failed to develop successfully for a number of reasons. First, the tradition of "privateering," that is, providing the services of an armed vessel and crew for money and prizes, overshadowed efforts like those described in this broadside to recruit a regular navy. But more important, the British Navy failed to capitalize on their tremendous advantage over the Colonial Navy, so that decisive victories were won or lost on land, rather than at sea. Mark Boatner points out that the American colonies were extremely vulnerable to attack along their coasts, and from within via the many deep rivers that penetrate the continent so that the British could have quashed the rebellion early if they had used their naval force effectively. By the time France sent part of her navy to support the colonies in 1778, it was too late for England to press a maritime war. Britain's many defeats had crippled her army, and although the Royal Navy could still be used to support the remaining troops, the advantage had already been lost. Thus, "the naval battles of the Revolution were secondary in strategic importance to the land operations," and the Americans managed to win the war without ever developing a strong navy of their own.

NATIONAL INDEX 15648
FORD 2061
ESSEX INSTITUTE, SALEM
38.1 x 25.1 cm.

# G R E A T
# ENCOURAGEMENT
# F O R
# SEAMEN.

ALL GENTLEMEN SEAMEN and able-bodied LANDSMEN who have a Mind to diſtinguiſh themſelves in the GLORIOUS CAUSE of their COUNTRY, and make their Fortunes, an Opportunity now offers on board the Ship RANGER, of Twenty Guns, (for FRANCE) now laying in PORTSMOUTH, in the State of NEW-HAMPSHIRE, commanded by JOHN PAUL JONES Eſq; let them repair to the Ship's Rendezvous in PORTSMOUTH, or at the Sign of Commodore MANLEY, in SALEM, where they will be kindly entertained, and receive the greateſt Encouragement.---The Ship RANGER, in the Opinion of every Perſon who has ſeen her is looked upon to be one of the beſt Cruizers in AMERICA.---She will be always able to Fight her Guns under a moſt excellent Cover; and no Veſſel yet built was ever calculated for ſailing faſter, and making good Weather.

Any GENTLEMEN VOLUNTEERS who have a Mind to take an agreable Voyage in this pleaſant Seaſon of the Year, may, by entering on board the above Ship RANGER, meet with every Civility they can poſſibly expect, and for a further Encouragement depend on the firſt Opportunity being embraced to reward each one agreable to his Merit.

All reaſonable Travelling Expences will be allowed, and the Advance-Money be paid on their Appearance on Board.

IN C O N G R E S S, MARCH 29, 1777.

RESOLVED,

THAT the MARINE COMMITTEE be authoriſed to advance to every able Seaman, that enters into the CONTINENTAL SERVICE, any Sum not exceeding FORTY DOLLARS, and to every ordinary Seaman or Landſman, any Sum not exceeding TWENTY DOLLARS, to be deducted from their future Prize-Money.

By Order of CONGRESS,

JOHN HANCOCK, PRESIDENT.

*DANVERS*: Printed by E. RUSSELL, at the Houſe late the Bell-Tavern.

## 36. Oppression: A Poem
[Boston?, 1777]

IN 1765, on September 19, an advertisement appeared in the *Pennsylvania Journal* for "Oppression, a Poem: by an American." This refers to a poem printed by C. Moran in London in 1765, with notes "by a North Briton," and the text of that "Oppression" poem is the source for "Tom-Cod Catcher" [plate 5]. It is not, however, the same poem that appears here.

The illustrations depict an astronomer, on the left, and a village beset by lightning, on the right. The figure of the astronomer is a crude adaptation of a 1767 woodcut by Isaiah Thomas. Ezekiel Russell used this cut at least twice, in 1782 and 1783, on the cover of Bikerstaff's *Boston Almanack for 1783* and on a broadside, "Predictions for the Year 1783." It is possible, therefore, that Russell also printed this "Oppression" broadside. Curiously, neither of the cuts bears any close relation to the text. Printers frequently used any ornamentation that was on hand, in order to make their broadsides more striking and appealing.

NATIONAL INDEX 10114
FORD 2114a
WEGELIN 705
NEW-YORK HISTORICAL SOCIETY
34.9 x 19.7 cm.

# OPPRESSION:

## A P O E M.

Or, NEW-ENGLAND's LAMENTATION on the dreadful EXTORTION and other Sins of the Times. Being a ſerious EXHORTATION to all to repent and turn from the Evil of their Ways, if they would avert the terrible and heavy JUDGMENTS of the ALMIGHTY that hang over AMERICA at this alarming and diſtreſſing Day.

COME all you Friends to Goodneſs, I pray you to attend,
I'll tell to you a Story on which you may depend,
If you will not believe it, I think you muſt be blind,
When it appears ſo evident to ev'ry ſerious mind.
There wants a Reformation throughout AMERICA,
And deep Humiliation, for it's a ſinful day;
But how can we deſire, or look for better times,
So long as we aſpire to multiply our crimes!
The Law has been deſpiſed, the Goſpel trampled on,
And we have been ſurpriſed by powerful *Briton*;
But they can go no farther than the length of their chain,
JEHOVAH is their Maſter, who can their Power reſtrain.
But while we are complaining of *England*'s Uſurpation,
Iniquity is reigning throughout this Northern Nation;
So bad is our behavior, we grieve the Holy Spirit,
And if we ſlight our Savior, we cannot Heaven inherit.
We ſeem quite unconcerned about our ſouls ſalvation,
Nor [illegible] we yet alarmed, to Goſpel Regulation;
The houſe of *Saul* grows ſtronger, as *David*'s houſe grows weaker,
And ſatan will reign longer, if we are ſuch ſelf-ſeekers.
His kingdom is maintained and ſtrengthened by ſin,
By ſome the building's framed, and others drive the pins;
*New-England*'s Sons will venture to travel in the dark,
And do refuſe to enter the New-Teſtament Ark.
A ſtorm of wrath is promis'd, a flood will ſurely come,
And overtake the ſtrongeſt, and drown the wicked one;
Altho' they fly to mountains, and hide themſelves in rocks,
Of wrath there is a fountain to ſweep the mountain tops.
If we will not take warning, we muſt go down to hell,
Who take delight in ſcorning the great IMMANUEL;
Whoſe arms are always open, and bids us welcome there,
And ſhews the greateſt token of love and friendſhip dear.
We have had publications, from the OMNISIENT ONE,
A promis'd habitation, prepared by his SON;
At this Fountain of Treaſure men might forever dwell,
But they refuſe ſuch pleaſure, and damn themſelves to hell.
'Tis very melancholy to hear of ſo much cheating,
To ſee men briſk and jolly while they are over-reaching;
But fiſh delight in water, for that's their element,
And if men are not cheating they cannot be content.
Extortion has been uſed too much for to relate,
The Poor have been abuſed for to increaſe eſtates [illegible]
When Extortion's increaſing, and greedy Muckworms crawling,
By ſuch unlawful Fleecing the Public Wealth is falling.
Extortioners and Tories, which of them is the worſt,
One brings us a fair ſtory, the other a blunderbuſs,
And openly preſents it, a muſket or a gun,
The other acts more ſecret, and murders ten to one.
We need not much admire that there are ſuch commotions,
F[illegible]re not men's deſires unbounded as the ocean?
[illegible] more a man poſſeſſes, the more he really craves,
[illegible]onger are his wiſhes, voracious as the grave.
[illegible]e's no ſkilful Phyſician can eaſily invent,
[illegible]re deſtructive poiſon by long experiment,
Than ſome Merchants and Farmers in ev'ry State and Town,
Oppreſſion and Extortion make up [illegible]
If there's a combination among [illegible]
To ruin State and Nation, let us not join with them;
If Sea-ports firſt oppreſſed, the C[illegible] may'nt [illegible]
Tho' *Eve* ſhe firſt tranſgreſſed, *Adam* was not excus'd.
Let all with deteſtation abhor for to oppreſs,
Nothing exalts a nation ſo much as righteouſneſs;
We are not ſo ſhort-ſighted but we may ſee ſo far,
If CHRIST is ſo much ſlighted GOD will continue a war.
We have an invitation to ſave ourſelves and lands,
To practice invocations for this is GOD's command;
We hope to have ſalvation, yet from the Savior run,
If there's no reformation *New-England* is undone.
GOD gives us plain direction how we may come to awe,
And live in good ſubjection unto our MAKER's Laws;
But we are ſo impolitic, and there are ſuch out-breakings,
We are loth to be held [illegible] to Laws of our own making.
If we had juſt conceptions of ſin which ſo abounds,
Should follow GOD's direction and tread corruption down;
Without much pains or labor we may know our duty,
And do by all our Nabors, as we would be done by.
This law is juſt and equal, we cannot it deny,
'Twill prove ſo in the ſequel of life when we ſhall die;
If we believe the Story found in the Goſpel Plan,
No one can enter glory that's a diſhoneſt man.
Since GOD has given us reaſon let us uſe it for him,
And not commit high treaſon againſt the KING of KINGS;
Who is our LORD and MASTER, and him we ought to own,
He is our rightful SOVEREIGN, and to him we belong.
*New-England* has been ſickly, and many a one have dy'd,
We've buried Father Conſcience, and raiſed Mother Pride;
Faith is now languiſhing, Repentance given over,
Without a good Phyſician theſe two cannot recover.
Charity faſt is cooling and Virtue faints away,
Ignorance is prevailing, but Knowledge doth decay;
Profaneneſs is in faſhion, Religion loſes ground,
Holineſs is decreaſing, Covetouſneſs abounds.
Sincerity is wanting, Sagacity is fled,
And Wiſdom lays expiring, and Piety is dead;
When Mercy is forſaken, Diſhoneſty's elected,
Juſtice and Truth condemned, Morality rejected.
How beautiful and god-like, delightful for to ſee
Princes and People walking in Love and Unity;
Remembering their MAKER, whom they are bound to love,
And ſo be wiſe as Serpents, and harmleſs as the Doves.
If we would be forgiven and live in Peace and Reſt,
Be Favorites of Heaven, and be forever bleſt,
Then let us all be willing at this oppreſſive Day
To be juſt in our Dealings, and put our ſins away.
Behold the Invitation of GOD ALMIGHTY's SON,
Who promiſes Salvation [illegible]
Let every SON for LIBERTY [illegible] *American* Towns,
Accept the Invitation to an Immortal Crown.

## 37. A Proclamation for a Day of Public Thanksgiving and Prayer
[Boston: John Gill, 1777]

PROBABLY to everyone's relief, this broadside did not call for "Fasting, Thanksgiving, and Prayer," the most common pattern since the practice began in the early years of the Massachusetts Bay Colony. Thanksgiving proclamations are still printed in the Commonwealth of Massachusetts, and are issued by the Governor, from the State house in Boston. Though the purposes for which these thanksgiving proclamations were originally instituted have been lost, and the days themselves have become state holidays, the ritual of proclaiming a day for reflection and thanksgiving persists.

Specifically, this broadside also carries the exhortation, *"God Save the American States,"* another example of the transformation of a formula originally intended to invoke divine assistance for the king.

NATIONAL INDEX 15423
FORD 2096
AMERICAN ANTIQUARIAN SOCIETY
41.9 x 33 cm.

# State of Massachusetts-Bay.

## A
## PROCLAMATION
### For a Day of public THANKSGIVING AND PRAYER.

*IT having pleased Almighty GOD, the Father of Mercies, amidst the Calamities of the present War, to bestow upon this, and the other* UNITED AMERICAN STATES, *many great and invaluable Blessings,—it becomes a People so highly favour'd of the LORD, especially at the Close of a fruitful Year, to express their grateful Sense of the divine Goodness, by public* THANKSGIVING and PRAISE:

WE have therefore thought fit, with Advice of the Council, and at the Desire of the House of Representatives, to appoint, and do hereby appoint, THURSDAY the Twentieth Day of *November* next, to be observed as a Day of THANKSGIVING and PRAYER throughout this State; hereby calling upon Ministers and People, of every Denomination, to convene on the said Day, and with humble Devotion, Gratitude and Praise, acknowledge the many Mercies bestowed upon us by our munificent Benefactor; particularly, that he hath, notwithstanding our great Unworthiness, blessed us with Health in our Dwellings, our Army and our Navy; and that the Earth hath yielded her Increase in such uncommon Plenty; and that he hath so far supported us in our Exertions against the arbitrary Claims and military Violence of *Britain*; and especially in a late Instance of Divine Interposition, in which the Arm of the LORD of Hosts and GOD of Armies very conspicuously appears, hath given us a compleat Victory over a whole Army of our Enemies; hereby teaching us firmly to rely upon Him whose is the Power, and the Glory, and the Victory: That he hath preserv'd the Lives of so many of our Officers and Soldiers, and especially the important Life of our illustrious Commander in Chief; that the Union of the Independent *American* States is not only preserved, but appears more and more permanent; and above all, that we yet enjoy the glorious Gospel of JESUS CHRIST in meridian Brightness; a Compliance with the reasonable Requisitions of which will introduce us to the Freedom and Felicity of a far better Country.

AND we hereby recommend to, and enjoin it upon Ministers and People, deeply to abase themselves under a Sense of their Sins and Unworthiness; lamenting the many Offences by which this People have forfeited all Pretensions to the Divine Favor; humbly imploring Forgiveness, through the Merits of JESUS CHRIST our LORD, and that GOD would be pleased, by the Influences of his Spirit, to lead us to the Knowledge and Practice of Truth and Righteousness; that he would inspire our Enemies with the Spirit of that merciful Religion they profess; that he would continue to support our righteous Cause, and speedily, if it be his holy Will, establish, on a permanent Basis, our Independence, Peace and Happiness; that *America* may become for the Equity of its civil Government, the Purity of its Morals, and the Practice of the Religion of JESUS, the Glory of all Lands, and the Joy of the whole Earth;—that every Species of Tyranny may be abolished from the World, and all Mankind made happy in the Enjoyment of that Religion which is Righteousness and Peace, and Joy in the Holy Ghost.

AND all servile Labour is hereby forbidden on the said Day.

*GIVEN at the* COUNCIL-CHAMBER *in* BOSTON, *the Twentieth Day of October, in the Year of our LORD, One Thousand Seven Hundred and Seventy seven.*

JEREMIAH POWELL,
ARTEMAS WARD,
RICHARD DERBY, Jun'r.
THOMAS CUSHING,
SAMUEL HOLTEN,
JABEZ FISHER,
MOSES GILL,
JOHN TAYLOR,
BENJAMIN WHITE,
BENJAMIN AUSTIN,
HENRY GARDNER,
DAVID SEWALL,
DANIEL HOPKINS,
NATHAN CUSHING,
TIMOTHY EDWARS,
ABRAHAM FULLER.

By their Honor's Command,
JOHN AVERY, Dep'y. Secr'y.

GOD SAVE THE AMERICAN STATES!

38. A Letter to a Worthy Officer of the American Army
[Worcester?, 1777?] By Lydia Learned.

LYDIA Learned (1730–1792) was a schoolmistress and storekeeper in Framingham, Massachusetts. She also wrote verse of an occasional nature, from time to time. She is specifically mentioned in the *History of Framingham, Massachusetts, 1640–1880,* a volume written by J. H. Temple, and published in 1880. Lydia Learned was particularly noted for her funeral elegies, some of which she no doubt composed on commission.

A letter in the archives of the American Antiquarian Society from John M. Merriman, dated March 31, 1933, claims that this poem was written in honor of Brigadier General John Nixon. A native of Framingham, he was in the town during the winter of 1777 and 1778. It would have been logical for the local poet to celebrate his fame, and wish him God's blessings and victory. The broadside was probably printed in Worcester, though probably not by Isaiah Thomas, who would have provided his colophon.

NATIONAL INDEX 43480
BRISTOL 4708
AMERICAN ANTIQUARIAN SOCIETY
33.8 x 21 cm.

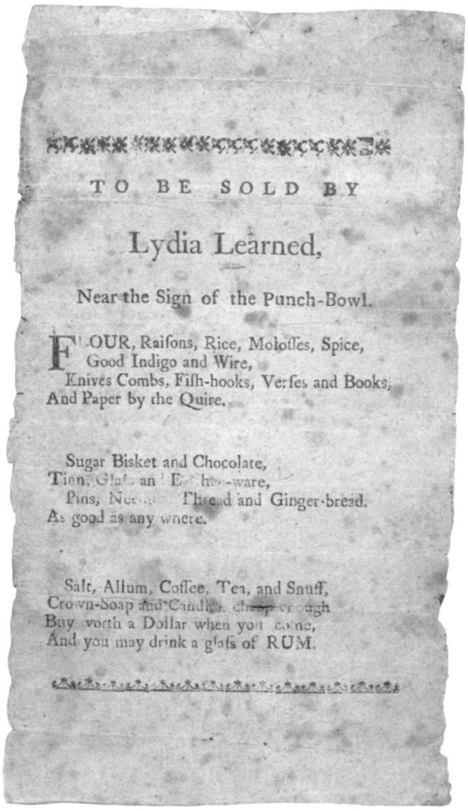
TO BE SOLD BY

Lydia Learned,

Near the Sign of the Punch-Bowl.

F[illegible]OUR, Raiſons, Rice, Moloſſes, Spice,
Good Indigo and Wire,
Knives Combs, Fiſh-hooks, Verſes and Books,
And Paper by the Quire.

Sugar Bisket and Chocolate,
Tinn, [illegible]-ware,
Pins, [illegible] Thread and Ginger-bread.
As good as any where.

Salt, Allum, Coffee, Tea, and Snuff,
Crown-Soap and Candl[illegible]
Buy [illegible]orth a Dollar when you [illegible],
And you may drink a glaſs of RUM.

# A
# LETTER
## TO
## A worthy Officer of the American Army.

YOUR Honor, Sir, is call'd to lead forth those,
Who are engag'd to go against our Foes;
I hope you go, not in your Strength or Pow'r,
But in his Name, whose Name is a strong Tow'r.

I hope you're aiming at our just Defence,
More than obtaining a great Recompence;
I hope God's Glory is your highest Aim,
And the best good of those that fear his Name.

The pow'rful Aid of Heav'n may you obtain,
While in the important Service you remain;
May all your Army now live in God's Fear,
And for their Safety may his Pow'r appear.

O may God's Blessing be on all who are
Now under your most kind religious Care;
May God preserve you from your Enemies,
And may you prosper in your Enterprize.

If Enemies you face, in Woods or Field
May you cause them to fall, to flee or yield;
If you engage with Foes on Land or Seas,
May you destroy, or conquer them with Ease.

God grant you may gain Vict'ry over those,
That are your Earthly and your Ghostly Foes;
I wish the War may in a short Time cease,
And you return Home to your Friends in Peace.

Sir, if your Lot be order'd otherways,
And Wars continue yet for many Days;
And if our Sins displease our Maker so,
That he will not forth with our Armies go.

If you should fall into your Enemies Hand,
And Captive go into a foreign Land;
If you among your Foes should be confin'd,
To God's just Will, Sir, may you be resign'd.

I hope you may find Favour in the Eyes,
Of them that are our common Enemies;
May Heaven grant you ev'ry needful Grace,
And soon return you to your native Place.

But if in Wars it be your Lot to die,
And pass from Time into Eternity;
When you your Warlike Weapons lay aside,
May you through Him who for his People dy'd,

A glorious never fading Crown obtain,
When you shall leave this World of Sin and Pain;
When you your Body leave to sleep in Dust,
Having in your Redeemer put your Trust.

May your departing never dying Ghost,
Be guarded safely to the Heav'nly Host;
Where Wars and Fightings will forever cease,
Where Captain of the Host is Prince of Peace.

---

*Kind Sir, do not despise my Letter,*
*Because I could indite no better:*
*From your unfeigned Friend it came,*
*And so I write my worthless Name.*

Lydia Learned.

Framingham, March 17, 1778.

## 39. The Last Words of Ezra Ross, James Buchanan and William Brooks
[Worcester, 1778]

THE two "execution" broadsides in this collection are typical of those that were traditionally used to establish a moral example, at the occasion of a public execution for crime. Public executions were justified on the grounds of their didactic social value, and scaffold confessions, or speeches to the young, were not uncommon. Execution sermons were preached in the Massachusetts Bay Colony, and occasionally the minister would include in his sermon a confession written or dictated by the criminal. Invariably, these confessions were moral lessons for the community through which the criminal would trace his past history, showing how one form of sin led to another, culminating in the capital crime for which he was soon to be executed. Increase Mather, for example, preached *A Sermon on the Occasion of the Execution of James Morgan* (Boston, 1684), in which the sermon's lesson is developed from Morgan's penitent confession, dictated to Mather during the week preceeding the execution.

The following broadsides capture these tragic moments by recapitulating the events of each crime in narrative depositions which were obtained from the criminals themselves. The printers have carefully followed the texts of each account, and have refrained from delivering moral judgments, though each broadside acts as an *exemplum* to those who read the accounts in full. As Ezra Ross, James Buchanan, and William Brooks were soldiers in Burgoyne's regiment, this narrative recounts an intriguing episode in the revolutionary conflict, a human interest drama that broadside printers must have valued highly. Moreover, the seducer's name, Bathsheba, has all the allusory value that an assigned or fictitious name might have brought to the story.

NATIONAL INDEX 43424
BRISTOL 4792
AMERICAN ANTIQUARIAN SOCIETY
43.5 x 33 cm.

# The last Words and dying Speech

## Of *Ezra Ross*, *James Buchanan* and *William Brooks*,

## Who were executed at Worcester on Thursday the 2d Day of July 1778,

## For the Murder of Mr. *Joshua Spooner*, of Brookfield.

*Bathsheba Spooner*, who was convicted of being accessary to the Murder of her Husband, was also executed at the same Time.

I JAMES BUCHANAN was a Sergeant in the Army under General Burgoyne, born in Glasgow in Scotland, aged 36 years. I WILLIAM BROOKS was a private in said army, born in the parish of Wednesbury, in the county of Stafford, in England, aged 27. We together on February 8th 1778, left Worcester, with an intent to go to Springfield to work. In passing Mr Spooner's, we were called in by Alexander Cummings, whom we thought was a British soldier. Having stood some time by the fire, he told us his master was gone from home, but he would go and call his mistress, for she had a great regard for the army, as her father was in it and one of her brothers. He called her, and she came down, and appeared glad to see us. She asked us, whether we came from the Hill? We told her we had, and were going to Canada, as I Buchanan, had left my family there. She ordered breakfast for us, and as soon as it was ready we were desired to go into the sitting-room. We were very much surprized at this, for we should have thought ourselves well dealt by, to have received any favour she might see fit to bestow on us in the kitchen. However we all breakfasted together. The weather being very bad, we were asked to stay till it cleared up. As we had but little money, we accordingly stayed. The weather continued very bad, we stayed there that day and night, I (Buchanan) am not positive whether it was the first or second day, she told me, when by ourselves, that she and her husband did not agree—that he was gone a journey to Princetown, and that he would not be at home soon, that we should not go from thence until the weather was fair, there being a great fall of snow at this time. We very readily consented, and stayed from day to day, expecting Mr. Spooner home. Mrs. Spooner getting very free in discourse with me (Buchanan) one day told me that she never expected Mr. Spooner to return, as there was one Mr. Ross gone with him, who had an ounce of poison, which he had promised her he would give to Mr. Spooner, the first convenient opportunity. The reader must needs think this a very strange circumstance, that she should make such a discovery to an entire stranger. She said at the same time, we should stay, till we saw whether Mr Spooner returned or not. Accordingly we stayed, and were never in better quarters, little thinking of the bait, the seducer of souls was laying for us, we were then in a disposition to catch at it, having no fear of God before our eyes, and entirely forsaken of him. Having tarried ten or eleven days, as near as can be recollected, he at length came home, and seeing us there, asked her who we were. She told him that I (Buchanan) was cousin to Alexander Cummings. He took no further notice of it; but going out among his neighbours, it is likely he was informed how long we had been there, and probably heard at the tavern of the quantity of liquor he had to pay for since his going on his journey. Be that as it may, at night he came home, and seeing we were not gone, he desired us to go immediately. We begged he would let us stay 'till morning: He after some time consented, that we should stay by the fire all night. He was in the sitting room by himself, and Mrs. Spooner went to bed. There was one Reuben Old, came upon some business with Mr. Spooner, and after some time came out and told us that Mr. Spooner told him he was afraid we should rob him, adding, that he had lost a silver spoon, and a great deal of pewter. This vexed us, as we were conscious we had no thought of stealing from him. Had we been so inclined, we had as much oppportunity as we could have desired. The spoon, he found where he laid it, Cummings convinced him there was none of the pewter missing. Mr. Spooner went up stairs and brought down a box, which he had his money in, and laid down on the floor with it under his head. Every thing Mr. Spooner did or said, Old came and told us, and was out with us all the time he was asleep, and we were all merry together, sitting by the kitchen fire. Said Old declared in court, that I (Buchanan) said, if Mr. Spooner came out I would for two coppers put him in the well, which is false. In the morning, it not being convenient to see Mrs Spooner to take our leave of her, we, Buchanan, Brooks and Cummings, went to Mrs. Stratten's to pass the day, 'till we could get an opportunity to bid Mrs Spooner farewell. We stayed at Mrs. Stratten's the best part of the day, Cummings having received five dollars from Mr. Spooner, to treat his pretended cousin with, we went to Mr. Cooley's tavern and had some drink, from thence to Dr Foxcrofts, stayed there until Cummings came and told us Mr. Spooner was in bed. We then went to the house, and had supper and liquor, retired to the barn, and tarried all night. In the morning had breakfast sent to the barn for us. And as Mrs Berry and Mrs. Tufts had been there the day before, and wanted to see me (Buchanan) I said I would go and see them. Mrs. Spooner said she would also go, which was agreed on. Buchanan and Brooks went there, and we all stayed at Mr. Green's drinking 'till late; some distance from thence, she said she had given a handkerchief to a British soldier that had some words in anger with me, Buchanan, upon which, Brooks went back on her horse, and she and I went home.—Brooks miss'd his road on his return, but got to the house some time after us, but did not get the handkerchief, as the soldier would not deliver it, until he saw Mrs. Spooner. Buchanan and Brooks stayed that night in the barn, in the morning went to Gilbert's Tavern, and staid there some time, and on coming out from his house, we saw Cummings coming on one of Mr. Spooner's horses, he told us his master was gone to the tavern, and that his mistress desired we would come there, which we did, and had supper, we went to the barn that night, and in the morning she sent us word that her husband was gone abroad into the country to get some oats. The boy Parker, had proposed to Brooks, if he would come and meet Mr. Spooner and him on their return, he, said Parker, said he would help to take Mr. Spooner's life. We went over from the barn to the house, and found he was gone, and stayed there all day, and lived on the best the house afforded of meat and drink: Mr. Spooner came home in the dusk of the evening, so that we had like to have been seen; but we heard him come with the sley to the door, and Brooks ran into the cellar, and I went and stood on the back stairs, until he went into the sitting room. We then came out, and went to the barn, there stayed all next day, and at night, when Mr. Spooner was in bed, we were sent for to the house, and received supper and liquor, to encourage another plan, which Cummings and Parker (who have for this time escaped punishment) proposed to poor Brooks, which was, they all three to go up stairs, and Brooks to take his life from him, for which he was to receive one thousand dollars, Mr. Spooner's watch, his buckles, and as much cloth as would make a suit of cloaths; but Brooks's heart failed him; and Mrs. Spooner said she did not think he was so faint-hearted. Had this been done he was to be put into the well as he was taken out of bed; for she observed it would be thought he had fallen in, drawing water in the night; next day had breakfast brought us by Cummings. He informed us, there was another plan formed by her, which was to have been executed as follows. Either Cummings or Parker to tell Mr. Spooner one of his horses was sick, and as he came to the barn to kill him, and put him amongst the horses feet, to make people believe when he was found that [illegible] him, but to make her believe he would not go over. The boy conducted accordingly. We stayed all that day and night. Next day, being Sunday, we stayed there; she came over at night; we told her we would go away the next morning; she desired we would not; but we would not stay. We set out to go to Sgringfield, as we went thro' Western, on that road, we engaged to work with one Mr. Marks a smith; I Buchanan worked there two days; but as he had no files fit for the branch of trade, Brooks followed, we proposed to go to Worcester to get some, which was agreed to.

We set off on Wednesday about noon, and in going by Mr. Spooner's we called in and told her where we were going; she said she would follow us down next day as she wanted to see her sister, saying she was glad we had got work so near; and further added, that she had two notes, one of 20 pounds lawful, and another of 300 dollars, which she would endeavor to get changed, and let me, Buchanan, have one hundred dollars, to purchase any thing I might want. We staid in the barn till morning, and then set out for Worcester, and she followed us the same day and called at Mrs. Walker's for us, according to agreement; she came in and staid some time, and gave me, Buchanan, a note, as much cloth as made a shirt, and 6 or 7 dollars; observing to me they came from one McDonald, an acquaintance of mine; she then went to see her sister, and desired us to stay till she came back, which we did; she returned on Friday morning about 10 o'clock, and staid till night; she told me, Buchanan, at parting, that she had no more paper money, but what she had given me, but begged I would procure her some poison to give Mr Spooner; I accordingly that day got one drachm of Calomel, and made it into 20 papers. I desired her to give one in the morning; she told me she never gave him any; she went to her sister's late that night, and call'd on us in the morning, about 10 o'clock, I went to the door; she would not come in, but desired me to come up to Mr. Nazro's shop, and she would get files for us, as we had not money sufficient to get what we wanted; she ask'd me, when we would come through Brookfield. I told her if she would set up, we would call on Monday night at eleven o'clock, she said she would; I parted with her and sent Brooks up to the shop. But as he came in sight, he saw her ride from the door and therefore did not go there; we staid at Walker's until Sunday afternoon, and then left Worcester, and about 8 o'clock at night got to Mr. Spooner's; we saw Mrs. Stratten at the well, I Buchanan, spoke to her, she told me there was no company in the house, but she would let Mrs Spooner know we were there; Mrs. Spooner came out, and told us that one Mr Ross was in the house, who had a brace of pistols loaded, and that he had promised her he would kill Mr Spooner as he came home from the tavern, she desired us to come in, which we did, he shewed us a pistol, and said Mr. Spooner should die by that to night. Either Brooks or Buchanan said it would alarm the neighbours.

Brooks said, if Ross would help him he would knock him down, accordingly, it was agreed on, and there was a look out kept at the sitting room door for his coming, in the mean time there was some supper brought by Mrs. Stratten to us, we had some flip before, there was now some rum brought, which we drank, each of us by turns giving a look out. We are certain Mrs. Statten could not but know what was going forward. That we leave to the judgment of the public. Mr. Spooner was at length seen coming, and then was the time for the Devil to show his power over sinners who had forsaken God.

*An Account of the Murder as it was committed.*

William Brooks went out and stood within the small gate leading into the kitchen, and as Mr. Spooner came past him he knocked him down with his hand. He strove to speak when down, Brooks then took him by the throat and partly strangled him. Ross and Buchanan came out; Ross took Mr. Spooner's watch out and gave to Buchanan; Brooks and Ross took him up and put him into the well head first; before they carried him away, I, Buchanan, pulled off his Shoes: I was instantly struck with horror of conscience, as well I might; I went into the house and met Mrs. Spooner in the sitting room, she seemed vastly confused: She went immediately up and brought the money which was in a box. She not having the key desired me to break it open, which I did; at the same time Brooks and Ross came in: She gave two notes of 400 dollars each to Ross to change and give the money to Brooks; but there was found some paper money, which Brooks received, being 243 dollars, and the notes were returned.

At the same time she gave Ross four notes, each of them ten pounds, to purchase camblet for a riding dress. Ross gave Brooks his waistcoat, breeches and shirt. She went and brought Ross a waistcoat, breeches and shirt of Mr. Spooner's. When they were shifted, she gave me, Buchanan, three eight dollar bills, and asked me when she should see me again, I told her in fourteen days, but it pleased God to order it sooner, and in a dreadful situation. Had we all been immediately struck dead after the perpetrating so horrid a murder, and sent to Hell, God would have been justified and we justly condemned.

About 11 o'clock at night, we set off for Worcester. About 4 o'clock in the morning we reached Mrs. Walker's house; Mary Walker and a Negro girl were within; we told them a parcel of lies to excuse our sudden return; in the morning we went to drinking, to endeavour to drown the horrid action we had been guilty of; we tarried there all day, with a view to go off at night, but it pleased God to order it otherwise, for Brooks, being in liquor, went down to Mr. Brown's tavern, there shewing Mr. Spooner's watch, and the people seeing him have silver Buckles, became suspicious of him, and one Ensign Clark going to Mrs. Walker's and seeing what passed there gave information concerning us. The news of the murder had now reached the town, and we were all taken and brought to trial before the Committee, examined and committed to goal. On the 24th of April last we were brought to trial before the Superior Court, found guilty and received sentence of death.

JAMES BUCHANAN,
EZRA ROSS,*
his
WILLIAM + BROOKS,
mark.

We, Buchanan, Brooks and Ross, are conscious to ourselves that we are indeed guilty of the above murder, and that hereby we have forfeited our lives into the hands of public justice, and expos'd ourselves to have our part in the lake which burneth with fire and brimstone. We desire to give glory to God by a free and full confession of our heinous guilt. We trust we have, with deep penitence and contrition of soul, confessed it to God, hoping in his infinite mercy and compassion, through the atoning blood of his Son Jesus, that our scarlet and crimson guilt may be done away, that we may be saved from eternal damnation, which we know we justly deserve, and obtain eternal life and salvation. We would, as dying men, who have been made to feel what an evil and bitter thing sin is, earnestly warn all, especially young people, that they would avoid the vices we have been addicted to, and which prepared the way for our committing the heinous wickedness for which we are to suffer an immature and ignominious death: That they would avoid bad company, excessive drinking, prophane cursing and swearing, shameful debaucheries, disobedience to parents, the profanation of the Lord's day, &c. That they would be pious, sober and virtuous, that so they may be in favour with God and man.

And now we commend our departing souls into the hands of a merciful God and Saviour, earnestly desiring that all who may be spectators or hearers of our tragical end, while we are the subjects of prayer, would lift up their hearts in fervent supplications for us, that God would receive us to his everlasting mercy.

---

* *A soldier in the Continental army, born at Ipswich, in the parish of Lynaebrook (New England) aged 18.*

---

¶ Mrs. *Spooner* said nothing at the Gallows.——

## 40. The Last Words and Dying Speech of Robert Young [Worcester: Isaiah Thomas, 1779]

UNLIKE the Spooner, Buchanan, Brooks and Ross narrative, this broadside traces the life history of a single person, up to and including the crime for which he was to be executed. The moral or didactic value of this type of confession is heightened by the dramatic way in which the capital crime is shown to climax a life blighted by weakness, particularly for women, as Young describes himself as "inclined to the company of women, but an absolute hater of all sorts of strong liquor." A British soldier, his career narrative is given continuity by a subordinate account of his movement with the British army, but the central focus is a sensational relation of his obsession with women, and his uncontrollable passion, which was the cause of this current predicament.

Young's confession is a more eloquent and dramatic statement than the legal deposition recounting the Spooner affair. And while the autobiographical statement on this broadside develops the character of a rogue, he is a picaresque rogue, of the type usually cast as hero in the popular literature of the eighteenth century, such as Fielding's *Tom Jones*. The conclusion of Young's amorous adventures, however, shows a calloused deceit which forces the brief narrative to come full circle, to a resolution in justice.

The illustration, depicting the scene at the gallows, was a standard motif on such broadsides. This one was also used on other broadsides printed by Isaiah Thomas.

NATIONAL INDEX 19448
FORD 2212
AMERICAN ANTIQUARIAN SOCIETY
51 x 40 cm.

THE

# LAST WORDS

AND

# DYING SPEECH

OF

## ROBERT YOUNG,

**Who is to be EXECUTED at Worcester this Day, November 11th, 1779, for a RAPE committed on the Body of Jane Green, a Child, eleven years of age, at Brookfield, in the County of Worcester, on the third Day of September last,**

I WAS born in *Carrick* on *Shannon*, in the County of *Leytrim*, in *Ireland*, and am now twenty-nine Years of age.

My father was a merchant, and I, being the youngest of his children then living, was intended for the same business, for which purpose I was kept at school until I was about fifteen years of age, and then my father thought proper, in order to have me well instructed in the business, to send me, in quality of a clerk, to a wholesale merchant in the city of *Dublin*, Mr. *George Reilly*.

At that early age I was much inclined to the company of women, but an absolute hater of all sorts of strong liquor. I made large promises to one of my employer's servant maids, if she would yield to my unlawful embraces, to which, by constant importunity, she consented; afterwards to prevent discovery, I studied all means to have her discharged, which I soon after got accomplished, being much in favour with the merchant and his wife. I then got acquainted with several lewd women, and being much in their company, in a short time learned to drink to excess.

I lived with Mr. *Reilly* about ten months, when he began to find out my way of spending my time and money when absent from the shop, for which he reprimanded me, and declared he would inform my parents of my conduct, if I would not quit such company and apply myself to the necessary callings of my business; on which I left him, and went to *Liverpool*, in *England*, where I staid twelve or fourteen days, and returned to *Dublin* again.

Soon after my return to *Dublin*, I inlisted and joined the 5th regiment, and then gave myself up to all manner of debauchery. The regiment lay ten months in *Dublin* after I had joined it, during which time I was sent to the hospital, being bad with a disorder, I had never before experienced, but was no stranger to it afterwards.

I was stationed for three Years in the *Isle-of-Man*; there *I* betrayed three girls, but after leaving them, have scarce thought of them to this fatal period. *I* was afterwards seven Years in the garrison of *Gibralter*, and then went to *England*.

On my return to *England*, finding a body of troops that were bound to *Canada*, under the command of General *Burgoyne*, *I* joined them as a volunteer, and we were landed at *Quebeck*, and there wintered. At *Quebeck*, *I* drew but little money, which induced me to study how *I* should procure more. At length I cast my eyes on a widow, paid her several visits, and strove to deceive her; she was for some time deaf to my protestations, but so closely did I pursue my purpose of deceiving her, that at length she gave heed to my request, and believed my falsehood: She supplied me with money, and I was enabled to get plenty of liquor, spending much of my time with lewd companions: The widow's affection became so great, that she requested me to stay behind; however, I left her and went with the troops against Ticonderoga, I was then doing duty with the artillery, but belonged to the 33d regiment. I was in the two principal engagements, but received no wound.

After the surrender of the British army, I marched with them as far as Hadley, were I became acquainted with a girl, who advised me to desert; I spent a night with her, and agreed to go as far as Western, and then return back, which I accordingly did.

Afterwards I went to *Pelham*, where *I* lived three months and then went to *Shelburne*, where *I* continued five months, at both these last mentioned places, *I* studied to deceive the fair sex, and betrayed a young woman in each of them. My rambling inclination continuing *I* soon left them as *I* had done many others, and went to *Greenfield*, where *I* kept school to teach reading and writing: After keeping school here about two months I began my old practices of seducing the young women, I gained the consent of one in particular, who I often went to see in private; she liked me so well that she promised to go with me: Her parents tried all means to keep her from me but to little purpose; they denied me admittance to their house; I tarried better than five months in *Greenfield* and when I left that place, the girl left her friends in order to see me which she often did. I afterwards lived in *Montague*, *Sunderland* and *Greenwich*, and kept school in several places to good acceptance.

Whilst I was keeping school in *Greenwich*, I was informed by Mr. *Green's* sister, that a school master was wanted in *Brookfield*; and when my time was out in *Greenwich*, I went to *Brookfield*, and denied belonging to the British troops, in order to avoid as much as possible any discourse on that subject.

I opened a school at Mr. *Samuel Green's*, which I duly and faithfully attended; I was not long there before I got acquainted with *Anne Green*, and kept her company some time before her parents knew of it, which when they did they strongly opposed it, knowing me then to be doing the same with others, and that I was many nights from home. I promised to quit all other company in that way, and offered marriage to *Anne*; she agreed: I then told her I belonged to the British army, but would never join it. Many arguments were used, and means tried, to diswade her from my company, but nothing could shake her constancy: When I was sick, she shewed such cordial affection that I loved her without deceit, and against much opposition we were published, and intended to be married in a few days.--- I now declare to the world, that I wronged her in court, and hope no one will think ill of her on my account. Her sister *Jane* was basely used by me; I humbly ask her forgiveness, and all others whom *I* have offended.

I freely forgive the world as *I* hope for forgiveness through CHRIST JESUS, and hope my unhappy end will be a warning to all others to forsake their evil ways and seek the LORD while he may be found, and not persist in those pernicious courses that will inevitably end in the destruction of their bodies and endanger their precious souls.

ROBERT YOUNG.

Printed and sold at the Printing Office, in *Worcester*.

## 41. This Day was Published by Isaiah Thomas
Thomas's Almanac for 1780
[Worcester: Isaiah Thomas, 1779]

SOME of Thomas's earlier almanacs contained much political matter in the form of illustrations, essays, and poems. The almanac for 1780 contains "Verses on Freedom" which are very general and do not relate to the Revolution in any particular way.

This advertisement for Thomas's almanac is typical of his annual pronouncements proclaiming the availability of the following year's pamphlets "by the Thousand, Hundred, Groce, Dozen, or Single." This copy, however, is especially interesting because it contains elegantly printed information about the historical importance of 1780, the "Bissextile" or Leap Year. Moreover, the "Planting of Massachusetts Bay" and the "Building of Boston" are given prominent historical association with important events of ancient history, particularly Biblical history, such as "Noah's Flood." This association is neither light-hearted nor without contemporary precedent; Puritan historiography since the early years of the Massachusetts and Plymouth colonies had stressed the importance of these colonies as a fulfillment of biblical prophecy. This historical sense was emphasized—though not by secular businessmen like Isaiah Thomas—when Revolutionary writers and ministers began to see independence from Britain as the commencement of the long-awaited millennium. An almanac would appeal to one's sense of history and to one's curiosity about the future because it contained information about both the past and the future of the colony.

NATIONAL INDEX 19439
FORD 2209
AMERICAN ANTIQUARIAN SOCIETY
43.2 x 36 cm.

This Day was publiſhed,

And to be SOLD by

ISAIAH THOMAS, at his Printing-Office, in Worceſter,

By the Thouſand, Hundred, Groce, Dozen, or Single,

As cheap as any in the ſtate,

# THOMAS's

Maſſachuſetts, New-Hampſhire, and Connecticut

# ALMANACK,

For the Year of our Lord Chriſt

# 1780,

Being Biſſextile, or Leap Year,

And the fourth Year of the INDEPENDENCE of AMERICA, which began July 4th, 177

| | |
|---|---|
| From Creation according to the beſt of Profane Hiſtory, | 5729 |
| But by Account of Holy Scriptures | 5742 |
| Julian Period, | 6493 |
| From Noah's Flood, | 4074 |
| From the Deſtruction of Sodom, | 3682 |

| | |
|---|---|
| From the building of Rome, | 2931 |
| From the Deſtruction of Troy, | 2662 |
| Hegira, or Flight of Mahomet, | 1189 |
| Firſt planting of New-England, | 171 |
| Planting of Maſſachuſetts-Bay, | 152 |
| Building of Boſton, | 150 |

Calculated for the Meridian of Boſton, Lat. 42.25. N. But will ſerve without any eſſential Variation for either of the N. E. States.

CONTAINING,

Sun's riſing and ſetting, Moon's riſing and ſetting, Changes of the Moon, Moon's Place, Time of high Water morning and evening, Calendar, Times of holding the Superiour and Inferiour Courts in the four New-England States, remarkable Days, Judgment of the Weather, Eclipſes, Vulgar Notes, Roads to the principal Towns on the Continent, Friends yearly Meetings in New-England, Vacations at Harvard College.

*To which are added for Inſtruction and Entertainment,*

Maxims and Sentences worthy of Obſervation.

The Wiſdom of Providence: an apologue from the German of the celebrated Gellert.

The good natured Huſband.

On Bluntneſs.

The different Stages of Life, phyſically conſidered; from the celebrated Dr. Cullen's Lectures.

Force of Imagination very powerful.

Fearful Death of a Popiſh Biſhop who was guilty of Oppreſſion.

A moſt remarkable Viſion.

Character of the French.

Egyptian Anecdote.

Account of ſome uncommon Burnings of Human Bodies, lucid appearances, &c.

Story of King John.

Repartee of a married Young Lady.

Verſes on Freedom.

By PHILOMATHES, An Independent Whig.

*N. B. This ALMANACK is pronounced by able judges to be equal in goodneſs to any publiſhed.*

Great allowance to thoſe who buy to ſell again.

## 42. By His Excellency John Hancock, Esq.
[Boston: Benjamin Edes & Sons?, 1781]

AS the years of revolutionary warfare dragged on, the colonists settled into a routine of victory and defeat, which required periodic assessment. Moreover, retrospective meditation and thanksgiving, both public and private, was a habit of mind that had persisted from Puritan New England. The individual would assess his day and record its events in a diary or journal, expressing thanks to God for providential guidance through the perils of his earthly journey. The colonial leaders were continuously declaring gratitude to God, for his leadership of the community through the perils of their errand into the wilderness, and now, for divine assistance in the establishment of divinely-instituted freedom for the American colonies.

John Hancock echoes this emphasis here by declaring that he feels compelled to commend to the "good people of this State, . . . the Goodness of *God,* in the Year now drawing to Conclusion . . . ," in "Retrospect on the Events which have taken Place since the Beginning of the War." Hancock lists the evidence supporting this enthusiasm, again following the example of leaders of the Bay Colony in Puritan times. And like many of the American broadsides in this collection, this one concludes with an exhortation in which the colonial emphasis is substituted for royal sentiment.

NATIONAL INDEX 17217
FORD 2302
AMERICAN ANTIQUARIAN SOCIETY
51.4 x 38 cm.

By His EXCELLENCY

# JOHN HANCOCK, Esq;

Governor and Commander in Chief in and over the Commonwealth of *Massachusetts.*

## A PROCLAMATION for a Day of THANKSGIVING.

WHEREAS it hath pleased Almighty GOD, the Father of Mercies, remarkably to assist and support the United States of *America*, in their important Struggle for Liberty against the long continued Efforts of a powerful Nation; it is the Duty of all Ranks of People to observe and thankfully acknowledge the Interpositions of his Providence in their behalf.

Through the whole of the Contest, from its first Rise to this Time, the Influence of Divine Providence may be clearly perceived in many signal Instances, of which but a few are mentioned.

In revealing the Counsels of our Enemies, when the Discoveries were seasonable and important, and the Means seemingly inadequate or fortuitous.—

In preserving and even improving the Union of the several States, on the Breach of which our Enemies placed their greatest Dependence.—

In increasing the Number and adding to the Zeal and Attachment of the Friends of Liberty.—

In granting remarkable Deliverances, and blessing us with the most signal Success when Affairs seemed to have the most discouraging Appearance.—

In raising up for us a powerful and generous Ally, in one of the first of the European Powers.—

In confounding the Counsels of our Enemies and suffering them to pursue such Measures as have most directly contributed to frustrate their own Desires and Expectations.—

Above all,

In making their extreme Cruelty to the Inhabitants of these States, when in their Power, and their Savage Devastation of Property, the very Means of cementing our Union, and adding Vigor to every Effort in Opposition to them.

And as, therefore, it is the incumbent Duty of the good People of this State, as well as of those of the other States, to take a Retrospect on the Events which have taken Place since the Beginning of the War, so I cannot but recommend, in a particular Manner to their Observation, the Goodness of GOD in the Year now drawing to a Conclusion.

In which,

The Confederation of the United States has been compleated.—

In which,

There have been so many Instances of Prowess and Success in our Armies, particularly in the Southern States, where, notwithstanding the Difficulties with which they had to struggle, they have recovered the whole Country which the Enemy had over-run, leaving them only a Post or two on or near the Sea.—

In which,

We have been so powerfully and effectually assisted by our Allies, while, in all the conjunct Operations, the most perfect Harmony has subsisted in the Allied Army.—

In which,

There has been so plentiful a Harvest, and so great Abundance of the Fruits of the Earth of every Kind, as not only enables us easily to supply the Wants of our Army, but gives Comfort and Happiness to the whole People:—And,

In which,

After the Success of our Allies by Sea, a General of the first Rank, with his whole Army, has been captured by the allied Forces under the Direction of our Commander in Chief.

I Do therefore, by and with the Advice of the Council, appoint, and do hereby appoint the Thirteenth Day of *December* next (the Day recommended by the Congress to all the States) to be religiously observed as a Day of Thanksgiving and Prayer; that all the People may assemble on that Day, with grateful Hearts to celebrate the Praises of our gracious Benefactor; to confess our manifold Sins; to offer up our most fervent Supplications to the God of all Grace, that it may please Him to pardon our Offences and incline our Hearts for the future to keep all his Laws, to comfort and relieve all our Brethren who are in Distress or Captivity; to prosper our Husbandmen and give Success to all engaged in lawful Commerce; to direct all our public Counsels, and to impart Judgment and Fortitude to our Officers and Soldiers; to protect and prosper our illustrious Ally, and favour our united Exertions for the speedy Establishment of a safe, honourable and lasting Peace; to bless all Seminaries of Learning, and cause *the Knowledge of GOD to cover the Earth, as the Waters cover the Sea.*

Given at the Council-Chamber in *Boston* the Twenty Second Day of *November*, in the Year of Our LORD One Thousand Seven Hundred and Eighty one, and in the Sixth Year of the Independence of the United States of America.

By His Excellency's Command,
*John Avery*, jun. Secretary.

*John Hancock.*

GOD SAVE THE UNITED STATES OF AMERICA.

## 43. Advertisement for *The Temple* [Newburyport: John Mycall, 1782]

THE American Revolution was not an isolated phenomenon. The far-reaching revolution in thought, now called the Enlightenment, stressed a new humanism which gave dignity to individual integrity and recognized the central role of human reason. If the Puritans had perceived "right reason" to be the guiding principle of divine providence in human psychology, the rationalists argued that reason itself was a divine principle and that the human mind, like the natural creation, was a supreme manifestation of God's creative power. The liberation of thought from the shackles of ecclesiastical authority had begun with the Reformation, two hundred years earlier. During the eighteenth century, revolutions throughout Europe expressed the acceptance of a new authority, that of a government formed by the consent of the governed, rather than a monarchy imposed through the traditions of divine right.

Throughout America, magazines and journals appeared which carried developments in the Enlightenment doctrine, and *The Temple*, advertised here by the printer John Mycall, was to have been an attempt to show that "the Interests of Liberty are inseparable from those of Learning and of Virtue." Thus, the Revolution was to have been seen as part of a much larger movement: the advancement of learning and the growth of human value. However, the time was not yet right for a new periodical, and *The Temple* was never published. Soon after the Revolution, such publishing ventures would again prove successful.

NATIONAL INDEX 44225
BRISTOL 5548
FORD 2337
MASSACHUSETTS HISTORICAL SOCIETY
40 x 37 cm.

# To the Public.

THE Interests of Liberty are inseparable from those of Learning and of Virtue---------- Born of the same celestial Origin, and animated by one life—they rise and fall—they languish and revive—they live and die together. The dear-bought experience of every Country known to Fame has inscribed this maxim, as with a Sun-beam, on the annals of Society, in almost every page.

IMPRESSED with sober conviction of its truth, the friends of human nature in America cannot but regard, with anxiety and distress, the emaciated visage of true Science—the pallid gloom with which the face of Literature is overcast, and the rapid advances of a fatal consumption on the vitals of substantial virtue.

WITH the progress of this decay, the return of a darkness which may be felt, and the revival and growth of the vices most baneful to Society, have kept equal pace. Among all the omens of the continuance of the public distress, this the TRUE PATRIOT feels to be the most alarming—partly as it is considered the immediate Source of the general torpor which has benumbed the senses of the Community, and diffused that fatal languor now manifest on every limb of the body-politic, at this serious crisis of its struggle for life—but chiefly on account of its ensuring the defeat of the most vigorous exertions, by entailing on them the insupportable frown of the offended Parent of Virtue, whose omniscience looks, with jealous eye, on whatever weapon is formed against the interest of useful knowledge; and, in whose omnipotent arm, Liberty has ever found her only stable and effectual GUARDIAN.

A SPEEDY remedy of this public distemper seems indispensible——without it, the case threatens very soon to become desperate————Every heart, friendly to mankind, or truly so to itself, now wishes in earnest to see the effectual application of some Panacea without delay———In the investigation of it, all virtuous minds should now UNITE their efforts—and to the efficacy of such researches it becomes the most respectable orders of men on the Continent, to contribute to the extent of every talent they possess.

STIMULATED by sense of duty to the Greatest of Patrons, and prompted by genuine zeal for the best of causes, a number of Gentlemen of liberal education, in diverse learned professions, and in various parts of the land, have generously engaged, without prospect of any emolument to themselves, freely to devote some part of their time weekly to the service of the Public, in laying before them, according to their best abilities, such observations as may appear most necessary in the exigences of the times, for the revival of VIRTUE and PUBLIC SPIRIT; and for the restoration of LITERATURE to its merited regard.

AND that the laudable design of the worthy undertakers may be brought to effect, the Publisher hereof has dedicated a FREE PRESS to the sole use of Publishing, if suitable encouragement is found,

## The TEMPLE,

A Weekly Paper, sacred to the interest of LEARNING and VIRTUE, of LIBERTY and RELIGION, on the following Plan.

ARTICLE I. Nothing personal, or of mere party-concern, shall be admitted; nor any thing but what is deemed interesting to the Public.

II. ARTICLES of mere News, Advertisements, or Public Lists, shall have no place

III. ESSAYS and Dissertations, in prose or verse, on Subjects of general utility, shall take up the body of the Work.

IV. DEBATES on Questions of importance in the political, literary, or religious world, will be exhibited with candor and impartial disregard of party.

V. CANDID and sober Remarks will be made on such manners, customs, measures and events, as appear to have general influence on the public welfare.

VI. ALL improvements in useful knowledge will be gladly circulated as they rise: and no branch of Learning or Science will be excluded.

VII. BRIEF Systems of the several Sciences will be laid down in their order, in a method calculated to make them plain to every reader of ordinary capacity.

VIII. AT proper intervals will be given brief Histories of the chief sects among Philosophers and Christians—short schemes of their opinions—with sketches of the lives of their Founders and principal Abettors.

IX. PLAIN abridgments of the general history of the world, both natural, political, and ecclesiastic, together with Anecdotes and Lives of eminent characters, and particular Histories of particular Nations and æras will be sometimes inserted.

THIS Paper will contain eight octavo pages—will be Printed on good Paper, and a new Type, nearly the size of that on which these Proposals are printed——Each Paper will be paged and numbered, in much the same manner as the Spectator, for the convenience of binding into one volume at the end of each year————

THEY will be ready to be delivered at the Printing-Office on Tuesday morning, weekly; and shall be sent by the Post to any Post-office in the United States, the Subscribers in each town agreeing with the Post, and paying the postage of their Papers.

THE price of the Paper shall be only one Dollar per annum, to be paid on receiving the first Number, (which is but about one penny sterling for each Number) and the Publication shall begin as soon as 3000 are subscribed for.

Subscriptions for the TEMPLE will be received by most of the Printers and Post-masters on the Continent, who are requested to make these Proposals public, and return a List of the Subscribers as soon may be, that the Publication may speedily commence.

N. B. *All Letters or packets directed to the Publisher of the Temple, and left at the Post-office in Newbury-Port, in the Common-wealth of Massachusetts, post paid, will be duly noticed.*

The performances of the ingenious, of all parties, adapted to this design, will be gratefully received: and the correspondence of all friends to Learning, Liberty and Virtue is earnestly sollicited, and shall be honorably regarded, by the Public's devoted and very humble Servant,

*JOHN MYCALL.*

*Newbury-Port, February 19th, 1782.*

*WE the SUBSCRIBERS, engage to take, and pay for the above-mentioned Publication, for the Term of one Year:—*

| Subscriber's Names. | Places of abode. |
| --- | --- |

## 44. Proposals for Circulating Thomas's Massachusetts Spy
[Worcester: Isaiah Thomas, 1782]

THIS broadside, dated May, 1782, and printed in Worcester, is a proposal issued by Isaiah Thomas concerning his famous newspaper, "a publick paper that was well known throughout these states before the Revolution." *The Massachusetts Spy* was to move into the Boston area, as competition for the equally famous *Boston Gazette.* This broadside advertisement is important because of what it reveals about Thomas as a printer, aside from its tangential connection with the American Revolution. Thomas justified the wider circulation on the grounds that while "there are publications of the like kind, and not without merit, in our capital; . . . at this all-important crisis there cannot be too many, nor we be too much enlightened." Richard Steele, the current editor of the *Worcester Telegram,* states that Isaiah Thomas was primarily a businessman, rather than a revolutionary or patriot, and that his vigorous opposition to the Stamp Tax on newspapers may have been motivated more out of practical understanding of the high cost of this tax to his business than out of disapproval of taxation in principle. This broadside advertisement seems to support Steele's view of Thomas. The events of the Revolution are used, not very convincingly, to develop a rationale for the wider circulation of the Worcester-based newspaper.

NATIONAL INDEX 19440
FORD 2340
AMERICAN ANTIQUARIAN SOCIETY
39 x 25.5 cm.

# Worceſter News-Paper---FREE and Uninfluenced.

## PROPOSALS for CIRCULATING

# THOMAS'S Maſſachuſetts Spy

## In the Town of BOSTON and its Vicinity.

A NUMBER of gentlemen in the metropolis of this Commmonwealth, friends to Science, encouragers of a FREE PRESS, and promoters of the publick good, having expreſſed their deſire that the MASSACHUSETTS SPY, a publick paper for news, politicks, &c. now printed and publiſhed in Worceſter, might be circulated in Boſton EVERY THURSDAY; the Editor of that paper begs leave to lay before the reſpectable inhabitants of Boſton, and the adjacent towns, the following PROPOSALS, viz.

I. THE Massachusetts Spy ſhall be a FREE paper, "open to all parties but influenced by none." Every gentleman who writes with DECENCY and CORRECTNESS ſhall have his writings properly attended to, and publiſhed in their turn; and care will be taken to prevent *typographical errors.*

II. The Spy ſhall be printed with fair new types, on good large demy paper, to contain four large folio pages, and every page four columns.

III. All Eſſays, Letters, &c. from gentlemen in Boſton, directed to the Editor for publication, ſhall be brought to him *free of all expence to the authors.*

IV. A Poſt-Rider for the particular purpoſe of conveying the Massachusetts Spy to Boſton, and bringing all matters for publication to the Editor, ſhall be eſtabliſhed, provided 300 papers are ſubſcribed for in the town of Boſton.

V. The Poſt-Rider ſhall arrive every THURSDAY (the day on which the Maſſachuſetts Spy is publiſhed) about noon, with the papers, in Boſton; he ſhall lodge them with a gentleman (whoſe name ſhall be made known, if a ſufficient number of ſubſcribers appear) in a publick part, and near the centre of the town, where attendance will be given for delivering them; but if the number of ſubſcribers in Boſton ſhould amount to Four Hundred, the papers ſhall be regularly left at the houſes of the reſpective cuſtomers on the day of publication, without any additional expence.

VI. As GENTLEMEN in TRADE may find it to their *advantage to* ADVERTISE *in an inland paper*, which will alſo circulate in the capital; all advertiſements ſent to the editor ſhall be punctually inſerted, at the ſame rates as they are in the News-Papers publiſhed in Boſton. A Gentleman of FIDELITY, reſiding in Boſton, will receive them and all Letters, &c. directed to the publiſher, and forward them, free of any additional expence for poſtage.

VII. Advertiſements ſhall never exclude matters of more importance to the publick: If at any time there ſhould happen to be too large a proportion of advertiſements to be inſerted, an additional paper will be publiſhed on that account.

N. B. Thoſe who ſend advertiſements are to accompany them with the pay.

VIII. The price of the Massachusetts Spy to the Subſcribers in Boſton, to be EIGHTEEN SHILLINGS per annum, *free of poſtage.* Nine Shillings to be paid on the delivery of the firſt paper, and Nine Shillings, at the end of every ſix months.

IX. No Subſcriptions to be received for leſs than ſix months.

X. Gentlemen who live in towns adjacent to Boſton, may be ſupplied with any number of papers, weekly, at the rate of Nine Shillings for every Twenty-Six papers, and ſo in proportion for a larger or ſmaller number, by applying *to the Gentleman* in Boſton who will deliver the ſaid News-Papers, or to the publiſher in Worceſter.

XI. If theſe propoſals ſhould meet with encouragement, a Poſt will commence riding from Worceſter to Boſton with the Massachusetts Spy, on the Third Thurſday of June next; but ſhould the Editor fail of encouragement by that time, the plan will be declined for the preſent. *Subſcriptions are now received at the Poſt-Office in Boſton.*

---

WHEN we are contending with a powerful nation, of which we were once a part, and ſucceeding in a glorious revolution, aided by a brave and generous ally—When we are eſtabliſhing a Conſtitution of Government, which, taken in all its parts, is the beſt that a free people were ever bleſſed with, and ought to be defended againſt the baſe attempts of lawleſs wretches, who delight in anarchy and confuſion—At ſuch times a train of *intereſting matters* are ever on the political carpet, and every well-wiſher to the proſperity of America, and the inhabitants of this Commonwealth in particular, will be deſirous to be made acquainted with the circumſtances of ſuch important tranſactions,

It is the deſign of the Editor of the MASSACHUSETTS SPY, to continue to *regiſter* in his paper, IMPARTIALLY, the particulars of ſuch intereſting events as are daily taking place, and which ought to be handed down to future generations—To point out *Errors* which may endanger the publick weal—To fruſtrate as much as poſſible the *Arts of deſigning men* againſt our happy conſtitution—To *expoſe the conduct of traitors* to their country—To convey *plans for publick benefit* to the knowledge of our citizens in general; and when DEBATES ariſe concerning *men in office*, or *meaſures* reſpecting the publick, to inſert them *freely* on *both ſides* the queſtion.

True it is, that there are publications of the like kind, and not without merit, in our capital; but at this all-important criſis there cannot be too many, nor we be too much enlightened. It has been ſuggeſted to the Editor of the Massachusetts Spy (a publick paper that was well known throughout theſe States before the Revolution) that, for obvious reaſons, it might be MORE SERVICEABLE to the inhabitants of this Commonwealth, if properly attended to, at the diſtance it is *now* publiſhed from the capital, than if it was printed in Boſton. Some of thoſe reaſons are—That *Eſſays* might be inſerted with MORE FREEDOM at a diſtance from the capital—That there would be *more room* in an *inland paper* for intelligence, &c. than in other papers printed in ſea-ports, which are much crouded with Advertiſements—That Eſſays reſpecting the publick good would be *better circulated* in this populous part of the country—That it might have a good tendency to *expel prejudices* which too often ſubſiſt *between town and country*, as the ſentiments of each other could be much better communicated, and might have a happy effect in *preventing trifling jealouſies*, which from want of proper information are often productive of much evil—That the Editor, from his ſituation in Worceſter, would have *more time* than his brethren in Boſton, *to collect intelligence*, and intereſting political productions, &c. from the weſtern and ſouthern news-papers brought by the Hartford Poſt—In ſhort, That if the Massachusetts Spy ſhould be well conducted, it would be likely from theſe and other circumſtances, to be of *more general utility* than any other news-paper in this Commonwealth. The want of ſuch a publication has been long complained of.

The Editor on his part will be happy in collecting and properly arranging every material circumſtance of news or entertainment, and in preſenting them to his readers in *due ſeaſon.* As his correſpondence is ſomewhat extenſive, and many gentlemen of abilities, *both in Town and Country*, have REALLY promiſed him their *aſſiſtance*, he has a proſpect of giving ſatisfaction to all thoſe who may encourage the propoſed undertaking of *circulating the* Massachusetts Spy in Boſton and its vicinity.

In order the better to be able to execute this plan to general acceptance, he has enlarged the ſize of the Massachusetts Spy, and it is now printed in the ſame form as it was in the year 1774 in Boſton—and is larger than any other news-paper publiſhed in this or the neighbouring States.

The Editor craves the aſſiſtance of ſuch Gentlemen in Boſton, and elſewhere, who may have from time to time European or Weſt-India News-papers fall into their hands, or thoſe which are publiſhed by the enemy on this continent, and begs that (after they have peruſed ſuch papers themſelves) they would be ſo very obliging as to forward them to him, that he may collect from them ſuch intelligence as will be intereſting to the publick, or entertaining to his readers; after which, if deſired, they will be returned to their owners.

If Gentlemen who meet with *new diſcoveries in Arts and Sciences* will communicate them to the world, for the benefit of mankind, the Editor of the Massachusetts Spy will always receive pleaſure in introducing them through the channel of his paper.

As *remarkable* Anecdotes, Advertisements Extraordinary, and Bon Mots, when *wrote with decency*, and *embelliſhed with ſentiment*, are generally entertaining, if Gentlemen who poſſeſs materials will compile them agreeable to the foregoing obſervation, due attention will be paid to them; and alſo to *advices* from the *Sentimentaliſts* who viſit the *Parnaſſian Mount.*

If thoſe Gentlemen who approve of theſe propoſals, ſhould become ſubſcribers for the ſame, they may be aſſured that to make the Massachusetts Spy worthy the peruſal of its readers will continue to be exerted the beſt endeavours of their, and the Publick's,

Moſt obedient, humble Servant,

*Worceſter, May* 1782.

ISAIAH THOMAS.

## 45. A Poem Spoken Extempore, by a Young Lady
[Boston: Ezekiel Russell, 1782]

LIKE much wartime verse, these poems are not as important for their literary qualities as they are for their historical significance. Both poems here are occasional, celebrating the victory of Washington over Cornwallis at Yorktown, but approaching the conflict from two different points of view.

The victory at Yorktown was, of course, strategically important for the Continental Army. The surrender of Cornwallis, British Commander at Yorktown, was the actual if unofficial end of the American Revolution as a military conflict of any major importance. Mark Boatner notes that, "although the campaign was a long one, extending from May to October, 1781, and the total forces numerous (approximately 30,000), casualties were light, roughly 400 continentals and 600 British. Thus Yorktown was a lengthy and difficult climax to the Revolutionary war."

NATIONAL INDEX 44247
BRISTOL 5572
AMERICAN ANTIQUARIAN SOCIETY
34.5 x 20.9 cm.

A

# P O E M,

Spoken Extempore, by a YOUNG LADY, on hearing the Guns firing and Bells chiming on account of the great and Glorious Acquiſition of their Excellencies Gen. WASHINGTON and the C. de GRASSE, by the Surrender of *York-Town*, in which were Lord *Cornwallis* and Army, conſiſting of Nine Thouſand Troops, a Forty Gun Ship, a Frigate, an armed Veſſel and One Hundred Sail of Tranſports.

HONOR commands great WASHINGTON I ſing,
The noble feat of Count deGRASSE muſt ring,
Who has *Cornwallis* now within his power,
With all his Army in an evil hour.
Brave GREENE I ſing, with all the Patriot SONS,
But moſt adore Great Godlike WASHINGTON ;
YORK-TOWN once more is freed from Britiſh chains,
Rejoice AMERICA now FREEDOM reigns :
FREEDOM is Our's ; vain Britons boaſt no more
Thy matchleſs ſtrength by ſea, nor on the ſhore.
Great WASHINGTON doth thunder thro' the plain,
And piles the field with mountains of the ſlain ;
His foes they tremble and his name adore,
Confeſs his might 'till time ſhall be no more ;
BraveCount de GRASSE! Nine thouſand men did fall
Into the hands of this brave Admiral ;
Captur'd by him, how wondrous 'tis to tell,
Beſides a frigate and an arm'd veſſel.
A ſhip of forty guns then met the fate
Of cruel war, and own this Hero great ;
hundred ſail of tranſports then did yield,
onfeſs him brave by ſea as in the field.
Let the brave VICTORS on their conqueſt ſmile,
And ſafe enjoy the triumph of their toil.
Let FREEDOM's DAUGHTERS weave a garland white
Of pureſt Lillies with ſupreme delight ;
Thro'out the world may it be ever ſaid,
They plac'd this chaplet on their Heroes HEAD.

---

Printed by E. RUSSELL, near Liberty-Stump.--At the ſame Place may be had, RUSSELL's AMERICAN ALMANAC, and BICKERSTAFF's BOSTON do.

# HIS LORDSHIP HUMBLED: OR, CORNWALIS's LAMENTATION.

GREAT Mars, thou god of battles won,
Why ſmiling view great WASHINGTON?
While I neglected lie forlorn,
A by-word for all—by you a ſcorn ?
Was mine his *fate*, and his'en mine,
I'd conquer all the ſouthern Clime :
That was the plan I had in view,
The States around me to ſubdue.
And from New-York our courſe we bent,
To Carolina firſt we went ;
The State was conquer'd we all thought,
But greater conqueſts ſtill I ſought.
Great confidence in me was plac'd,
I therefore was for making haſte,
In doing buſineſs of this kind,
I form'd the following deſign.
Towards York-Town to bend my way,
Make forced marches night and day ;
And join the *Traitor Arnold* there,
To conquer all—no lives to ſpare.
As did *Burgoyne*, when on his way,
'Till he came to Saratoga,
Where he was *nab'd*—his is my *fate*,
Nought can be done—it is too late.
Great WASHINGTON has took his poſt,
Has *humbled* me and all my hoſt ;
The Britiſh flag he has pull'd down,
The *honor* of the Britiſh crown ;
And the ALLIES reſumes it's place,
To my confuſion and diſgrace :
I'd rather in my cradle dy'd,
Than have been *humbled* in my pride.
I dread, I fear, I dare not ſee,
That Hero's face, that's *humbled* me :
O ! muſt I go with bended knees,
For him to do juſt as he pleaſe ?
My honor's gone—no titles now,
No more than *Gage*, *Burgoyne*, or *Howe* ;
They're gone and fled—there's none that ſays,
There's the great *chief*—let's give him praiſe.
The praiſe is due to WASHINGTON,
Whoſe *glory now, and ever ſhone* :
See that great CHIEF, triumphant ſtands,
Smiles at my loſs—defies my bands.
It pierces me—I feel the ſmart,
Juſt like a dagger to my heart ;
To think I brag'd and made ſuch boaſts,
What I'd do 'mongſt rebel hoſts.
That with my Britiſh German bands,
Would ſpread the *terrors* of my hands,
And cruſh rebellion from this ſhore,
Ne'er to be heard amongſt them more.
My brags are now come to an *end*,
I wiſh to find ſome *honeſt* friend,
That would aſſiſt me in my trouble,
And help me out of this bad *hobble*.

## 46. Important Intelligence of Peace! [Worcester, 1783]

THIS broadside expresses a sense of urgency in the exclamatory headline, but paradoxically, its news is dated, even including summaries of the stages of negotiation which led to the final peace treaty. Following the defeat of Cornwallis at Yorktown [plate 45], military operations in America virtually ceased. Mark Boatner notes that the British proclaimed a cessation of hostilities on February 4, 1783, and Congress issued a similar proclamation on April 11, 1783. For nearly two years, various stages of peace negotiations were in progress, so that the final proclamation of peace was anticlimactic, legalistic, and much less dramatic than the heroic victory of Washington over Cornwallis at Yorktown had been. The peace negotiations were actually begun as early as 1780, before Yorktown, and the treaty was finally signed in Paris on September 3, 1783, and ratified by Congress on January 14, 1784. This broadside carries some of the highlights of the negotiated settlements, and an announcement of the end of hostilities.

NATIONAL INDEX 44389
BRISTOL 5730
AMERICAN ANTIQUARIAN SOCIETY
29.8 x 22.2 cm.

# Important Intelligence of PEACE! Between America and Great-Britain, and all the European Powers at War.

## SURE and CERTAIN.

NEW-YORK, March 26.

A GENERAL PEACE.

LATE on Monday night, arrived an expreſs from New-Jerſey, which brought the following account:—That on Sunday laſt the 23d inſt. a veſſel arrived at Philadelphia from Cadiz, with diſpatches to the Continental Congreſs, informing them, That on TUESDAY the 21ſt of JANUARY, the PRELIMINARIES to a GENERAL PEACE, between Great-Britain, France, Spain, Holland, and the United States of America, were ſigned at Paris, by all the Commiſſioners from thoſe powers; in conſequence of which, hoſtilities, by ſea and land, were to ceaſe in Europe, on Thurſday the 20th of February; and in America, on THURSDAY the 20th of March, in the preſent year, one thouſand ſeven hundred and eighty-three.

This very important intelligence was on Monday night announced by the firing of cannon, and great rejoicings at Elizabeth-Town.

Late laſt night arrived Lewis Morris, Eſq; expreſs from Philadelphia, who brought a printed paper, from which the following are copied.

PHILADELPHIA, March 24, 1783.

Yeſterday arrived after a paſſage of 32 days from Cadiz, a French ſloop of war, commanded by M. du Queſne, with the agreeable intelligence of PEACE.

The particular articles reſpecting this happy and glorious event are as follows:

*The principal* ARTICLES *of the* PRELIMINARIES *of* PEACE, *of the 21ſt of January 1783.*

FRANCE to retain Tobago and Senegal.

France to reſtore to Great-Britain, Grenada, Saint Vincents, Dominica, and Saint Chriſtophers.

St. Euſtatia, Demerara, Barbice, and Iſſequibo, to be reſtored to the Dutch.

Great-Britain to reſtore to France, Goree, St. Lucia, St. Pierre, and Miquelon.

The Fiſhery of France and England, on the Coaſt of Newfoundland, to remain on the ſame footing on which they were by the Treaty of 1763, except that part of the Coaſt of Bonaviſta, at Cape St. John's, ſhall belong to the Engliſh.

France to be re-eſtabliſhed in the Eaſt-Indies, as well in Bengal, as on the Eaſt and Weſt Coaſt of the Peninſula, as regulated by the Treaty of 1763.

The Articles of the preceeding Treaties, concerning the demolition of Dunkirk, to be ſuppreſſed.

Spain to retain Minorca and Weſt-Florida.

Great-Britain cedes Eaſt-Florida to Spain.

An agreement to be entered into between Spain and Great-Britain, about the cutting of wood in the bay of Honduras.

Great-Britain to retain the Dutch ſettlement of Negapatnam, in the Eaſt-Indies.

Great Britain to reſtore Trinquemale to the Dutch if not retaken.

St. Euſtatia, Demarara, and Iſequebo, to be reſtored by the French to the United Provinces.

Great-Britain acknowledges the *Sovereignty* and *Independence* of the *Thirteen United States of America.*

The limits of the United States to be as agreed upon in the Proviſional Articles between them and Great Britain; except that they ſhall not extend further down the river Miſſiſippi than the 32d degree of North latitude from whence a line is to be drawn to the head of the river St. Mary [illegible]long the middle of that river down to [illegible]s mouth.

WORCESTER, April 1, 5 o'Clock, P. M. 1783.

We have this moment received the above truly intereſting and pleaſing intelligence by a Gentleman directly from Boſton. The Intelligence arrived there yeſterday in four days from the City of New-York.

Great rejoicing has been manifeſted whereever the above glorious intelligence came.

The preliminaries with America nearly as publiſhed laſt Thurſday.

*Copy of a letter from* Elias Boudinot, *Eſq; Preſident of the Continental Congreſs, to* William Livingſton, *Eſq; Governor of New-Jerſey.*

"An expreſs has juſt arrived from on board a ſloop of war in the river, which left Cadiz February 14.—She announces that the definitive treaty, having been ſigned by all the belligerent powers, on the 21ſt of January, all hoſtilities had ceaſed in Europe; and that the ſame happy event was to take place in this country on the 20th of March inſtant. The Count d' Eſtaing, who was ready to ſail with ſixty ſhips of the line, a very formidable armament, had given up the attempt, and was diſperſing his fleet to the different ports. This ſhip does not bring us official diſpatches, having been ſent by the Count d' Eſtaing, and the Marquis de la Fayette, in hopes that ſhe might by accident (as ſhe has done) be the fortunate medium of the earlieſt communication.—Although the ſtage goes to-morrow morning, I could not with ſatiſfaction to my own mind, ſuffer your Excellency and my friends in Trenton, to be deprived of the knowledge of ſo happy an event, one moment longer than abſolute neceſſity required.

I have the honor to be, &c. &c.

# LAUS DEO.

## 47. Boston, April 18, 1785
## [Boston: Peter Edes, 1785]

NAVIGATION Acts, and Acts of Trade, had always regulated commerce between England and her colonies including America. However, as this broadside proclaims, "no commercial treaty is at present established between these United States and Great-Britain . . . ," that is, no regulations had been established that the merchants of America would now be willing to recognize as valid. Therefore, the merchants of the town of Boston met and voted on some proposals toward the establishment of a suitable agreement, one which would serve commercial interests specifically, and the political interests of both nations generally. Until such an agreement was officially made, the merchants of Boston pledged that they would not trade with the British. Following the cessation of active hostilities, the re-establishment of commercial ties with Britain developed as an important aspect of recovery from the war, though reconciliation—the alternative to independence often proposed before Lexington and Concord—was never a goal of these commercial proposals.

NATIONAL INDEX 44652
BRISTOL 6028
FORD 2405
AMERICAN ANTIQUARIAN SOCIETY
42.3 x 33.6 cm.

*BOSTON, April 18, 17*

# The Minds of the People being greatly and juſtly agitated by the apparent Intention of the Government and the Merchants of Great-Britain to deprive the induſtrious Trader of every Benefit of our Commerce, by the entire Monopoly of the ſame to themſelves; and this Apprehenſion being increaſed by authentic Advices received by the laſt Ships---A numerous and reſpectable Meeting of the Merchants, Traders, and others, convened at Faneuil-Hall, on Saturday the 16th Inſt. to conſider the alarming State of our Trade and Navigation, the following Votes were unanimouſly agreed to:---

WHEREAS *no commercial treaty is at preſent eſtabliſhed between theſe United States and Great-Britain: and whereas certain Britiſh merchants, factors, and agents, from England, are now reſiding in this town, who have received large quantities of Engliſh goods, and are in expectation of receiving farther ſupplies, imported in Britiſh bottoms, or otherways, greatly to the hindrance of freight in all American veſſels; and as many more ſuch perſons are daily expected to arrive among us, which threatens an entire monopoly of all Britiſh importations in the hands of all ſuch merchants, agents, or factors, which cannot but operate to the eſſential prejudice of the intereſt of this country:*

THEREFORE, to prevent, as far as poſſible, the evil tendency of ſuch perſons continuing among us (excepting thoſe of them who ſhall be approbated by the Selectmen) and to diſcourage the ſale of their merchandize—WE the merchants, traders, and others, of the town of Boſton, DO AGREE,

THAT a committee be appointed to draſt a petition to Congreſs, repreſenting the embarraſsments under which the trade now labours, and the ſtill greater to which it is expoſed; and that the ſaid committee be empowered and directed to write to the merchants in the ſeveral ſea-ports in this State, requeſting them to join with the merchants in this town in a ſimilar application to Congreſs, immediately to regulate the trade of the United States, agreeably to the powers veſted in them by the government of this Commonwealth; and alſo to obtain inſtructions to their repreſentatives at the next General Court, to call the attention of their delegates in Congreſs, to the importance of bringing forward ſuch regulations as ſhall place our commerce on a footing of equality.

VOTED, That the ſaid committee be requeſted to write to the merchants in the ſeveral ſea-ports of the other United States, earneſtly recommending to them an immediate application to the Legiſlatures of their reſpective States, to veſt ſuch powers in Congreſs (if not already done) as ſhall be competent to the intereſting purpoſes aforeſaid; and alſo to petition Congreſs, to make ſuch regulations as ſhall have the deſired effect.

VOTED, That we do pledge our honor, that we will not directly, or indirectly, purchaſe any goods of, or have any commercial connections whatever with, ſuch Britiſh merchants, factors, or agents, as are now reſiding among us, or may hereafter arrive either from England, or any part of the Britiſh dominions (except ſuch perſons as ſhall be approved as aforeſaid)—and we will do all in our power to prevent all perſons acting under us, from having any commercial intercourſe with them until the ſalutary purpoſes of theſe reſolutions ſhall have been accompliſhed.

VOTED, That we will not let or ſell any warehouſe, ſhop, houſe, or any other place for the ſale of ſuch goods, nor will we employ any perſons who will aſſiſt ſaid merchants, factors or agents by trucks, carts, barrows or labor (except in the reſhipment of their merchandize) but will DISCOUNTENANCE all ſuch perſons who ſhall in any way adviſe, aid, or in the leaſt degree, help or ſupport ſuch merchants, factors or agents, in the proſecution of their buſineſs, *as we conceive all ſuch Britiſh importations are calculated to drain us of our currency, and have a direct tendency to impoveriſh this country.*

VOTED, That a committee be appointed to wait on thoſe perſons who have *already let* any warehouſe, ſhop, houſe, or any other place, for the diſpoſal of the merchandize of ſuch merchants, agents, or factors, and inform them of the reſolutions of this meeting.

VOTED, That we will encourage, all in our power, the manufactures and produce of this country, and will, in all caſes, endeavour to promote them.

VOTED, That a committee be appointed to make immediate application to the Governor and Council of this Commonwealth, requeſting them, if they think proper, to direct the ſeveral Naval-Officers in this State, to grant no permit for the landing of goods from the dominions of Great-Britain conſigned to, or the property of perſons of the aforeſaid deſcription, until the meeting of the Legiſlature.

VOTED, That copies of theſe reſolutions be printed and diſperſed among the inhabitants, that they may be adopted and carried into execution, with that temper which is conſiſtent with the character of good citizens.

☞ *ON our public virtue muſt depend the ſucceſs of the meaſures propoſed; and relying on that zeal for the public ſafety, which has been ſo often and effectually exerciſed by this town, they cannot fail of meeting the warm and unanimous approbation of the State in general, and of all thoſe who are well-wiſhers to the proſperity and laſting happineſs of America.*

[PRINTED BY PETER EDES.]

## 48. British Lamentation. Together with Bunker-Hill Ode
[Boston?, 1786]

BOTH of these poems were probably occasional verses, though only the second poem is designated as such, for it was composed in honor of the grand opening of the Charles River Bridge, which connected the peninsula of Boston with the mainland. Thomas Dawes (1757–1825) was the son of Colonel Thomas Dawes. After graduating from Harvard in 1777, he became a lawyer, and was later appointed as a justice in the Massachusetts Court System.

Following the declaration of peace in 1783, the Constitutional Conventions began the arduous task of forming a new government and recovering from the active hostilities of the Revolutionary War. In some respects, the war continued until 1815; however, the events of 1770–1781 were already subjects for heroic balladry and folk legend. Thus the first of these poems, "British Lamentation," views the events of the war from the perspective of a disillusioned British soldier, who "set sail for America" in the first quatrain and in the last, exhorts the Americans to "Fight on, fight on,/ . . . Fear not old England's thund'ring noise,/ Maintain your cause from year to year,/ God's on your side, you need not fear." Similarly, the theme of liberty is proclaimed by the "Bunker Hill Ode," but both poems are more important for their expression of colonial pride and enthusiasm than they are for their limited merits as artistic creations.

NATIONAL INDEX 44861
BRISTOL 6252
FORD 2433
WEGELIN 505
AMERICAN ANTIQUARIAN SOCIETY
34.5 x 20.5 cm.

# BRITISH LAMENTATION.

Together with

BUNKER-HILL ODE.

'TWAS on that dark and dismay day,
When we set sail for America;
'Twas on that fourteenth day of May,
When we set sail for America.

'Twas on that dark and dismal time,
When we set sail for this northern clime;
Where drums do beat and trumpets sound,
And unto Boston we were bound.

And when to Boston we did come,
We thought by our British drums
To drive those rebels from that place,
And fill their hearts with sore disgrace.

But to our sorrow and surprise,
We saw them like grasshoppers rise;
They fight like heroes much inrag'd,
Which did affright old General Gage.

Like lions roaring for their prey,
They fear no danger nor dismay.
Bold British blood runs thro' their veins,
But still with courage they sustain.

We saw those bold Columbia's sons
Spread death and slaughter from their guns.
FREEDOM or DEATH! those heroes cry,
I'm sure they're not afraid to die.

We sail'd to York, as you've been told,
There the loss of many a Briton bold,
For to make those rebels own their king,
And daily tribute to him bring.

In York was many traitors found,
They said that they could win the ground;
They said they could win the day—
There was no danger they did say.

New-York it was a garden place,
They said they could in a short space,
Pull down your towns, lay waste your lands,
In spite of all your Boston bands.

A garden place it was indeed,
And in it grows a bitter weed,
Which will pull down our highest hopes,
And sorely wound our British troops.

'Tis now September, the seventeenth day,
I wish I'd ne'er come to America—
Full fifteen thousand has been slain,
Bold British heroes every one.

Now I receiv'd my mortal wound,
I bid adieu to old England's ground;
My wife and children mourn for me,
But never more can they me see,

Fight on, fight on American boys,
Fear not old England's thund'ring noise,
Maintain your cause from year to year,
God's on your side, you need not fear.

ODE composed by T. Dawes, jun Esq.—
Sung on Bunker-Hill, June 17th, 1786,
at the opening of Charles River Bridge.

NOW let rich music sound,
And all the region round,
With rapture fill;
Let the full trump of Fame,
To Heav'n itself proclaim
The everlasting name
Of BUNKER HILL.

Beneath this sky-wrapt brow,
What Heroes sleep below!
How dear to Jove!
Not more belov'd were those
Who foil'd celestial foes,
When the old Giants rose
To arms above.

Now scarce eleven short years
Have roll'd their rapid spheres
Thro' Heav'ns high road;
Since o'er yon swelling tide,
Pass'd all the British pride,
And water'd Bunker's side
With foreign blood.

Then Charlestown's gilded sphires
Felt unrelenting fires,
And sunk in night;
But Phœnix like she'll rise
From where her ruin lies,
And strike astonish'd eyes
With glories bright.

Meand'ring to the deep,
Majestic Charles shall weep
Of war no more;
Fam'd as the Appian way,
The worlds first Bridge to day,
All nations shall convey
From shore to shore.

On our bless'd mountain's head,
The festive board we'll spread,
With viands high;
Let Joy's broad bowl go round,
With public spirit crown'd;
We'll consecrate the ground
To LIBERTY!

## 49. Procession. Boston, Oct. 19, 1789
[Boston, 1789]

THE era of the American Revolution is traditionally closed with the inauguration of George Washington as the first president, April 30, 1789, in New York City. Already a hero of the Revolution for his masterful strategies as Commander-in-Chief of the continental forces, Washington was instantly made a heroic figurehead in the public imagination, and was therefore a natural choice for first president.

The present broadside proclaims a forthcoming visit to the town of Boston, indicating the preparations and order of procession attending that occasion. The image of Washington was widely dramatized as that of a Greek God or Roman Emperor; the classical influence in American culture during the early federal period is amply manifest in descriptions of great leaders, as well as in the architecture of the period. Another contemporary broadside, for example, celebrates Washington's visit to Boston in this way:

> Behold the man! whom virtues raise
> The highest of the patriot throng!
> To him the muse her homage pays,
> And tunes the gratulary song . . .
> May health and joy a wreath entwine,
> And guard thee thro' this scene of strife;
> Till seraphs shall to thee assign,
> A wreath of everlasting life.

[Ode/ to the President of the Uni-/ted States on his arrival at/ Boston, 1789; National Index 45496; Bristol 7018; Wegelin 693]

NATIONAL INDEX 21701
FORD 2552
AMERICAN ANTIQUARIAN SOCIETY
39.8 x 26.7 cm.

# Proceſſion.

Boston, Oct. 19, 1789.

AS this town is ſhortly to be honoured with a viſit from THE PRESIDENT of the United States: In order that we may pay our reſpects to him, in a manner whereby every inhabitant may ſee ſo illuſtrious and amiable a character, and to prevent the diſorder and danger which muſt enſue from a great aſſembly of people without order, a Committee appointed by a reſpectable number of inhabitants, met for the purpoſe, recommend to their Fellow-Citizens to arrange themſelves in the following order, in a

## PROCESSION.

It is alſo recommended, that the perſon who ſhall be choſen as head of each order of Artizans, Tradeſmen, Manufacturers, &c. ſhall be known by diſplaying a WHITE FLAG, with ſome device thereon expreſſive of their ſeveral callings—and to be numbered as in the arrangement that follows, which is alphabetically diſpoſed, in order to give general ſatisfaction.--- The Artizans, &c. to diſplay ſuch inſignia of their craft, as they can conveniently carry in their hands. That uniformity may not be wanting, it is deſired that the ſeveral Flag-ſtaffs be SEVEN feet long, and the Flags a YARD SQUARE.

### *ORDER OF PROCESSION.*

MUSICK.

The Selectmen,
Overſeers of the Poor,
Town Treaſurer,
Town Clerk,
Magiſtrates,
Conſuls of France and Holland,
The Officers of his Moſt Chriſtian Majeſty's Squadron,
The Rev. Clergy,
Phyſicians,
Lawyers,
Merchants and Traders,
Marine Society,
Maſters of veſſels,
Revenue Officers,
Strangers, who may wiſh to attend.

| | |
|---|---|
| Bakers, - - - | No. 1. |
| Blackſmiths, &c. - - | No. 2. |
| Block-makers, - - - | No. 3. |
| Boat-builders, - - - | No. 4. |
| Cabinet and Chair-makers, - | No. 5. |
| Card-makers, - - | No. 6. |
| Carvers, - - - | No. 7. |
| Chaiſe and Coach-makers, - | No. 8. |
| Clock and Watch-makers, - | No. 9. |
| Coopers, - - - - | No. 10. |
| Copperſmiths, Braziers and Founders, | No. 11. |
| Cordwainers, &c. - - - | No. 12. |
| Diſtillers, - - - | No. 13. |
| Duck Manufacturers, - - | No. 14. |
| Engravers, - - - | No. 15. |
| Glaziers and Plumbers, - - | No. 16. |
| Goldſmiths and Jewellers, - - | No. 17. |
| Hair-Dreſſers, - - - | No. 18. |
| Hatters and Furriers, - - | No. 19. |
| Houſe Carpenters, - - | No. 20. |
| Leather Dreſſers, and Leather-Breeches Makers, - - | No. 21. |
| Limners and Portrait Painters, - | No. 22. |
| Maſons, - - - - | No. 23. |
| Maſt-makers, - - - | No. 24. |
| Mathematical Inſtrument-makers, | No. 25. |
| Millers, - - - - | No. 26. |
| Painters, - - - | No. 27. |
| Paper Stainers, - - | No. 28. |
| Pewterers, - - - | No. 29. |
| Printers, Book-binders and Stationers, | No. 30. |
| Riggers, - - - | No. 31. |
| Rope-makers, - - - | No. 32. |
| Saddlers, - - - | No. 33. |
| Sail-makers, - - - | No. 34. |
| Shipwrights, to include Caulkers, Ship-Joiners, Head-builders and Sawyers, | No. 35. |
| Sugar-boilers, - - - | No. 36. |
| Tallow-Chandlers, &c. - - | No. 37. |
| Tanners, - - - | No. 38. |
| Taylors, - - - | No. 39. |
| Tin-plate Workers, - - | No. 40. |
| Tobacconiſts, - - - | No. 41. |
| Truckmen, - - - | No. 42. |
| Turners, - - - | No. 43. |
| Upholſterers, - - - | No. 44. |
| Wharfingers, - - - | No. 45. |
| Wheelwrights, - - - | No. 46. |
| Seamen, | |

N. B.—In the above arrangement, ſome trades are omitted—from the idea, that they would incorporate themſelves with the branches mentioned, to which they are generally attached. For inſtance—it is ſuppoſed, that under the head of *Blackſmiths*, the Armourers, Cutlers, Whiteſmiths and other workers in iron, would be included; and the ſame with reſpect to other trades.

Each diviſion of the above arrangement is requeſted to meet on ſuch parade as it may agree on, and march into the Mall—No. 1 of the Artizans, &c. forming at the South-end thereof. The Marſhals will then direct in what manner the Proceſſion will move to meet the Preſident on his arrival in town. When the front of the Proceſſion arrives at the extremity of the town, it will halt, and the whole will then be directed to open the column—one half of each rank moving to the right, and the other half to the left—and then face inwards, ſo as to form an avenue through which the Preſident is to paſs, to the galleries to be erected at the State-Houſe.

It is requeſted that the ſeveral School-maſters conduct their Scholars to the neighbourhood of the State-Houſe, and form them in ſuch order as the Marſhals ſhall direct.

The Marine Society is deſired to appoint ſome perſons to arrange and accompany the ſeamen.

50. By His Excellency John Hancock, Esquire
[Boston: Adams and Nourse, 1789]

THIS thanksgiving proclamation follows the form of earlier ones, but it has several distinctive features. The date set for the day of Thanksgiving, November 26, 1789, is a paradigm for the more recent custom of celebrating Thanksgiving Day on the fourth Thursday in the month of November. The rhetoric of the broadside reflects the strong influence of Enlightenment doctrine, e.g., the exhortation to God "to promote the Knowledge and Practice of True Religion and Virtue, and the encrease of Science . . . and generally to grant unto all Mankind such a degree of temporal prosperity, as he alone knows to be best." Like the earlier royal proclamations and government documents, the broadside carries a seal, but this is the new seal of Massachusetts. Instead of featuring a coat-of-arms, the central motif of this design is the figure of an Indian. The broadside also contains an apostrophe which follows the pattern seen in a number of colonial broadsides in this collection, substituting America, Massachusetts, the People, or some form of early national identity for the loyalist rubric, "God Save the King." The printing was done by Adams & Nourse, official printers for the General Court of the Commonwealth of Massachusetts Bay.

NATIONAL INDEX 21947
FORD 2544
AMERICAN ANTIQUARIAN SOCIETY
50.5 x 41.3 cm.

Commonwealth of Massachusetts.

By his EXCELLENCY

# JOHN HANCOCK, Esquire,

GOVERNOUR OF THE COMMONWEALTH of MASSACHUSETTS.

By the President of the United States of America: A Proclamation

# A Proclamation,

## FOR A DAY OF THANKSGIVING.

HAVING received from THE PRESIDENT of the UNITED STATES, the following PROCLAMATION, viz. "WHEREAS it is the Duty of all Nations, to acknowledge the Providence of Almighty GOD, to obey his Will, to be grateful for his Benefits, and humbly to implore his Protection and Favour: And whereas both Houses of Congress, have, by their joint Committee, requested me to recommend to the People of the United States, a Day of Public Thanksgiving and Prayer, to be observed by acknowledging with grateful Hearts, the many and signal Favours of Almighty GOD, especially by affording them an Opportunity peaceably to establish a Form of Government, for their Safety and Happiness. Now THEREFORE I DO recommend and assign THURSDAY, the TWENTY-SIXTH day of NOVEMBER next, to be devoted by the People of these States, to the service of that great and glorious BEING, who is the beneficent Author of all the good that was, that is, or that will be: That we may then all unite in rendering unto him our sincere and humble Thanks for his kind care and protection of the People of this Country, previous to their becoming a Nation;—for the signal and manifold Mercies, and the favourable interpositions of his Providence in the course and conclusion of the late War; for the great degree of Tranquility, Union and Plenty, which we have since enjoyed; for the peaceable and rational Manner in which we have been enabled to establish Constitutions of Government for our Safety and Happiness, and particularly the National one now lately instituted;—for the civil and religious Liberty, with which we are blessed, and the means we have of acquiring and diffusing useful Knowledge;—and in general, for all the great and various Favours, which he hath been pleased to confer upon us. AND ALSO, That we may then unite in most humbly offering our Prayers and Supplications to the GREAT LORD and RULER of Nations, and beseech him to pardon our National and other Transgressions;—to enable us all, whether in public or private Stations, to perform our several and relative Duties properly and punctually;—to render our National Government a Blessing to all the People, by constantly being a Government of wise, just and constitutional Laws, discreetly and faithfully executed and obeyed;—to protect and guide all Sovereigns and Nations, (especially such as have shewn Kindness unto us) and to bless them with good Government, Peace and Concord;—to promote the Knowledge and Practice of true Religion and Virtue, and the encrease of Science among them and us;—and generally to grant unto all Mankind such a degree of temporal Prosperity, as he alone knows to be best." given under my hand at the City of New York, the third day of October in the year of our Lord 1789 George Washington

*AND whereas it has been the laudable Practice of our Ancestors, and continued from the first Settlement of this Country, to set a part a Day in the Year, for public and social THANKSGIVING and PRAISE:*

I DO THEREFORE, by and with the Advice of the COUNCIL, appoint THURSDAY, the TWENTY-SIXTH Day of *November* aforesaid, to be religiously observed as a Day of THANKSGIVING and PRAISE, within this Commonwealth: Calling upon Ministers and People to assemble on the same Day, and join with the other States in the Union, in rendering Thanks to ALMIGHTY GOD, for the great Blessings bestowed upon these confederated States. And to acknowledge his manifold goodness to the People of this Commonwealth;—in particular, in that he has been pleased to favour us with so good a measure of Health, the Year past;—to prosper in so great a degree our Husbandry, our Fishery, Trade and Manufactures; but more especially that we still enjoy that most invaluable Blessing, the Gospel of Peace—at the same Time accompanying their Thanksgiving with humble Supplication, that we may ever live mindful of our Obligations to our Divine Benefactor; that his Favours may still be continued to us, and that the Christian Religion in its true Spirit, may prevail amongst us, and be extended to all People upon the Earth.

*GIVEN at the* COUNCIL-CHAMBER, *in* Boston, *this Fourteenth Day of* October, *in the Year of our LORD, One Thousand seven Hundred and Eighty-nine, and in the* Fourteenth *Year of the INDEPENDENCE of the* UNITED STATES *of* AMERICA.

JOHN HANCOCK.

*By his Excellency's Command,*
*With the Advice and Consent of the Council,*

JOHN AVERY, jun. Secretary.

GOD *save the* COMMONWEALTH *of* MASSACHUSETTS!

---

BOSTON:—PRINTED by ADAMS & NOURSE, PRINTERS to the Honourable GENERAL COURT.

# Afterword

THE first printing press was established in the British colonies of North America late in 1638, in Cambridge, Massachusetts. At that time in England, printing was confined to London, York, and the universities; it was not widespread. The Reverend Jose Glover was the man responsible for the establishment of the printing press in North America. What induced him to sail to the colonies with such a venture in mind? In *The Colonial Printer,* Lawrence Wroth theorizes that two motives were at work: the potential usefulness of the press to the newly founded college and for the propagation of religious faith among the Indians, and the possibility of financial gain. He was never to see his ideas carried to fruition, for he died during the voyage. Stephen Daye, a locksmith, set up the press and issued "The Freeman's Oath" and an almanac by William Pierce in late 1638 or early 1639. No copies of these two publications are extant, so the first product of that press which is available today is *The Whole Book of Psalmes,* a metrical setting of the Psalms edited by Richard Mather and printed by Daye in 1640. This was followed by a variety of religious and secular publications—catechisms, sermons, religious tracts, laws, publications from Harvard, and almanacs. Samuel Green acquired the press in 1649, and continued the traditional publications which Daye had issued.

A second press arrived in Cambridge in 1655, from the Corporation for Propagating the Gospel in New England, and a third was sent in 1659. The purpose of this organization, based in London, was to convert the natives to Christianity. A major step in this program was the translation of the Bible into the Indian tongue and the publication of this translation. John Eliot was the individual responsible for translating the Bible, and Samuel Green began the task of printing the two-volume work in 1660. In 1663, Marmaduke Johnson finished the task. This was a mammoth undertaking for a small provincial press, and the Eliot Indian Bible stands as one of the great milestones of the colonial press.

During the first thirty years of printing in Massachusetts, the output was controlled by the General Court, which delegated the power of censorship to the officials of Harvard College in 1662. The General Court strengthened its domination of the printing press in 1664 by forbidding the establishment of a press elsewhere in the colony. The power of censorship was used infrequently. But in 1677, for example, the General Court halted the publication of Thomas à Kempis's *Imitation of Christ,* although the licensees had approved the printing.

Marmaduke Johnson tried unsuccessfully several times to obtain permission from the General Court to establish a press in Boston. In 1674, he finally was granted leave to do so, but he died and it was left to John Foster, a graduate of Harvard, to establish the press across the Charles

River from Cambridge. Among John Foster's publications was William Hubbard's *Narrative of the Troubles with the Indians in New England* (1677), for which Foster supplied a wood cut map of New England. Almanacs, books, pamphlets, and proclamations from the General Court were among the other products of his press.

Samuel Green continued printing in Cambridge until his death in 1702, at which time the press belonging to Harvard ceased publishing. In Boston, Foster printed until his death in 1681, when the management of his press fell to Samuel Sewall. Samuel Green, Jr., printed for Sewall, as did James Glen. From then on, there were several printers active in Boston in any given year.

Lawrence Wroth explains that it is difficult to characterize precisely the output of the colonial press, because a large percentage, possibly as high as seventy-five percent, of the publications have vanished. Yet enough survives, even from the period from 1640 to 1700, to provide a glimpse into the products of the press. Significantly, the types of publications issued in this early period continued to appear throughout the eighteenth century. Literature, both secular and religious, almanacs, and government documents form the bulk of the early publications.

Surprisingly, during the first years of the press in Cambridge and Boston, several important pieces of literature were produced, including *The Whole Book of Psalmes* and John Eliot's translation of the Bible. Michael Wiggleworth's *Day of Doom,* a poem revealing his harsh theology, was printed in Cambridge in 1662. Two groups of "native" poems were printed by John Foster in 1676 and 1678. First came Benjamin Thompson's *New Englands Crisis,* about the Indian wars. The later volume was *Several Poems,* written by Anne Bradstreet. Sermons were another form of literature particularly popular in New England, since religion was at the center of New England life. Another form of literature popular in the late seventeenth century, and throughout the eighteenth, was the elegy. Generally printed as broadsides, elegies dating from the seventeenth century are very scarce. Fortunately, Nathaniel Morton included many of them in his *New-England's Memoriall,* printed by Samuel Green and Marmaduke Johnson in 1669.

Of an entirely different nature were more ordinary publications, such as almanacs. During the colonial era, almanacs were widely read and found their way into almost every home. Even Cotton Mather took notice of them, stating in the preface to his own almanac for 1683 that "such an anniversary composure comes into almost as many hands as the best of books." Published each autumn, almanacs served as calendars and contained much useful information on diverse topics as well.

Also prominent in the early press were documents issued by the colonial government: proclamations for fast and thanksgiving days, and laws of the General Court and the town of Boston. The proclamations were issued as broadsides, the format still in use today. Government printing was lucrative and steady, and provided the financial stability necessary to carry on the precarious business of printing.

The first newspaper to be published on a regular basis was *The Boston News-Letter.* Established in 1704, it was followed by others, so that by 1730 there were seven different journals being published in four of the colonies. Again, publishing a weekly newspaper was a risky venture, dependent on labor, availability of paper and other materials, and distribution. As the eighteenth century progressed, these problems became less difficult to manage, at least until the Revolution when paper was in short supply, and many of these early newspapers flourished. The editorial content of the newspapers was frequently drawn from English and European journals, or from those of the other colonies. Relatively little of the content, other than the numerous advertisements, was of a local nature. Often broadsides filled this void, as elegies on the deaths of prominent men, the confessions and last words of criminals, ballads on news worthy events, advertisements for stolen goods, and so on attest.

A broadside, "The Freeman's Oath," was the first item printed in the British colonies, and the broadside format continued to be popular. Even today, broadsides and handouts abound. Being ephemeral by nature, only a small proportion of the earliest broadsides exists today. Since they were blank on one side and frequently large in size, broadsides were handy for wrapping objects and for scrap paper, uses hardly suitable for preservation into the twentieth century. There are still in existence, however, seventeenth century copies of the Harvard College commencement *theses* and *quaestiones* printed as early as 1642, ballads, elegies, government proclamations and taxbills, advertisements, documents pertaining to the religious controversies, and a few other miscellaneous broadsides. In *Broadsides, Ballads &c. Printed in Massachusetts 1639–1800,* Worthington C. Ford listed only 238 broadsides printed before 1700; and in many cases, he was unable to locate copies in public or private repositories.

Many more broadsides are extant from the eighteenth century. As the press expanded, more broadsides were printed and more managed to be preserved by individuals sensitive to their value as history, by town governments, and by the ministers who received the proclamations issued by the colonial and state governments. Finally, at the end of the eighteenth century and in the early nineteenth, state and national historical societies, such as the Massachusetts Historical Society, the New-York Historical Society, and the American Antiquarian Society were founded, and collecting began in earnest.

As the eighteenth century progressed, the broadside format began to be used as a means of expression in the context of the growing turmoil between Great Britain and her American colonies. The Stamp Act affected the printers in particular, so they lashed out to protect their profits in a business that was still a precarious one. Newspapers were the obvious forum for such discussion, yet anonymously written and printed broadsides were also useful, particularly for the printing of ballads or arguments on a given topic, which were so inflammatory that no one wanted either the credit or the blame. The broadside format was also useful for announcements and the proceedings of meetings.

Broadsides were distributed in a variety of ways. Ballads were generally sold by hawkers or pedlars in town and country, for only a few cents. Advertisements, such as those for *The Temple* or Isaiah Thomas's almanac, would have been sent to prospective customers and to postmasters, and would have been posted in public places. Government proclamations, whether for thanksgiving or fast days, or for the declaration of martial law or independence, were read from the pulpit in each parish. The copies were then deposited with the town clerk or retained by the minister. Broadsides printed for executions or other special events were probably sold at the time, passed around among friends, and then destroyed either wilfully or by the passage of time.

During the eighteenth century, printers gradually became aware that illustrations could enhance the attractiveness and hence the popularity of broadsides. Yet, the timely nature of broadsides frequently precluded the design and execution of a cut specifically for a particular broadside. And, even in Boston, there were few artisans regularly occupied in such endeavors. The boot on "Liberty, Property, and no Excise" [plate 1] was made for that specific broadside, but most of the illustrations were already on hand in the printer's shop. Hence, the illustrations often bear little or no relation to the subject of the broadsides that they adorn. Instead, the illustrations, crude as some of them are, serve merely to decorate the printed sheet.

Throughout the eighteenth century, broadsides were printed in substantial numbers for many different purposes. During the Revolutionary War era, this format was particularly well suited as a forum for the popular response to the political and social turmoil of the years between the Stamp Act and the ratification of the Constitution. The existence of these documents facilitates the understanding of this important phase of the nation's history.

Georgia B. Bumgardner

# Biographical Sketches

THE careers of many of the colonial Massachusetts printers were dislocated by the American Revolution. Some, like Isaiah Thomas, were forced to move their printing presses to places beyond British control. Others remained muted in Boston. Some printers who were loyal to the British government also saw their businesses change radically. Most tradesmen and craftsmen could keep a low profile, although their lives were also affected by the Boston Port Bill and non-importation agreements. Printers, however, along with the other leaders of the Revolution, were often the targets of British tyranny. General Gage, for example, in his proclamation of martial law [plate 20], declared that "The Press, that distinguished Appendage of public Liberty, and when fairly and impartially employed it's [*sic*] best Support, has been invariably prostituted to the most contrary Purposes."

The purpose of this section is to provide brief sketches of the printers represented in this collection. Most of the material presented here is taken from Isaiah Thomas's *The History of Printing in America.* First published in 1810, it remains the best source for information on the printing and printers of the eighteenth century. Isaiah Thomas was well acquainted with the printers of his generation and therefore his comments are particularly cogent. Other information on these printers has been taken from the Printer's File at the American Antiquarian Society, and the *Dictionary of American Biography.*

## ADAMS AND NOURSE

Thomas Adams (1757?–1799) and John Nourse (1762?–1790) were partners in Boston from 1783 to 1790, during which time they printed for the State of Massachusetts in addition to running their own general printing business. Adams began printing in 1778 and published several newspapers, including the *Independent Chronicle* from 1784 to 1799. John Nourse entered the printing business in 1783, and died at an early age. An example of their work is illustrated as plate 50.

## NATHANIEL COVERLY (1744?–1816)

Located in Boston from 1767 to 1775, Nathaniel Coverly then moved to Chelmsford, Concord, Boston (1777–1784), Plymouth, Middleborough, Boston (1788–1794), Concord, Amherst, and several other towns. He finally ended his peripatetic career in Boston, where he worked from 1803–1816. Never involved in publishing a newspaper, he issued broadsides, almanacs, and pamphlets of a popular nature. He printed in Chelmsford the broadside illustrated as plate 24.

## MARGARET DRAPER (1727–1807)

After the death of her husband, Richard, Margaret Draper continued to publish the *Massachusetts Gazette and Boston News Letter,* and also printed for the governor and the council, with the assistance of John Boyle and then John Howe. The *Massachusetts Gazette* was loyal to the British government, and was the only newspaper published in Boston after the commencement of the hostilities. When the British Army left Boston, Margaret Draper went to Halifax with other Loyalists, and then to England, where she received a pension from the government.

## RICHARD DRAPER (1727–1774)

The son of a printer, Richard Draper was brought up in the trade, eventually taking control of the *Boston Weekly News Letter,* which had been published by his father since 1732. In addition to publishing almanacs, pamphlets, and books, he became the printer for the governor and council of the colony, issuing proclamations such as that shown as plate 4. Samuel Draper formed a partnership with his brother in the early 1760's, but died in 1767 at the age of thirty. Although the brothers published the newspaper together, only Richard Draper's name was allowed to appear on the government's publications. The Drapers were involved in the publication shown as plate 3, which announces the end of the Stamp Act.

## EDES AND GILL

Benjamin Edes (1732–1803) and John Gill (1732–1785) formed their partnership in 1755, and published the *Boston Gazette and Country Journal* from 1755 to 1775. They also printed political pamphlets and publications for the General Court of the colony. They were both staunch patriots, and Edes was forced to escape to Watertown with the printing press. Gill was arrested on August 4, 1775, for "printing treason, sedition, and rebellion." Fortunately, he was not imprisoned, but it was not possible for him to resume printing until the British had evacuated the city. He then began printing sermons, state documents, almanacs, and the *Continental Journal,* which he sold to James D. Griffith shortly before his death. Gill was the brother of Moses Gill, who during the Revolution was a member of the Council of Massachusetts, which acted in lieu of a governor until the state constitution was framed in 1780.

In Watertown, Benjamin Edes printed for the Provincial Congress, and continued printing for the state during the Revolution in addition to issuing almanacs, books, and pamphlets. After the evacuation of the British troops, Edes returned to Boston and continued the publication of the *Boston Gazette.* His two sons, Peter and Benjamin, worked with him for several years until 1784. His newspaper suffered, and his own finances were equally depressed by the depreciation of paper money. However, Isaiah Thomas recorded that "no publisher of a newspaper felt a greater interest in the establishment of the independence of the United States than Benjamin Edes; and no newspaper was more instrumental in bringing forward this important event than *The Boston Gazette.*"

Edes and Gill together published the broadsides shown as plates 3, 6, 7, 10, and 15; Edes alone, plates 26, 27, and 34; Gill alone, plate 37.

## PETER EDES (1756–1840)

The son of Benjamin Edes, Peter joined his father for about five years, from 1779 to 1784, and then printed his own broadsides and pamphlets. A participant in the Boston Tea Party, Peter Edes was imprisoned by the British in September of 1775 for concealing fire-arms in his house, a blatant offense against Gage's proclamation of June 19, 1775, reproduced as plate 21.

After 1787, Edes worked in Newport, Boston, Haverhill, Augusta, Maine, and then in Baltimore from 1818 to 1832. His last years were spent in Bangor, Maine. The only broadside in this collection printed by Peter Edes is reproduced as plate 47.

## THOMAS FLEET, JR., AND JOHN FLEET

Thomas Fleet, Jr., (1732–1797) and John Fleet (1734–1806) succeeded their father at his death in 1758, and published the *Boston Evening Post* until the beginning of the Revolution. Their other publications include pamphlets, books, and almanacs. They remained in Boston after Lexington and Concord, but their printing business came to a standstill. The American Antiquarian Society lists only one publication from their press in 1775, an almanac. Their printing business picked up in 1776, but they did not continue their newspaper. The Fleets were two of the publishers of the broadside of plate 3, and that of plate 28 may be attributed to them on the basis of the illustration used by their father in 1745.

## JOHN HOWE (1754–1835)

For a short time, John Howe assisted Margaret Draper in the publication of the *Massachusetts Gazette,* but left Boston with other Loyalists in 1776. He was probably in New York for a short period with two other Loyalist printers from Boston, Nathaniel Mills and John Hicks. From 1777 to 1780, he was the publisher of the *Newport Gazette,* but then emigrated to Halifax, where he published a newspaper and was printer to the Nova Scotia government. The broadside reproduced as plate 25 has been attributed to John Howe.

## JOHN MYCALL (1750–1833)

Born in Worcester, England, John Mycall was a school teacher in Amesbury in 1775, the same year in which he entered the printing business as a partner of Henry Walter Tinges, in Newburyport. From 1776 to 1799, Mycall remained in Newburyport as a printer of almanacs and pamphlets and the publisher of the *Essex Gazette*. He probably published the edition of the Declaration of Independence reproduced as plate 32. He also tried to publish a magazine, *The Temple*, but this venture failed although the prospectus remains [plate 43]. In 1800, Mycall became a storekeeper in Harvard, Massachusetts, and then moved to Cambridge, where he resided from 1808 to 1826. He spent the last years of his life in Newburyport.

## EZEKIEL RUSSELL (1743–1796)

After serving as an apprentice to his brother, Joseph Russell, Ezekiel printed in Portsmouth, New Hampshire, with Thomas Furber. Returning to Boston in 1767, he procured his own press and issued pamphlets and a few books. From November 1771 to May 1772, he published *The Censor*, which was supported by the British government.

About 1774, he moved to Salem and then to Danvers, where he remained from 1777 to 1781. He returned to Boston and located his shop near the great elm known as the Liberty Tree, which is mentioned in "Liberty, Property, and No Excise," the first broadside in this collection. Russell's business consisted of popular publications–almanacs, pamphlets, and broadsides, which he sold to individuals and to pedlars. Plates 19, 29, 31, 33, 35, 36, and 45 represent works that either bear Russell's imprint, or can be attributed to him.

## ISAIAH THOMAS (1749–1831)

Probably the most famous printer of this group, Isaiah Thomas began his protest against the British in 1766, when he opposed the Stamp Act while printing for the owner of the *Halifax Gazette*. After he returned to his native Boston in 1770, he established the *Massachusetts Spy*, which he used to support the cause of liberty. The British occupation of Boston drove him from the city at the time of the battle of Lexington and Concord. He fled westward to Worcester, where he established that town's first printing press, and resumed publication of the *Massachusetts Spy* on May 3, 1775. Times were difficult for printers everywhere, so Thomas leased his paper and moved to Salem in 1776, but he returned to Worcester in 1778. Eventually conditions improved, and Thomas emerged from the Revolution as a large scale publisher and bookseller, with partners up and down the Atlantic coast. After retiring from business in 1802, he turned to scholarship, and accumulated materials for *The History of Printing in America*. In 1812, he founded the American Antiquarian Society, to which he devoted the rest of his life. Among the broadsides in this collection, Thomas's are shown in plates 9, 14, 40, 41, and 44.

# Further Reading

## EDITIONS AND COLLECTIONS


Bumgardner, Georgia, ed. *American Broadsides, 1680–1800.* Barre, Massachusetts: The Imprint Society, 1971.

Heartman, Charles F., ed. *The Cradle of the United States, 1765–1789, Five Hundred Contemporary Broadsides, Pamphlets, and a Few Books. . . .* Perth Amboy, New Jersey: privately printed, 1922.

Winslow, Ola Elizabeth, ed. *American Broadside Verse.* New Haven: Yale University Press, 1930.


## SECONDARY WORKS


Bailyn, Bernard. *The Ideological Origins of the American Revolution.* Cambridge: Harvard University Press, 1967.

Becker, Carl. *The Declaration of Independence: A Study in the History of Political Ideas.* New York: Harcourt-Brace & Co., 1922. Reprint. Alfred Knopf, Inc., 1958.

Boatner, Mark Mayo. *Encyclopedia of the American Revolution.* New York: David McKay, Inc., 1966.

Brigham, Clarence S., *Paul Revere's Engravings.* Worcester: American Antiquarian Society, 1954. Reprint. New York: Atheneum, 1969.

Davidson, Philip. *Propaganda and the American Revolution, 1763–1783.* Chapel Hill: University of North Carolina Press, 1941.

*Dictionary of American Biography.*

Ford, Worthington C. *Broadsides, Ballads, &c., Printed in Massachusetts, 1639–1800.* Boston: Massachusetts Historical Society, 1922.

Greene, Jack P. *The Reinterpretation of the American Revolution, 1763–1789.* New York: Harper and Row, 1968.

Heimert, Alan. *Religion and the American Mind: The Eighteenth Century.* Cambridge: Harvard University Press, 1966.

Hitchings, Sinclair. "A Broadside View of America," *Lithopinion* (Spring, 1970), Issue 17, Vol. 5, No. 1, pp. 65–71.

Jensen, Merrill, ed. *Tracts of the American Revolution, 1763–1776.* New York: Bobbs-Merrill Company, 1967.

Labaree, Benjamin Woods. *The Boston Tea Party.* New York: Oxford University Press, 1964.

Major, A. Hyatt. *American Printmaking, the First One-Hundred and Fifty Years.* New York: New York Graphic Society, 1969.

Miller, John C. *The Origins of the American Revolution.* Palo Alto: Stanford University Press, 1959.

Moore, Frank. *Ballads and Songs of the American Revolution.* Boston, 1886.

Morgan, Edmund S. *The Birth of the Republic, 1763–1789.* Chicago: University of Chicago Press, 1956.

Morgan, Edmund S., and Morgan, Helen M. *The Stamp Act Crisis.* New York: Collier Books, 1963.

Shipton, Clifford K., and Mooney, James E. *National Index of American Imprints through 1800: the Short-Title Evans.* Worcester: American Antiquarian Society and Barre Publishers, 1969.

Silver, Rollo G. *The American Printer, 1787–1825.* Charlottesville: University Press of Virginia for the Bibliographical Society of Virginia, 1967.

Thomas, Isaiah. *The History of Printing in America, with the Biography of Printers and an Account of Newspapers.* Edited by Marcus McCorison. Barre, Mass.: Imprint Society, 1970.

Tyler, Moses Coit. *The Literary History of the American Revolution.* New York: G. P. Putnam's Sons, 1897.

Vaughan, Alden, ed. *Chronicles of the American Revolution.* New York: Grosset & Dunlap, 1965.

Walsh, Michael. "Contemporary Broadside Editions of the Declaration of Independence," *Harvard Library Bulletin,* 3 (1949): pp. 31–43.

Winsor, Justin. *The American Revolution: A Narrative, Critical, and Bibliographical History.* Reprint. New York: Sons of Liberty, 1972.

Wroth, Lawrence C. *The Colonial Printer.* Portland, Maine: The Southworth-Anthoensen Press, 1938. Reprint. Charlottesville: University Press of Virginia, 1964.

Zobel, Hiller B. *The Boston Massacre.* New York: The Norton Company, 1970.

Library of Congress Cataloging in Publication Data
Main entry under title:
Massachusetts broadsides of the American Revolution.
Bibliography: p.
1. Massachusetts—History—Revolution, 1775–1783—Sources. 2. Broadsides. I. Lowance, Mason I., 1938– II. Bumgardner, Georgia B.
E263.M4M54 974.4'03 75–32488
ISBN 0–87023–208–8